Living with Lupus

Book Thirty
LOUANN ATKINS TEMPLE WOMEN & CULTURE SERIES

Living with Lupus

WOMEN AND CHRONIC ILLNESS IN ECUADOR

By Ann Miles

University of Texas Press   *Austin*

The Louann Atkins Temple Women & Culture Series is supported by Allison, Doug, Taylor, and Andy Bacon; Margaret, Lawrence, Will, John, and Annie Temple; Larry Temple; the Temple-Inland Foundation; and the National Endowment for the Humanities.

Copyright © 2013 by the University of Texas Press
All rights reserved

First edition, 2013

Requests for permission to reproduce material from this work should be sent to:
Permissions
University of Texas Press
P.O. Box 7819
Austin, TX 78713-7819
utpress.utexas.edu/index.php/rp-form

♾ The paper used in this book meets the minimum requirements of ANSI/NISO Z39.48-1992 (R1997) (Permanence of Paper).

LIBRARY OF CONGRESS CATALOGING-IN-PUBLICATION DATA
Miles, Ann (Ann M.)
    Living with lupus : women and chronic illness in Ecuador / by Ann Miles. — First edition.
        p.   cm. — (Louann Atkins Temple women & culture series; book thirty)
    Includes bibliographical references and index.
    ISBN 978-0-292-76200-8
    1. Systemic lupus erythematosus—Ecuador.   2. Women—Diseases—Ecuador.   I. Title.
    RC924.5.L85M55   2013
    362.1967′72009866—dc23   2012035775

doi:10.7560/744653

Contents

Acknowledgments

THE ORIGINS OF THIS BOOK GO BACK TO A COLD
Michigan January day in 2001 when I received an email from
the daughters of one of my long-term informants in Ecuador, telling me that
their mother, Rosa, had been diagnosed with lupus. Rosa had been sick for
quite some time, and so the diagnosis came as a bit of a relief to me. At least
they knew what she had, I thought. I knew very little about lupus then, and
so I did what we all do these days when we want to learn about something we
know nothing about. I googled it. I did not like what I learned. I wondered
how someone in her precarious financial position could afford the medications; I worried that she would not understand what she needed to do to take
care of herself; and although it seemed like a very small thing, it made me
profoundly sad to learn that the sun sensitivity associated with lupus meant
that Rosa might never again be able to take the chill out of her bones by sitting in the warm sun. I couldn't imagine how she could make the adjustments, financial and otherwise, to keep her lupus in check.

Although it took some time, indeed years, Rosa did get her lupus under
control, and today she is, thankfully, in quite good health. This book would
not have come about without Rosa and her family and the other Ecuadorian
women with lupus who opened up their hearts and homes to me with gra-
ciousness and honesty in the face of very difficult life challenges. Theirs is
not an easy road. I can only hope that I have done them justice.

I owe an enormous debt of gratitude to the Fulbright Foundation for
awarding me a U.S. Senior Scholar grant to conduct this research, and I especially wish to thank the Fulbright Commission in Ecuador, and its director
Susana Cabeza de Vaca, for allowing me the flexibility to use that grant over
a two-year period. This research was also funded by a Western Michigan
University Faculty Research and Creative Activity Award and the Dean's
Office of the College of Arts and Sciences. Over the years this book was in

preparation I had the pleasure of working for three remarkably supportive department chairs at WMU, Robert Ulin, LouAnn Wurst, and especially my *compañero de clase* David Hartmann, who gave both real and symbolic assistance.

Among those in Ecuador who made this project possible are two old friends, Dr. Jaime Astudillo Romero, the Rector of the University of Cuenca, and most notably Dra. Ana Luz Borrero. I have known both of these scholars since my first trip to Ecuador in 1988, and their support of my endeavors has never wavered. Ana Luz provided some of my initial contacts with Ecuadorian physicians, thus moving this project forward in untold ways. Several Ecuadorian physicians generously shared their time and expertise with me including Dr. Sergio Guevara Pacheco, Dr. Claudio Galarza Maldonado, Dra. Maria Kourilovitch, Dr. Holger Dutan, and Dra. Jenny Guiñansaca. I must especially thank Dra. María del Cármen Ochoa Palacios, as this project would not have been possible without her generosity of spirit and mind. Others in Ecuador who assisted me include María Elena Ramírez, Carmella Gavilanes, José Cardenas, and Sandra Torres. Warm-hearted Leonor Crespo and her family provided my family with a kind of home away from home, as did my dear friend Blanca Mendoza. The many afternoons and evenings spent in their company and eating their wonderful food enlivened our experiences. Finally, I wish to thank my very faithful friend and colleague Lynn Hirschkind, whom I depend upon to help sort through the pragmatic details of coming and going, but who also is by far the most astute and perceptive analyst of Ecuadorian culture. When I am in doubt, I ask Lynn.

In a project of this length there many people who knowingly or unknowingly see you through the process by sharing ideas, expertise, and friendship. Several people read all or parts of the manuscript or the grants on which this research is based and gave me invaluable advice. These include Lenore Manderson, Carolyn Smith-Morris, Robert Ulin and especially Jason Pribilsky. Cleothia Gill selflessly plowed through a very early version of the manuscript providing me with much needed guidance and immeasurable social support, as did Katya Gallegos, who carefully read every word and offered an extremely valuable insider/outsider perspective. University of Texas Press reviewer, Elizabeth Roberts, challenged me to push my thinking beyond where I may have been comfortable going at first. Her thoughtful but kind critique has made this a much better book. My graduate school buddy Kathleen Skoczen remains one of my most thorough readers and reliable supporters, and I can think of very little that does me as much good as spending an afternoon in her company. I would also like to thank the very patient George Lockwood, who gravely listened as I endlessly talked through chapters and who helped me to see where my strengths may lie.

Finally, I cannot imagine working in Ecuador without having my very beloved family, my husband Rich and my "mostly companion" Isabel, there with me. I am inestimably grateful for their enthusiasm for accompanying me every year and for good-naturedly embracing whatever comes their way. For my intrepid Isabel, this has included diving sloppily into an ice-cold swimming pool just after dawn to the jeers of her Ecuadorian classmates, suffering through bouts of ringworm and endlessly itchy flea bites, politely eating things she would really rather leave alone, and enduring countless hours listening to adults talk. She and Rich have made Ecuador much more to me than a place where I work; it is a place where we build family ties.

Living with Lupus

CHAPTER ONE

Introduction

*I*N 2000, ROSA QUITASACA, AN ECUADORIAN WOMAN of "humble" rural origins living in the third largest city in the country, fell seriously ill. Rosa, who was in her forties, was known to be emotionally sensitive and physically delicate, and she often complained about the sadness and exhaustion she felt because of the multiple trials and burdens in her difficult life. Given this, at first, no one in her family really paid too much attention to her complaints. Her symptoms came on rather slowly, starting with fatigue and the seemingly normal aches and pains of aging. But then, almost overnight, things spiraled out of control. She was unable to get out of bed unassisted, lost weight very rapidly, complained of relentless pain, and often seemed dazed and confused.

Rosa's children, ranging in age from seven to twenty years old, grew increasingly alarmed as they watched their mother's health decline precipitously. Terrified that she would die, they took her to several doctors who tested her for a range of cancers, including lymphoma and leukemia, but for months she was left undiagnosed and with little medical reassurance. She was given multiple blood transfusions and an assortment of medications, and despite temporary improvements accompanied by hope that the doctors had finally found the cause, nothing helped for very long. These false diagnoses embittered both Rosa and her children, all of whom became disillusioned and distrustful of doctors.

Eventually her kidneys began to fail; her heart tissue inflamed, making it difficult for her to breathe; and she had several frightening seizures, one of them at home with only her three youngest children present. Then, more than a year after her first symptoms and several months of very serious health complications, Rosa was diagnosed with systemic lupus erythematosus (SLE), a chronic autoimmune disorder. Once diagnosed, it took more than two years for Rosa's condition to fully stabilize, and she was in and out of hospitals several times during that period. Like most lupus patients, she was put on a complicated daily regimen of prescription medications, including the steroid prednisone and immunosuppresants. She was instructed to watch her diet and encouraged to avoid direct sunlight, as sometimes lupus patients can have a severe reaction to ultraviolet (UV) radiation.

SLE or lupus is an autoimmune disorder whereby the body's immune system loses the ability to recognize the difference between foreign bodies (antigens) and healthy cells and tissues. Unable to differentiate self from foe, as it were, the immune system then attacks healthy body tissue, particularly connective tissue. Lupus usually starts with fatigue and joint pain, but if left untreated, it can cause irreversible tissue damage. SLE is "systemic" in that tissues throughout the body can be affected, including internal organs and the brain. Given how long Rosa went untreated, she was very fortunate that her kidneys recovered from the sustained inflammation.

Under the best of circumstances, lupus can be difficult to diagnose, as there is no single test that confirms its presence, and the course it takes in any individual is unpredictable. No two cases of lupus look exactly alike, and the range of possible complications is so vast that the illness creates confusion and frustration. As Rosa's daughter describes it, "First it was one thing, and then it was everything. You never know where it will go next." Even with treatment, lupus is characterized by periodic "flares" and remissions, and patients can go days, weeks, or even months in relatively good health, followed by a "flare" that has them exhausted and in pain. Factors that can trigger flares are idiosyncratic and can include too much exposure to UV radiation, a viral or bacterial infection, or physical or emotional stress. While there is some evidence that a tendency for lupus runs in families, the evidence is also clear that the genetic connection is a complicated one.

By the time that Rosa was diagnosed with lupus, her family had already been torn apart by the forces of transnational migration. In 1995, looking for economic opportunities that never seemed possible in Cuenca for those without social standing and *palanca* (leverage), her eldest son Vicente joined the thousands of poor Cuencanos who had moved to New York in search of work. Rosa never seemed to emotionally recover from her son's departure, as he had long been her closest and most trusted confidant. The early years of Rosa's marriage had been especially difficult, and Vicente filled the emotional gap left by that sometimes tense and unfulfilling relationship. While the family had great hope that their economic lives would be transformed by Vicente's migration and the remittances he sent home, in the end that did not happen. Vicente struggled to make it in New York, and despite some grand gestures in the form of impressive gifts for holidays like Mother's Day, he was not able to send much money home to his family.

Then, in late 1999, Rosa's husband Lucho left Ecuador for the United States. In the 1990s Ecuador faced a protracted economic downturn, and Lucho found it increasingly difficult to make ends meet in Cuenca on his earnings as a taxi driver. Some days he came home with little to show for his labors, as gasoline prices rose at the same time that the economy was stagnating. He often felt like his sixteen-hour workdays were in vain; he began to worry he would never be able to "retire" and that he would be compelled to work until the day he died. He rejected as ridiculously old-fashioned the notion that his children could financially care for him as he aged and was determined to go to the United States for a few years, save his money carefully, and return with enough capital to build his own home and maybe start a small business. Rosa's illness disrupted that plan completely, as her medical expenses mounted and strained the family budget.

The question, of course, for Lucho and Rosa and for millions of Latin American families is how to pay for the continual and specialized care that chronic illness usually requires, now that they have eked past the acute threats that had until recently typified the health profile in the developing world. Chronic illness taxes financial and emotional resources over the long haul, stressing budgets and emotional resilience. In the Quitasacas' case, it means that Lucho remains the phantom husband, father, and citizen, staying in New York far longer than he ever intended and participating in what is now one of the most important of Ecuadorian economic enterprises, sending home remittances.[1]

By the time Rosa was diagnosed, I had known the Quitasacas for close to fifteen years, and I had watched how the family's concerns changed as they adjusted first to city life and then to the absence of transnational family members. I frequently spoke to Lucho in New York, especially in the early months and years of Rosa's illness as he struggled to understand it. It was clear to me that Rosa's illness continued to puzzle Lucho. I was never sure that he fully grasped the idea that lupus is truly lifelong. The cognitive, and actual, distance between New York City and Cuenca surely contributed to Lucho's inability to understand the basics of his wife's chronic illness suffering. For years when he and I spoke on the phone, he quizzed me about when I thought Rosa's lupus would be cured. He always seemed a little surprised when I explained again that he should prepare himself for a lifetime's worth of illness burdens. Sometimes he questioned her treatments with me, "They don't know what they are doing, they must be giving her the wrong pills," he proposed one day. At another time he misinterpreted the side effects of steroid use—in Rosa's case, a swollen face—as physical evidence of her robustness. Despite what she said to him, he thought she looked well. "*Mi mujer* (my woman) looks good. She is fat!" he exclaimed triumphantly after examining pictures I had sent him of my visit to her. It simply was not yet within the range of his personal experience that someone could live for an indefinite period of time with a very serious, medically managed health condition.

By the summer of 2004 Rosa's lupus was well in control, and the family had returned to a fairly normal routine. Lucho stayed in New York and sent money home regularly, which helped pay the hospital debts from Rosa's illness and purchase the medications she needed on a daily basis. Fortunately the costs of those were declining over time as her health continued to improve. The children too had all returned to their normal school and work routines, as Rosa no longer needed regular care. By late August, however, it was clear that something was wrong with their youngest daughter, Cecilia, aged sixteen, as her normally easygoing nature suddenly shifted, and she became moody, taciturn, and lethargic. Soon she broke out in a rash across her face and arms and complained of searing pains in her shoulders, arms, and legs. She was quickly diagnosed with lupus by Rosa's rheumatologist, and she was immediately put on a high dose of corticosteroids to stabilize her condition and control the inflammation. Despite the early diagnosis, quick medical intervention, and the family's familiarity with the condition, shockingly, Cecilia died of lupus only four months after she was diagnosed. The reasons for her quick decline are complicated, convoluted, and sketchy, and I discuss her death in more detail in Chapter Five.

Rosa and Lucho's family story, as dramatic as some elements of it are, is in fact not a completely singular one. There is little argument that as Ecuador and other Latin American countries continue to urbanize (63% of the Ecuadorian population resides in urban areas) and as the standard of living increases especially in cities and towns, the national health profile will reflect a greater incidence of more "modern" health problems such as obesity, diabetes, heart disease, and cancer (PAHO 2007; Waters 2006:119).[2] Hypertension and diabetes are already among the top ten causes of mortality in Ecuador (PAHO 2007). To be sure, lupus and other autoimmune disorders like rheumatoid arthritis are not as common as the diseases listed above, but their intractability and unpredictability might make their personal and social costs even greater than those of more well understood conditions. Given the relatively poor circumstances of her life and the lack of local knowledge about lupus, Rosa has been very fortunate to survive her chronic illness. The vigilance of her daughters played no small part in her recovery. Given the state of local knowledge about lupus, it is, sadly, not all that surprising or unusual that Cecilia did not survive.

The story I tell in this book is not only about Rosa and her family; it is a far more expansive treatment of the lives of many Ecuadorian women who are living with lupus. Rosa's illness experiences are, like everyone's, mediated by her life and disease trajectory, by her culturally constructed understandings of self and body, and by her relationships with others. The illness experience is simultaneously intensely idiosyncratic, as no two cases of any illness play out in exactly the same way, and it is fundamentally shared. While our bodies may indeed suffer individually, that suffering resonates with cultural understandings about life, and it reverberates through our social worlds as others are affected by and participate in some aspects of the illness experience. How we understand and enact illness is mediated by who we are and the models of social and symbolic life in which we live and communicate.

While my concerns for understanding illness focus on the social and cultural dimensions of it, there is no getting around the fact that "lupus" is a biomedical category. As a disease, it has a number of subjective symptoms, but it is generally defined by a set of established criteria, including some that are measurable only through biomedical testing. In the end, a diagnosis of lupus is firmly in the hands of biomedically trained professionals. As far as I know, there are no "indigenous" or Ecuadorian understandings of lupus that are separate from or exist outside its biomedical existence. A diagnosis of lupus therefore implies some kind of engagement with biomedicine. That does not mean, however, that lupus as a disease classification moves across cultures in a singular fashion, that it is understood in the same way wherever it is diagnosed, or, importantly, that even the measurable biological manifestations of it are identical across time and place (see Lock and Nguyen 2010).[3]

This book examines Ecuadorian women's experiences with lupus by taking a meaning-centered approach that recognizes the lived experiences of individuals, privileges the multiple possibilities and meanings inherent in situated daily life, and probes how these come together to inform the ways that understandings about a biomedically determined chronic illness are constructed. The reader will find that while I do identify some important themes that reoccur in women's understandings of their illness, I do not attempt here to construct a singular model of the "Ecuadorian chronic illness experience" or even "women's lupus experiences." Rather, I focus on the multiple meanings that illness has for women within the Ecuadorian contexts. The Ecuadorian contexts include an understanding of the always changing worlds that modern women navigate daily, which are shaped by, among other things, the locally generated gender and class configurations, the available health care options and treatment possibilities, knowledge about the body and health, and the values and morals promoted by both religion and popular culture. I am less concerned with finding the rationale for chronic illness behavior, that is, why patients pursue one course of action or another, than I am with exploring the ways that people think about their experiences, including at times the irreconcilable contradictions that illness can create (see Young 1981).

In keeping with this orientation, the book has been designed to juxtapose important thematic concerns with the lived experiences of individuals with an eye towards exploring how women understand lupus in their lives. In other words, "cultural" beliefs and practices about health, bodies, gender, God, families, a good life act like centripetal forces that orient the direction but do not wholly determine how an individual woman comprehends her illness experience. Moreover, because chronic illness takes multiple forms and meanings, I do not try to rectify or resolve the contradictions and reversals that may appear between different women's accounts and, indeed, the different orientations that can occur in a single woman's account over time. Rather, this book seeks to explore the ambiguities of lives lived precariously on the margins between sick and well.

One of the goals of this book is to bring together, in the form of an extended case study of one illness, the literature on women, emotion, and illness in Latin America and the broader anthropological literature on chronic illness. The growing body of work from Latin America documents the ways that (primarily poor) women's health and their perceptions of health are framed at least in part by their life circumstances as women. Much of that literature centers on examining culturally specific illnesses, like *nervios* or nerves, among several others and it explores how the vicissitudes of women's precarious lives create emotional stress that ultimately leads to culturally understood expressions of physical illnesses (see Finerman 1989; Finkler 1994; Rebhun 1994; Tousignant 1989). This literature attempts to link an understanding of women's bodily experiences and complaints, undifferentiated headaches or diffuse pains, to their social roles as women in circumstances of patriarchy and poverty. While the illnesses described are often "chronic" in nature, as they can be present for an indefinite period of time, for the most part they are explained as though they are culture-bound syndromes or in other words in ways that emphasize their "folk" qualities and therefore their cultural specificity. When reciprocity between kinsmen weakens, rural Ecuadorian women experience *pena* ("pain, grief"; Tousignant 1989) and when poor women in the northeast of Brazil have stayed silent too long in the face of interpersonal failure, they have "swallowed frogs" (Rebhun 1994). In other words, emotional or psychosocial conditions are manifest in secondary somatic, culturally specific complaints.

This book expands our understandings of women's experiences with longterm illness in Latin America and explores the intersections between a biomedically determined illness category (SLE) and women's culturally mediated lived experiences (see Ots 1990).[4] In doing so, I hope to dispel some of the implicit, if not always explicit, dichotomies that emerge from the literature between "real or not real" (biomedical or "folk"), "mind or body" (emotional or somatic), and even "marginal or modern" (poor and rural and not poor and urban). For example, women suffering from lupus are biomedically legitimized in ways that women suffering from "folk" or culturally specific syndromes may not be, yet we will see that their experiences as sick women, whether they are well-to-do or poor, are undeniably troubled in similar sorts of ways. Moreover, the institutional authority of biomedicine to name and assign an illness (a presumed natural category) does not remove that illness from the realm of the cultural (see Kleinman 1988). Scientific categories such as "autoimmune" or "lupus" are not only imbued with cultural and social assumptions (see Napier 2003), they are also differentially interpreted as they move across cultural and personal domains. Having an illness biologically "legitimized" does little, in the end, to mitigate suffering.

Similarly, the literature on chronic illness is increasingly questioning how we create analytic and cultural categories and what that means for ethnographic research, including examining the very dichotomies that have defined it as a discrete area of research. Indeed, Manderson and Smith-Morris problematize our dichotomous biomedical categories of acute and chronic and stress that for chronic illness sufferers, health and illness form part of, and are integrated into, an individual's lifelong understandings of self, body, and experience (Manderson and Smith-Morris 2010; Smith-Morris 2010). Manderson and Smith-Morris argue for using the term "lifelong" illness instead of "chronic" as a means of moving away from the understanding that illness categories like acute and chronic are wholly distinct, especially for the sufferer. While there may in fact be a diagnostic moment that defines, at least biomedically, a "before and after" understanding of illness temporality, an interpretive lens that equally privileges continuity as well as disjuncture may be more analytically useful as well as reflective of how patients really think. In other words, Manderson and Smith-Morris' argument urges us to understand illness experiences not solely for the ways that chronic illness disrupts lives but also for the ways that sufferers integrate life events; understandings of self, body, and illness; and the struggles of daily life into a coherent "continuum" (see also Smith-Morris 2010:26). In part, this is a question of interpretive emphasis, but I think it is an important one. As we will see in later chapters, while the diagnosis of lupus was often a disruptive shock to women, like a "cold bath," as one woman described it to me, and while lupus clearly altered their life trajectories and understandings of self, we can also see how over time women try to incorporate their lupus experience into their more expansive life stories.

The approach that I take to understanding Ecuadorian women's illness experiences in this book is one that explores the narrative experience. Field work primarily consisted of meeting with women who have lupus and, with minimal prompting, allowing them to tell me the story of their illness. Sometimes it took a while for the stories to become elaborated, while in other cases I was barely able to sit down before my informant began to speak. While I carried a standard list of questions with me, I generally let the speaker guide the direction of the discussion and referred to the questions only when our conversation stalled (see Briggs 1986). By encouraging women to take the conversations where they wished, I was able to see more clearly how women individually understand their illness and the impact it has on their lives.

I attempted whenever possible to conduct interviews in women's homes (eighteen of twenty interviews were in homes) because women are often most comfortable there and therefore freer to talk, but also because it allowed me to assess to a limited degree my informants' economic status. Homes, and what they are filled with, often tell a great deal about the resources in a household, and I learned about women's unspoken life circumstances by seeing where they live and what they surround themselves with. Because most of the interviews occurred in women's homes, it was not at all unusual for family members to join our conversations; their comments as parents, children, and spouses reflect how much they are invested in the illness experiences of their loved ones. Given the importance of family, I welcomed participation by family members if the informant seemed to desire it, and they frequently did. Often the participation of family members provoked greater discussion of some topics by the lupus patient herself, who then elaborated on a family member's point, but it also provided a glimpse of how chronic illness directly affects loved ones. The perspectives of mothers, fathers, husbands, sons, and daughters are crucial to the experiences of lupus patients as their lives are deeply embedded in family relationships.[5]

The economic range of my informants was broad, and I interviewed women from well-to-do households whose family members were professionals or successful entrepreneurs; women who were part of the growing urban working classes and who held low-wage clerical, sales, or service positions; and others who were maids or other menial workers. Some women I was able to interview on several occasions, spanning three years of data collection, while other women I spoke with only once. Many of the women (eleven) were patients of a single doctor, Dr. Solis, who graciously introduced her patients to me and in doing so made this project feasible. Some of them saw Dr. Solis in her private office, while others had health benefits provided by their employers and saw Dr. Solis at the Social Security Hospital (Ecuadorian Institute for Social Security or IESS), where she attends to patients weekday mornings. The remaining nine women came to my attention through various means; some were patients of other physicians whom I interviewed, some were relatives of patients, and some came to me, like Rosa, through longstanding relationships I had in the city. I interviewed women like Rosa who have had lupus for many years, and others who were fairly recently diagnosed, as well as women whose lupus is very well controlled and those who suffer from continual health problems and whose health status is precarious at best.

Narrative accounts have been long understood by medical anthropologists to be an important means for uncovering the lived experience of having a chronic illness (See Kleinman 1988; Mattingly 1998; Smith-Morris 2006), as they generally incorporate and elaborate on the idiosyncratic and personal dimensions of suffering as they are experienced in particular cultural and social worlds. According to Garro and Mattingly (2000:17), "The study of narrative becomes a place to explore cultural life as an unfolding personal and social drama." Illness narratives are stories constructed by sufferers about their condition and its impact on their lives; they are considered an important means for making sense of the chaos and disruption (Becker 1997) associated with a debilitating chronic illness. Not only can individuals with the same illness have radically different narratives depending on their life circumstances and disease severity, among other things, but the illness narrative of a single woman can vary over time as her illness symptoms wax and wane, as her life circumstances change, or as treatment options expand or contract.

In other words, illness narratives are discursively constructed by individuals at particular moments and reflect most closely what is on the mind of the sufferer at that moment. Often they are filled with contradictions and disjunctures; they can change on a dime. Moreover, because lupus is ambiguous and there are no definitive answers about the cause, the best approach to treatment, or the course it will take in any individual, patients often find themselves trying out different ideas as they seek to make sense of their experiences, or they look for some glimmer of hope. Rationally consistent personal narratives are rare (Young 1981).

In addition to highlighting aspects of the personal experience, narratives can also inform us more broadly about the culture in which the narrative is embedded. They help us to see the role of culture and social life in framing the illness experience. Mattingly calls stories or narratives "cultural scripts" because they encode meanings about the causes of illness (both broadly and specifically) and the socially understood meanings of the illness (Mattingly 1998:13). As such, illness narratives are unique to the individual at the same time that they include broader cultural and social understandings about sickness, pain, and suffering (Kleinman 1988).

Saris (1995) stresses that chronic illness narratives are linked to important cultural "institutions" that he problematizes and defines not as structures or networks but rather in the Bourdieuian sense of conceptual "fields" that "set up discourse or practice" (42). For Bourdieu (1977), institutions are part of forming *habitus*, the unconscious, historically constructed and learned "dispositions" and suppositions that generate and organize both thought and action. Thus, individual illness narratives, both in what they say and what they leave silent, necessarily are "imprinted" by these institutions or conceptual schemas (Saris 1995:65). The experience of the individual, both in sickness and in health, is mediated through (usually in consonance with but sometimes in dissonance to) the conceptual fields allowed by the prevailing institutions (Saris 1995). Saris is concerned not just to discuss the personal dimensions of the illness experience but also to "distribute the responsibility for the production of this experience to presences beyond the experiencing self" (Saris 1995:43). We must work between the personal and idiosyncratic and the social and cultural to reveal how each influences the expression and meaning of the other.

In much the same way, this book is an attempt to make sense of a collection of narratives and to find in them and balance appropriately the idiosyncratic and the cultural, the personal and the "institutional." To create understandable meaning in narrative, the teller generally follows a certain logical framework that guides the readers or listeners and helps to organize their interpretations of what is being told. However, narratives do not imitate life because they are structured in ways life is not (see Mattingly 2000). Narratives have "plots" and "arcs" that frame them, usually in predictable ways (see Charon 2006; Garro and Mattingly 2000).[6] In my interviews I found that the illness stories women constructed tended to follow a similar plot sequence from initial symptoms to diagnosis to management. Many were punctuated with crisis episodes that served as "turning points" in diagnosis or management. For some, resolution has yet to come. Sometimes women ended their narratives with a larger parable applicable for life in general, saying things like "*hay que seguir adelante*" ("one must move forward") or "*no hay otra cosa*" ("there's no other option").

But my concern here is not really to deconstruct the details of the emplotment of narratives as much as it is to decipher the ways that narrative broadly reveals culture. Women's stories of illness share a number of key elements between them at the same time that they are always provisional and emerging; the analysis of narrative consists of recognizing the various ways that common themes play out in individual stories but also in identifying the cultural meanings and social institutions that lie behind those commonalities. From explicit, personal talk emerges implicit, often taken-for-granted, understandings about culture and how the world is, or ought to be, constructed (Quinn 2005:45).

Of course, the listener also brings his or her own contingent understandings to the narrative. No doubt, my long experience in Cuenca and the years I have spent working with women and writing about gender, families, and health have influenced how I interpreted the narratives I collected. Over many years I have become aware both of the particular strains on women's lives and of the discourses they use to describe their lives, their families, and their understandings of what really matters. Those understandings of gender and social privilege provided the conceptual frames through which I interpreted what I heard.

This book spends a great deal of time exploring how gender has an impact on chronic illness suffering. In every way, women interpret their lives and their bodies, their illness trajectories and the ramifications of their illness, through their lived, culturally constructed, gendered experiences. Just as their lives have been fundamentally shaped by gender, so too are their illness experiences. However, the discussions of gender in Ecuador, the ways that it frames thinking and being in daily life and the ways that it intersects with illness, are spread throughout the book, rather than located in one place. I have done this very consciously since I want the reader to understand gender as it is enacted by real people, and not as an abstract concept or set of established relationships or social roles (see Butler 1999). Indeed, gender matters most as it plays out between individuals and between individuals and cultural and social institutions. By placing the discussions of various aspects of gender in each chapter, I seek to more closely align the abstract or conceptual with the real. I hope that by juxtaposing examples of how women enact and think about gender with the broader analyses of it in the literature, we can more easily understand the apparent contradictions and collusions that we see.

There have been tremendous shifts in women's social roles in the more than twenty years that I have been working in Ecuador, but at the same time that much has changed, much has also stayed the same. Although more women are attaining higher education and entering both the formal and informal workplaces where more women remain even after marriage, their roles in the family as daughters, wives, and mothers are still central to defining modern Ecuadorian femininity. By linking analytical discussions of gender to women's work and home experiences very directly, I hope to capture more honestly the interplay of gender and vulnerability both in everyday life and in the lives of the ill.

In many ways this was the easiest anthropological project that I have undertaken in Ecuador at the same time that it was the most difficult. Ecuadorians, although known for their friendliness, are fairly cautious with outsiders, and they have a healthy skepticism about the motivations and benefits of "research." I have learned over the years of working in Cuenca that it generally takes a good deal of time and patience to establish the *confianza* ("confi-dence," "trust") necessary for good ethnographic research. The poor in par-ticular have every reason to distrust those (like me) who represent powerful places and institutions since they have rarely done them any good. I have al-ways understood and respected people's reticence to open up and discuss sensitive topics. I usually take my cues from my informants, and I do not venture where someone seems unwilling to go at the moment. Therefore, I was quite taken aback at how quickly and easily I was able to establish rap-port with the women I interviewed for this book. While I would like to think it has all to do with the experience I have gained after working for nearly twenty years in the same place, I am more inclined to believe that it has to do with the state of mind of the women who have lupus.

Having a chronic illness is taxing on the body, on personal finances, and on relationships. Sometimes even loving friends and family grow weary of hearing the sufferer's complaints, and the chronically ill begin to shy away from talking about how they feel, lest they worry, vex, or irritate their loved ones. My visits to women's homes, therefore, were seemingly greeted as an opportunity, a chance to talk freely about how they feel and to express their fears and worries without any concerns that what they would tell me would change anything in their interpersonal lives. While some women have fairly upbeat stories to tell of how they manage their lupus, others have heartbreak-ingly sad ones. For some, lupus is a disruption in their life trajectory that sidetracked but did not derail them. These women occasionally feel tired, stiff, and sore, and they respond by monitoring their diets, medication, and stress levels. But for others, lupus, and caring for lupus, has become the central and dominating motif of daily life as a life-threatening flare always seems to be looming, even simple activities are often too much, and they find themselves constantly in and out of doctor's offices and hospitals in an attempt to control symptoms.

The "difficulty" that I encountered in this project was the all-too-human sadness that I experienced while listening to women's sometimes tragic sto-ries of pain and loss. Several women I interviewed have very serious cases of lupus and the illness reverberates through every aspect of their lives, in-cluding destroying marriages, threatening jobs, obliterating independence, altering child rearing preferences, and undermining self-esteem and compe-tency. There are indeed some women who can speak of the confidence they gained because they were able to "conquer" lupus to some degree; for those who have not, their precarious health status has bled into every other domain of their lives, altering women's "expectations of life choices" and therefore their self-identity (see Mendelson 2009:70). For women who cannot get their lupus under control, the constancy of their infirmities and the unpredictable nature of their lives wear on their hearts and bodies, making them physically and emotionally exhausted all of the time. For others, the intermittent nature of their lupus flares puts them on a debilitating emotional roller coaster ride as periods of good health and hopefulness are ruptured overnight and plans and dreams are seemingly impossible to achieve. As an anthropologist, all I really had to offer these agonized women was a sympathetic ear, which I can only hope was in some small way a comfort, and the promise to tell their stories accurately and carefully.

This book is fundamentally organized to highlight four major themes that emerge from an analysis of women's illness narratives: liminality, loss, suffering, and transformation. The book does not, however, employ an overarching explanation that then reconfigures the various themes into a single metanarrative. Rather, in each of the four chapters (Chapters Four–Seven), different theoretical ideas are introduced to help broaden the discussion about it, and then case studies are presented that illustrate how that theme is manifest in different women's experiences. Among the important ideas that I will elaborate on in relation to these themes are the ways that gender and class intersect in systems of subordination, the influence of biomedicine in framing illness understandings and the ways that biological and cultural logics intersect, and how notions of self and identity, in the past, present and future, are expressed and reworked. I hope to show both where Ecuadorian women's chronic illness narratives resemble those found elsewhere, and where they differ.

Chapter Two provides the reader with the broad background necessary for understanding the discussions that follow. The chapter describes the site of this research, the city of Cuenca, providing details about how social class and the centuries-old system of social privilege figure into Cuencanos' understandings of themselves and others. The chapter also offers detailed information about lupus from both biomedical and sociological perspectives, and it contrasts the biomedical and western knowledge of lupus with what is known in Ecuador by physicians and patients. The chapter further examines the literature on chronic illness in anthropology and elsewhere as a means for highlighting the questions that are examined more thoroughly in later chapters.

Chapter Three continues the discussion of the regionalized setting and focuses specifically on describing the Ecuadorian health care system, explaining the options that are available and the difficulties that many people face in accessing good care. Even in the Social Security System (IESS) where care should, theoretically, be egalitarian across classes because all subscribers have similar benefits on paper, there is a perception that the system works better for those with more social leverage.

The next four chapters (Four–Seven) illuminate the central themes I

identified in women's narratives: liminality, loss, suffering, and transformation, and each of these chapters is organized in a similar fashion. They begin with a short introduction; I then explore that theme as it is represented in
the literature, and then I present two case studies that offer variations on the
ways the theme is elaborated and experienced in women's daily lives. One of
the difficulties I had in writing up the case studies found here was in determining which chapter to place them in, as individual narratives invariably intersect with multiple themes, rather than one exclusively. While perhaps it
would be easier to digest the material if the case studies spoke only to one
theme or another, that is simply not the way things work on-the-ground. Indeed, quite the opposite is true. Therefore, the reader will find that the contents of one case study sometimes overlaps with themes addressed in other
chapters or that the two cases found in one chapter diverge considerably or
speak to multiple concerns at once. Real life is filled with ambiguities, half-
starts, and contingencies, and there is no honest way around that fact.

I do realize, however, that by placing a case study in one chapter or another, I have chosen to emphasize one theme in the narrative over another.
Those kinds of choices are an inevitable part of writing about complex human lives. In the end, I would like the reader to understand that these themes
do not exist independently of one another and that the examples I have se-
lected neither represent the complete range of possibilities nor circumscribe
all the possible permutations. So, for example, while I separate loss and suffering analytically in Chapters Five and Six, and present case studies that
speak directly to these themes independently, they are, quite logically, usually intertwined in multiple ways.

To some extent, chronic illness can be seen as "emerging" rather than entrenched in places like Ecuador, which means that cultural models for understanding them are still very much in the process of becoming. Indeed, I found
that women and their families often do not know what to make of an illness
that comes and goes without warning, nor could they easily reconcile themselves to the idea that long-term infirmity and disability can strike someone
in the prime of life. The reality is that a generation or so ago, many of the
women I interviewed would not have survived with lupus beyond a few years.
This book attempts to capture this emerging moment as women struggle to
find meaning for what is still a relatively new phenomenon in their worlds:
medically managed, long-term chronic illness. We will see here their efforts
to incorporate that reality into their daily lives as modern women with numerous school, work, and family obligations and responsibilities, as well as
their less tangible concerns about living up to the elusive and ever-changing
standards of contemporary Ecuadorian femininity. Operating in an unequal
society in terms of both gender and class and depending on a stratified health

care system that offers widely divergent treatment options, women wove these various threads together to construct narratives that represent and reflect their experiences. As we will see, sometimes women have far more questions than they do answers as they attempt to make sense of an experience that defies facile explanations.

CHAPTER TWO

Cuenca, Lupus, and Chronic Illness

*I*T IS UNCLEAR TO ME HOW MUCH ROSA REALLY UN-derstands about lupus. She knows, of course, from personal experience, that it is debilitating, that it can run in families, and that it can sometimes be deadly. Moreover, although she does not always do it, she knows that she is supposed to take care of herself, which means taking her medications, seeing her doctor regularly, and not allowing herself to become overtired. However, her knowledge of the specifics of her condition, for example, that it is autoimmune, is vague and frankly uninformed. She counts on her daughters, especially the eldest, Alejandra, to explain why she needs a certain test or medication, and then she promptly forgets what she has been told. When she discusses lupus with someone unfamiliar with the disease, she usually tells them that it is a kind of blood disorder. While there may be elements of truth to that description, it is too vague to be at all meaningful, and that is her intention. Like so many others with lupus, Rosa finds it easier to gloss over the details of her condition, especially since she really does not understand them in the first place. With only a third-grade education, Rosa's knowledge of biology is minimal, her abilities to comprehend the complicated dynamics of the immune system are limited, and her confidence to ask questions of her doctors is almost nonexistent.

Typical of women of her poor, rural background, Rosa is extremely shy and quite compliant with her doctors, and she therefore asks them very few questions. She is painfully aware of the class differences between herself and these more educated elites, and she simply smiles politely with her eyes averted, rather than appear to be assertive or leave the impression that she questions their medical authority (see Darghouth et al. 2006). The few times I went with Rosa to her doctors I was taken aback at just how passive she was in their presence, and I worried that far too little information was being exchanged. She asked very few questions of her doctors, and she responded to their queries with only minimal detail. I could not help thinking that these were less than ideal doctor-patient encounters.

For the most part, Rosa does some of what her doctors tell her to do with little real understanding, or perhaps even concern, for why, but worse than that, when she does not, usually for financial reasons, she generally keeps that information to herself. She does not want to disappoint her doctors, provoke them to order more expensive tests or medications, or appear to be ungrateful or ignorant for not following their advice. Outside their offices, however, Rosa reveals a profound suspicion of some of her doctors, and she questions if they are really *buena gente* ("good people"). The implication here is that *buena gente* are kind and patient people who practice medicine purely for humanitarian rather than financial reasons. Those doctors whom she would categorize as *buena gente* are sensitive to class differences and try whenever possible to make financial accommodations for their more "humble" patients like her. Those accommodations might include reduced charges for office visits, free drug samples, and a willingness to help find laboratories and clinics with the best pricing. Over the years Rosa has seen several physicians and has yet to find one with whom she is completely comfortable. She was most happy with the physician who cared for her daughter Cecilia, but since her daughter's death, she refuses to see him for fear that it would bring up too many sad memories. She does not blame him for Cecilia's death, but she does not want to see him either.

In contrast to chronic illness sufferers in Ecuador who are better educated and internet savvy, Rosa does not have much access to information about her illness. I saw no printed materials anywhere in Cuenca explaining lupus; there are no pamphlets or hand-outs that might help patients understand and communicate to others about their medical condition. Moreover, given Rosa's low literacy levels, the internet, which she could access inexpensively in a local internet café, is not really an option for her. Her daughters have occasionally consulted websites for information about lupus, but one of them told me what she found there was frightening rather than comforting. In contrast to what one finds in the United States, there are no support groups in Cuenca for lupus patients; except in very rare circumstances, there is no counseling of any kind available to help patients sort through the emotional, psychological, and even the logistical complications of having a serious chronic illness. For most women, doctor's consultations, for better or worse, are the only means of educating themselves about lupus, and their families are the primary source of assistance and counseling.

While Rosa may not have much abstract "knowledge" about her condition, she is very aware of the lived experiences of having a chronic illness.

Both her day-to-day activities and the larger meaning of her life have been profoundly altered by her experiences with lupus, provoking her to ask those difficult "Why me?" questions that have few satisfying answers. She cannot help but question why she was afflicted with lupus, why she survives with it, and, most troubling, why her daughter did not. She also knows that her illness is expensive and that the money spent on it could be very usefully spent on other family needs. So, much to her daughter's dismay, if Rosa is feeling well for a while, she will skip taking her medications and forego doctor's appointments so that she can save money. The family has just emerged from the debt accrued during Cecilia's final hospitalization, and Rosa has her sights set on moving out of her rented house and building a home of her own. Doctor's office visits cost $25 U.S.[1] out-of-pocket, and Rosa has a hard time justifying the expense while her health remains stable.

Finally, Rosa also knows that chronic illness can become very tiresome for those around her. While her children remain fiercely loyal to her and attentive to her needs, she is aware that her husband does not always understand her worries and that her always ambivalent extended family, including her siblings, has grown weary of her long struggle to stabilize her health. They were tapped dry, emotionally and financially, during Cecilia's illness, and for now Rosa does not tell them of her everyday worries nor does she feel that she can count on any of them should she fall seriously ill again.

CUENCA

Rosa's tentative relationships with her physicians closely mirror the dynamics of race and class in Cuenca that both constrain social possibilities and frame social relationships. When Rosa moved from a small rural town to Cuenca more than twenty-five years ago, she lived in two rooms in a rundown tenement house in the city's central historical district. Like many others, she moved to the city because land was scarce in the rural areas, and making a living was precarious, and she wanted to provide her children with better educational and, therefore, career opportunities. Today, she joins the thousands of others, most of them with relatives working abroad, who live in burgeoning working-class "suburbs" that ring the periphery of the city. Although these new neighborhoods are filled with brand-new, two-story homes packed with the latest appliances, many of the streets have yet to be paved by the municipality. Over the years I have written extensively about Cuenca, and I find that it is always difficult to describe the city fully, as it is often so very contradictory.

Cuenca is most certainly a charming place with a well-maintained colonial era downtown and a central plaza that has beautifully manicured trees, flowers, and ornamental shrubs. Recently the city has started piping classical music into the plaza, adding to the overall genteel ambiance. Old men still meet daily on park benches to smoke cigarettes, discuss the news, gossip, and watch the world go by. On Sundays folk ensembles often perform on the small stage in the plaza, and the park fills first with families coming from church and then later in the afternoon with young people in their very best clothes who awkwardly flirt with one another. Shoeshine boys ply their trade there, and families can have their child's picture taken atop a toy pony. Ecuadorian and foreign tourists usually enjoy Cuenca because it is clean and orderly, at least the parts they usually see, and while it has all the amenities of a big city, one can still see "traditional" charm in the form of local women dressed in the "folk" costume of the *Chola Cuencana* with their wide, gathered, knee-length *pollera* skirts and woven Panama hats, selling produce in the colorful municipal markets or washing clothes by the riverside.[2]

Cuenca likes to advertise that it represents the best of the old and new worlds, an ideal blending of past and present and historical markers point out the pre-Incan, Incan, and Spanish influences on the local culture (see Weismantel 2001). Most middle- and upper-class Cuencanos bemoan the migration to the United States that Rosa's family and so many others have engaged in, and they see it as a source of irretrievable culture loss. They worry that the rural and "folkloric" *chola* "culture" is being corrupted by fast money and loose morals brought back by migrants from the United States (Miles 2004). Cuencanos often have a romanticized vision of the region's Andean past, which they wish their rural peasants would embody forever, and they wonder whether some special "knowledge" is not lost as the city and the surrounding countryside modernizes. Cuencanos of all classes drink herbal teas for their healthful benefits, extol the virtues of the fresh air of the countryside, and believe, if only to a limited extent, that rural people are healthier because they live closer to nature and therefore "closer to God" (see Miles 1998b).

The city grows larger every time I visit, and today terrible traffic jams clog the narrow cobblestone streets of the central historical district and new neighborhoods are being carved out of the countryside. Buses rumble through city streets endlessly, linking the center to the growing periphery and spewing dense black exhaust that soils the thin air. In the twenty-two years that I have been working in Cuenca, the population has risen considerably.[3] Much of the growth is due to rural-to-urban migration, and it is increasingly difficult to figure out where the city ends and the countryside begins as new neighborhoods with substantial homes spring up out of what once was farm land. Most of the homes in these newer neighborhoods are *"hecho de dólares"* ("built from dollars"), in other words, funded through remittances sent by loved ones working in the United States. In an obvious display of its consumer modernity, there are now two full-fledged shopping malls in Cuenca, complete with an impressive array of specialty and big-box stores, multiple-screen movie theaters, bowling alleys and arcades, and food courts with free wireless internet access. The city has several major hospitals, both public and private, and countless smaller clinics. Because Cuenca is home to three universities, each with a medical school, the popular understanding is that the city has as comprehensive an array of medical facilities and specialties as anywhere in the country.

Although much has changed in Cuenca over the past two decades as the city has grown and become more cosmopolitan and commercial, it still retains much of the "old world" flavor that city officials like to market to tourists and for which the old-guard families take such pride. At its best, this means that the downtown historical district is now a UNESCO Cultural Patrimonial site, and loving care is taken to preserve its architectural character. A few years ago the city streets were repaired with each colonial-era brick painstakingly refitted even though they wreak havoc with today's cars, trucks, and buses. At its worst, the "old world" flavor also means that the centuries-old social customs that privilege those with "good names" (i.e., Spanish surnames) and historical ties to Spain are maintained; who you know, or *palanca*, still makes a tremendous difference in the available opportunities (see Hirschkind 1980; Miles 2004). Networking with powerful friends, family, and godparents is still the easiest way to get ahead and something of a prerequisite for most professional employment opportunities.

Rosa's grown children often complain to me that their "Indian" name signals that they are unimportant, if not inferior, and that a college education means a good deal less than they think it ought to since qualifications are often secondary to *palanca* when it comes to getting a job. This system of social exclusion plays no small role in fomenting the emigration from this region, as those marginalized by the system seek to circumvent it entirely. Many hope to return one day with enough capital to start a business that will make them financially independent.

In addition to having an entrenched elite, a very wealthy class of commercial entrepreneurs, and a disaffected rural and rural-to-urban migrant population, Cuenca also has a fairly well-established quasi-professional working class that fills many of the retail, clerical, and lower-level managerial positions in town. This group generally carries Spanish surnames but usually not those with known historical ties to power and influence, and they live in fairly modest homes in aging city neighborhoods. They think of themselves as "decent" people who work hard and respect the traditional values, and they are often equally critical of the poor and those who come from rural areas whom they see as uneducated, uncultured, and perhaps not as hard working as themselves, as they are of the elites, whom they rightly believe generally keep economic power to themselves (Hirschkind 1980). Indeed, the rural poor in some cases are economically leapfrogging over the old middle and working classes as the remittances they bring from their migration abroad allows them a kind of consumerism that the urban working classes can only imagine. Moreover, the elites, they are quite sure, mostly look out for themselves.

Cuencanos often refer to Cuenca as a small and closed-minded place where people talk and gossip about one another and where it is best if personal failings, ranging from health problems to financial difficulties, are well hidden from public view. Social standing and saving face are highly valued, among the rich and poor alike. For lupus sufferers, this means that concerns about what others think figure prominently in how the illness is understood. In general, families try to maintain a good social appearance in the face of unexplained illness, which implies that they share little potentially damaging information and seek help from a limited range of people. Sometimes the fear of censure that was expressed was as minor as Rosa not wanting her extended relatives to know when she has a flare, to a middle-class family fearing possible public scorn when they had no other option but to petition public and private organizations for financial help during a severe medical crisis.

The women I interviewed for this book come from the various strata of Cuencan society, including those with Indian and those with Spanish surnames, those who have relatives who have migrated to the United States and those whose families have worked in the city for generations, and those with *palanca* and those completely without it. When I began this project I assumed that there would be a clear relationship between social status and access to the best medical care for lupus. In other words, I presumed, for example, that the elites would have access to the very good care locally and would seek care outside Ecuador if need be and that the perceived quality of care would decline as social-class standing declined. For example, I figured that the rural population and rural-to-urban migrants like Rosa would have the least satisfaction with their medical care. To my surprise, this turned out not to be the case, mainly because, like Rosa, so many of the women in the countryside, the *cholas* marginalized by Cuencan society, have relatives in the United States who send remittances back home to help with medical expenses. Some of these women are seeing the best trained physicians in Cuenca.

While I have no doubts that the poorest of the poor in Cuenca, those socially marginalized and without access to foreign-earned capital, are the least likely to survive with lupus, beyond this very destitute group it appears that the working middle class may be in a more difficult position than the rural or rural to urban working classes. Indeed, most of the women in the working middle class earned only modest salaries, which were never enough to allow them to seek private medical care. In fact, many considered themselves fortunate to have their employers pay for their enrollment in the semipublic subscription health program known as Social Security or *Seguro*. This coverage, while far superior to the benefits available in the public health hospitals, can be difficult to access and is often inadequate for the needs of the chronically ill. Yet, even here *palanca* matters, and more upper-class women seemed to have better experiences with the Social Security system than did their more humble counterparts. I found that women without *palanca* who relied entirely on the Social Security system are often those whose access to care was most limited and circumscribed and that they are often the least content with their medical care. As I will outline in more detail in Chapter Three, the Ecuadorian public health system and the Ecuadorian Institute for Social Security (IESS) are both still woefully unprepared to cope with the structural burdens of increasing chronic illness management.

In the section that follows I discuss the illness of lupus from two contrasting vantage points. The first is primarily from the United States, and it describes the illness from the perspective of medicine and science, including what we know about lupus in relation to social inequality. The second will focus on lupus in Ecuador and discuss how biomedical knowledge there is intermingled with cultural and social knowledge. In this section I will focus on what Ecuadorian physicians and patients told me about what they know about lupus and lupus care. As we shall see, the biological manifestations of lupus vary widely under all circumstances, but there are some patterns to the common medical complications found in Ecuador as well as culturally specific ways that the illness is understood and managed medically and socially.

LUPUS IN THE UNITED STATES

While physicians described the name and some of the symptoms of lupus as early as the twelfth century, the name "lupus" was standardized in medical textbooks in the mid nineteenth century (Benedek 2002). The disease was distinguished by Ferdinand von Hegra, a Viennese physician, by the raised, red lesions "in a distribution not dissimilar to a butterfly which were noted on the bridge of the nose and across the cheeks" (Benedek 2002:3). The lupus malar rash called to mind the markings of the red wolf (*canis lupus*) and hence the name was given. Even though only a small percentage of lupus patients experience facial lesions, the name has persisted, as has the importance of von Hegra's early mention of the butterfly. Today, the butterfly is the unofficial symbol of lupus advocacy and support groups in Europe, Canada, and the United States. Although the disease was recognized early, treatment for lupus was slow in coming; until the 1960s and the extensive use of corticosteroids to control inflammation, survival rates for lupus did not reach much beyond a few years (Benedek 2002).

In lupus the "T" and "B" white blood cells are overstimulated, creating auto antibodies that attack healthy tissues, leading to inflammation and pain. Lupus is unpredictable, and patients can have periods of high disease activity, "flares," followed by periods of remission. While there is some evidence that lupus and other autoimmune disorders run in families, the evidence is also clear that the genetic connection is a complicated one. No single gene has been identified for lupus, and studies of identical twins show a discordance in disease incidence that indicates that others factors (broadly understood as social, economic, personal, and environmental) must play a role in activating lupus in one individual and not another (Wang et al. 2008; Zouali 2005).

The causes of lupus are still essentially unknown, but they are no doubt multifactorial. In the literature on lupus there is almost a mind-boggling array of factors being considered as potentially linked to the manifestation of lupus. For example, because the disease is far more prevalent in women, scientists are examining the role that estrogen may have in the development or expression of SLE and, more recently, how the "awakening" of a gene on the X chromosome may lead to autoimmune dysfunction and susceptibility (Hampton 2007). Other research topics include the potential role of viruses, especially the Epstein-Barr virus, in provoking B-cell activity and lupus (Greenstein 2002) and the possibilities of environmental and chemical contaminations as contributing factors (Mongey and Hess 2002). An article in *Clinical Rheumatology* even discusses lipstick use as potentially associated with lupus, and identifies the chemicals eosin, phthalate, and octynoic acid, which are commonly found in that cosmetic, as capable of negatively impacting immune function (Wang et al. 2008). In short, there is no known "cause" of lupus, and the disease is considered, like many autoimmune disorders, to be a combination of genetic, environmental, and social factors.

Diagnosing lupus is difficult, as the disease can mimic other conditions, and like many autoimmune disorders, there is no single test that confirms a positive diagnosis. Instead, a patient is believed to have lupus if she has four out of eleven diagnostic criteria. Among the criteria is the presence of the butterfly rash; photosensitivity; excessive protein in the urine, indicating kidney involvement; and a "positive" antinuclear antibody (ANA) test. The positive ANA test, which checks for auto antibodies to cell nuclei, is often considered a "hallmark" of lupus, and 97% of diagnosed lupus patients in the United States have high levels of ANAs (Weinstein and Kyttaris 2003). The test, however, is not definitive of lupus, as several other autoimmune conditions also present with a positive antinuclear antibody test and, moreover, the test results can sometimes be ambiguous, indicating a high, but not a "high enough," level. Does someone with a high but not-too-high ANA test with three other symptoms "qualify" as a lupus patient, or does she have scleroderma, rheumatoid arthritis, or any one of a number of related and equally difficult-to-diagnose autoimmune conditions? In the United States, it can sometimes take years before an accurate diagnosis of systemic lupus erythematosus (SLE) is made, as patients are put through a battery of tests, compounding the financial and emotional burdens of sufferers and their families (Mendelson 2009).

In the United States, rates of lupus are rising, but it is unclear whether this is an effect of better screening and diagnosis or whether environmental conditions contributing to autoimmune disorders are increasing. Determining the incidence and prevalence of lupus appears to be very difficult, as disease manifestations and study methodologies vary greatly (Lim and Drenkard 2008). Because of the difficulty and subjectivity in diagnosing lupus, actual prevalence rates of lupus probably far exceed reported rates, and researchers assume that mild cases of lupus are significantly underreported (Lim and Drenkard 2008). Best estimates are that in the United States, prevalence rates for lupus range from a low of 17–71 per 100,000 among Caucasian women to a high of 56–283 for African American women (Manzi 2001). Like many autoimmune disorders, lupus affects women at least seven to eight times more often than men (Manzi 2001). Lupus most often occurs in women of childbearing age, but it can also develop in fairly young women, some not yet in their teens.

In addition to higher prevalence among minorities, in the United States there are clear disparities in the morbidity and mortality of lupus in relation to race, ethnicity, and socioeconomic status (SES) (Alarcón 2001; Danchenko et al. 2006; Ward 2001). In general, lupus disease activity, organ damage, and functional disabilities vary by socioeconomic levels, with poorer patients experiencing greater disease burdens than wealthier ones (Rus and Hochberg 2002; Ward 2001). Since race and ethnicity are often linked to SES, and conflated in the literature, we find that African American and Hispanic populations in the United States who are generally of lower SES have higher rates of lupus incidence and do worse when they do have it (Alarcón 2001). Tellingly, the medical literature discusses concerns about genetic susceptibility to lupus and the psychosocial variables linked to low SES, such as low social support, individual health habits, and compliance with medical advice (Bae et al.

2001; García-González et al. 2008; Petri et al. 1991), but offers little discussion of how institutionalized racism and poverty impact health more generally, including the lifelong effects of social stress and how access to quality care is differentially apportioned. In short, the literature either tries to link higher disease activity to genetic variability or it "blames the victim" by assuming that higher disease burdens are a result of patient noncompliance with medical directives.[4]

Typical of the research that tries to connect ethnicity and SLE is work by Seldin et al. that examines if Amerindian ethnicity in Argentina is associated with greater risk of SLE (Seldin et al. 2008). While Amerindian identity was determined through genetic testing and found to be associated with greater risk of SLE and greater renal involvement, there was no discussion of how the Amerindian populations in Argentina might be socially and economically situated relative to the majority Euro-American population. In other words, risk was associated solely with ethnicity and discussed as though it could be extracted from socioeconomic influences.

One of the difficulties in treating lupus patients from all socioeconomic and ethnic backgrounds is that the illness is characterized by a great deal of unpredictability. The course and severity of the illness varies widely among patients, and each case has its own constellation of symptoms and complications. One patient may have a good deal of photosensitivity and experience angry red lesions after a brief dalliance in the sun, while others suffer from poor circulation, aching joints, or headaches, but have little photosensitivity. Lupus can affect multiple organ systems including the kidneys, the circulatory system, and the central nervous system. The disease can appear confusing and arbitrary as symptoms move throughout the body. While lupus often begins in an individual as inexplicable and debilitating fatigue, usually accompanied by joint pain, many patients report some central nervous system involvement, ranging from frightening delusions and seizures during severe lupus flares, to everyday forgetfulness that seems to wear away at everyone's patience. Moreover, the emotional toll of lupus is not insignificant, and many lupus patients find that the unpredictable nature of the disease, the sleep disruptions, and the social consequences of having a lifelong illness contribute to depression and despair, which often intensifies emotional stress, triggering a lupus flare.

There is currently no cure for lupus, only the ability to manage symptoms to some degree, and patients must be closely monitored throughout their lives. While every patient tolerates medications differently, the most common and affordable medications used in the management of lupus, including corticosteroids, chemotherapies, and immunosuppressants, carry significant risks and unpleasant and dangerous side effects. Long-term use of corticosteroids have been linked to significant increases in cholesterol levels and the concomitant health risks of high cholesterol and weight gain. Long-term steroid use is also associated with early and severe osteoporosis. Many women report finding steroids difficult to use because of the unexpected weight gain and the odd effect of inflammation of the lower face. Steroid users often develop a "moon face" as their lower jaw and cheeks expand and swell. Moreover, many women also complain that steroid use increases facial hair, leaving them with a coat of downy hair on their cheeks. While medically "benign," the moon face and hair growth associated with steroid use are psychologically and emotionally very difficult for many women (Hale et al. 2006).

Other common lupus medications include hydroxychloroquil (*Plaquenil*), which was developed for malaria but seems to reduce inflammation in lupus patients. If neither *Plaquenil* nor steroids are well tolerated by the patient, doctors may prescribe methotrexate, originally a cancer therapy, and/or azathioprine (*Imuran*), both of which act as immune suppressants. All these medications have a range of minor and major side effects associated with them, which can affect patient compliance with use (García-González et al. 2008). The average lupus patient usually takes a cocktail of medications on a daily basis to reduce inflammation, suppress the activity of the immune system, or counteract the side effects of steroid use. During a lupus flare, medication dosages are usually increased, and, often, symptom-specific new drugs are introduced.

Finally, a new and important class of medications called "biologics" has recently been introduced. Biologics are genetically engineered monoclonal antibody medications that target specific immune cells, known as "B" cells (Arkfeld 2008). Scientists are still unclear of the exact role that B cells play in autoimmune disorders, but recent evidence suggests that biologic therapy reduces B cells and inflammatory activity and severity (Arkfeld 2008). At the time I started this project in 2005 the biologics developed for rheumatoid arthritis had not been approved for use in treating lupus in the United States, where results of trials appeared dubious (Lateef and Petri 2010). These medications were, however, being prescribed "off-label" in the United States for lupus, and at least one physician in Cuenca has used biologic therapies extensively with his lupus patients. In 2010, after successful Phase II clinical trials, *Benylista* (belimumab), developed by the pharmaceutical company Human Genome Sciences Inc. was approved by the US Food and Drug Administration (FDA) to treat SLE that has not responded to other therapies. Benylista is very expensive, and cost estimates are at $30,000 per patient, per year (Pollack 2010).

Even in the United States where lupus support groups work hard to "raise awareness" of lupus, the illness is little known and poorly understood by the general public. Even more troubling, Napier writes that lupus is a socially "meaningless" disorder because it does not conform to established cultural stereotypes and facile meanings of what constitutes illness and suffering (Napier 2003).[5] As Napier points out, lupus patients sometimes do not appear ill and in fact are often told by others that they "look well" because of the flushed cheeks and weight gain associated with corticosteroid use. Worse yet, because the day-to-day symptoms of lupus can be so very subjective, such as pain, fatigue, and forgetfulness, women are often told, or it is subtly implied, that their problems are really all "in their heads" (Napier 2003:87). Indeed, the two most common symptoms of lupus, pain and fatigue, are impossible to measure by objective criteria and therefore their "validity" relies solely on the patients' own reports.

Because lupus afflicts women with so much greater frequency than men, many women report that they often have a hard time convincing their doctors that their symptoms of fatigue signal a physical and not an emotional problem (Napier 2003).[6] Unable to see any obvious visible signs of illness, others begin to question the legitimacy of the lupus patient's complaints and wonder how someone's health could possibly swing so wildly. Speculation begins, and friends, family, and co-workers wonder if the lupus patient is trying to get out of work and responsibility, or worse, if her symptoms are "real" at all (Miles 2009; Napier 2003). Because women are generally assumed to suffer more from "psychosomatic" conditions, sometimes even physicians are slow to believe and respond to the complaints of female lupus patients. Whitehead and Williams (2001) conclude that women with lupus in the United States are doubly burdened because of gender and the diagnostic uncertainty of their condition. They argue that women are in a continual struggle "to be heard and to have their symptoms and needs taken seriously" by their physicians who should be, but often are not, well aware of the vagaries of the condition (Whitehead and Williams 2001:118).

LUPUS IN ECUADOR

The diagnosis of lupus, whether in the United States or in Ecuador, is unquestionably a "biomedical" event, one that involves interpreting and then categorizing a set of symptoms and test results into a defined illness category. Yet the ways that lupus is known, understood, and experienced in Ecuador, by doctors and patients, is influenced by local understandings and conditions. Among the conditions affecting the experience of lupus in Ecuador may be elements of what Lock and Nguyen call "local biologies" (Lock and Nguyen 2010). Local biologies assumes that culture, environment, and

biology mutually interact with one another but also that "biological and social processes are inseparably entangled over time, resulting in human biological difference that may or may not be subjectively discernible by individuals" (Lock and Nguyen 2010:90).

Given the difficulties of collecting prevalence data in the developed
world, where morbidity and mortality statistics are generally of good quality,
it should come as no great surprise that there are currently no statistics on lupus morbidity and mortality in Ecuador, although one physician estimates
that in 2007 there were twelve thousand cases of lupus in Ecuador (*El Mercurio* 2007a). Medical record keeping in Ecuador in general is quite poor, and
deaths caused by lupus are not officially reported. According to one physician I spoke with, patients who die from lupus usually die from complications
such as kidney failure or pleurisy, and their deaths are reported as stemming
from these causes and not lupus. Moreover, local doctors have cumbersome
personal record-keeping strategies, and many felt that they could not give me
an accurate estimate of their own patient loads as patients come and go frequently, doctors see patients in multiple locations (often public and private
with unreconciled record-keeping systems), and many patients see multiple
doctors. They all agreed, however, that they are seeing an increasing number of patients. Of course, this may well be because the training of physicians and diagnostic procedures are better, hence cases that would have been
missed previously are now being diagnosed.

Extrapolating from what we do know about lupus epidemiology elsewhere we can probably make a reasonable assumption that rates are on the
higher, rather than the lower, end of the scale. Evidence for this statement is
drawn primarily from prevalence studies in the United States that point to
a number of variables that are associated with higher prevalence. Many of
these are present in Ecuador. These variables include having Native American or Hispanic ethnicity (Chakravarty et al. 2007; Sacks et al. 2002; Seldin
2008; Walsh and Gilchrist 2006), living in conditions of poverty or low socioeconomic standing (Walsh and Gilchrist 2006; Ward 2001) and, because of
the high altitude, increased exposure to UV light (Walsh and Gilchrist 2006).
There has also been some discussion of the possible contribution of environmental contamination to developing lupus, and a lupus cluster has been identified (although scientifically unconfirmed) among cut-flower workers in
Colombia. Presumably because of the growth in the cut-flower industry in
Ecuador, imports of pesticides rose 2.6 times between 1992 and 2004, as did
pesticide poisonings (PAHO 2007:313). In sum, local environmental conditions such as high altitude and pollution, in likely combination with the possible greater genetic susceptibility associated with Amerindian identity and

higher rates of poverty, may contribute to higher than average rates of lupus in Ecuador.

Because of the altitude, high exposure to UV radiation is far more likely in highland Ecuador than in many other places. The majority of the women (15 out of 20, or 75%) I interviewed described some problems with facial lesions, and many women suffered with serious rashes, especially before diagnoses or during a flare. This compares with lesion rates of about 35% in the United States (Sontheimer and McCauliffe 2002). These women describe feeling embarrassed and ashamed to leave their homes when their faces are red and inflamed, and several reported that they hate to look in the mirror because they feel "ugly" or like a "monster."

Others complained of the effects of the weight gain from steroid use, which often changed the shape of their faces and their bodies. As it so often is for Andeans, weight gain tended to be concentrated on the upper body, broadening shoulders, chests, and abdomens in particular. Altogether, weight gain seemed to be differentially valued by my informants; those like Lucho, who grew up poor, saw the weight gain as a positive sign, while those more economically fortunate associated thinness with attractiveness. Moreover, weight gain, whether it is deemed attractive or unattractive, is almost always associated with good health and well-being and convincing people not to believe the "evidence" in front of them is a challenge. In a country where food insecurity is only a generation or a neighborhood away, if that, for many, being overweight continues to imply economic security and wealth.

Compared with non-Hispanic white women in the United States, Ecuadorian women may be at higher risk of serious renal disease with lupus. The literature notes Hispanic populations in the United States generally have significantly higher rates of kidney dysfunction with lupus than non-Hispanic whites and are more likely to develop lupus nephritis, inflammation of the kidneys (see Alarcón et al. 2002; Bastien et al. 2002). The reasons for this may have to do with a lack of access to quality clinical care and timely early treatment, but they are also thought to be linked to possible genetic differences among Amerindian populations (Bastien et al. 2002).[7] Both delayed care and Amerindian identity are common among Ecuadorian lupus patients, and the doctors I spoke with considered renal involvement the most serious risk for their lupus patients.

Physicians expressed concern to me about educating their patients, especially about how to take care of themselves with lupus. Their advice includes taking all medications as prescribed, not allowing oneself to become overly tired or to work too hard, staying out of the sun when possible, and carefully watching one's diet. Staying out of the sun is a recommendation that patients find difficult to follow. Cuenca is located at about 2,500 meters (about 8,400 feet) above sea level, and nights and mornings can be quite chilly. Central heating is practically unheard of, and the sun is usually the only way to warm homes. Sitting briefly in the sun to warm up is one of life's small pleasures, as are trips to the coast to go to the beach, a common and inexpensive vacation for many families. Indeed, for some, avoiding the sun is a daily challenge as they use public transportation and must stand at unsheltered bus stops, sometimes in full sun.

Aside from avoiding alfalfa supplements, which have been associated with lupus flares, there is little in the popular or scientific literature in the United States about specific dietary restrictions in relation to lupus. Mostly the advice is to eat a "healthy diet," and it is not generally believed that any particular food can provoke a flare. In contrast, doctors in Ecuador believe that diet is essential to lupus control, and they advise patients to watch their diets carefully, reduce their meat consumption, and especially avoid two highly valued special-occasion foods: guinea pig and roasted pork. Doctors reported to me that these foods simply were "very fatty" and "not healthy" for their patients. Patients were quick to pick up on dietary advice, and many patients made a point of explaining in detail how their diet changed after their diagnosis with lupus. Overall they now try to eat more vegetables, "*todo verde*" ("everything green"), as one woman called her diet, and avoid eating too many meat products. Several women unhappily mentioned that they never touched any of the "good things" anymore, especially *cuy* (guinea pig), and two women told of debilitating flares they experienced after eating *cuy*. "I had *cuy* for Mother's Day," one woman reported, "and I was sick for a week afterwards."

Curiously, guinea pig has a high protein content (20%) and lower fat content (about 7%) than many other meat products, yet it was classified with pork by doctors and patients as a potential source of ill health, because it was deemed to be "*pura grasa*" ("pure fat"; Archetti 1997:31). While pork is indeed a fatty meat (about 40% fat content), it is unclear why guinea pig is thought to be unhealthy and fatty. It is possible that Cuencanos are simply mistaken in viewing *cuy* as "fatty," but I think much more is going on here. Both *cuy* and roasted pork are generally special-occasion foods, associated with parties where dancing, drinking, and overindulgence generally rule. It could be that the "party" associations of excess in general have led both doctors and their patients to see *cuy* as a symbol of unhealthiness. Alternatively, while eating guinea pig on special occasions is an established part of middle-class life in Cuenca and even the upper classes raise and eat them, *cuy* is, nonetheless, the "peasant food *par excellence*" (Archetti 1997:31). Guinea pig originates in Indian, rather than Spanish culture, and it is most associated with rural peasant life rather than modern urban life. Given Cuencanos' ambivalent relationship with Indian culture, seeing *cuy* as unhealthy for some may be considered as a sign of modernity.

However, the idea that *cuy* can be a deleterious food is not wholly a "modern" or urban idea, and under some circumstances, Indian and peasant groups have traditionally avoided consuming guinea pig. Archetti argues that in both indigenous and mestizo populations in Ecuador, food, diet, and health have long been linked through an understanding of a diffuse humoral system of balancing "hot" and "cold" (Archetti 1997). In this system, certain illnesses or conditions (like childbirth) are thought to be either "hot" or "cold," and the remedy for them includes eating foods or drinking infusions that counterbalance the condition. In other words, "hot" illnesses are treated with "cold" foods and vice versa. Hot and cold are not thermal properties but intrinsic ones, although a concern for thermal properties of the body is important, and people do avoid too much heat or cold.

The historical origins of humoral concepts are unclear, as they appear in many places in the old and new worlds (Colson and Armellada 1983; Foster 1953). In Ecuador it is in not a comprehensive system at all, even among indigenous groups where the concepts are most fully elaborated; not all illnesses are understood to be either hot or cold, nor are all foods classified (Archetti 1997). According to Archetti, however, guinea pig is classified as the hottest meat (pork is very hot too) and therefore is counterindicated for people experiencing "hot" conditions, including menstruation and childbirth. This does not mean that *cuy* is considered unhealthy, only that one must take care when eating it if one is already in a "hot" condition.

No one I spoke with in Cuenca used the humoral categories to understand lupus or to explain the "unhealthy" properties of *cuy*. In fact, for years I have questioned people in Cuenca about humoral concepts, and very few could articulate any kind of systematic understanding of them. These ideas are associated in Ecuador most strongly with rural "traditional" households (Archetti 1997), and they have become increasingly vague and diffuse as they move from rural to urban sites. To be sure, most Cuencanos are concerned about thermal temperature, and they try not to shock the body by changing temperatures too quickly. Ice-cold drinks are generally avoided, moving from a warm room into the cold night air is thought to be harmful, and baths are best taken in the afternoon when the sun can warm the body. The phrase a "cold bath" means a severe shock, as we have seen in the previous chapter when a woman referred to her diagnosis in that way. But most Cuencanos have no clear understanding of humoral properties and how balancing them results in well-being.

So, if no one described lupus as having humoral properties, and no one described *cuy* as too hot, and if guinea pig really is not a fatty food, why then is *cuy* considered a dangerous food for lupus patients? My answer is that I believe a kind of hybridization of ideas about food and health has occurred. Cuencanos have retained the idea from the humoral system that *cuy* is "special" or distinctive (it is the hottest meat) and that it should be consumed with some care. But, they have lost the humoral rationale for the caution and substituted in its place a more "modern" understanding about the dangers of a high-fat diet. In a country where heart disease is the third cause of death, public health warnings about cholesterol and fat are fairly well understood in urban settings.

In addition to particular food restrictions, Ecuadorian doctors believe that socioeconomic status has a significant impact on options for patient care, and a patient's socioeconomic position may very well mean the difference between life and death. As one physician explained, he occasionally treats extremely indigent patients who are admitted to the hospital experiencing what he believes might well be serious lupus flares. They often cannot afford the tests that suggest a diagnosis of lupus, and they leave the hospital with no diagnosis and a minimal supply of steroids. He never sees those patients again, and he assumes they do not live very long.

The financial burdens of lupus vary widely depending on the severity of the case, the medications needed, and the patient's economic and insurance status. Only a few of my informants carried private insurance (coverage changed from year to year of the study), which usually pays up to 80% of medication costs. Those who have coverage with the IESS generally have some medications like *Plaquenil* and corticosteroids covered completely, while other more specialized medications must be purchased out-of-pocket. Patients reported a broad range of direct expenses for medications from no costs for those with mild cases and IESS coverage, to those who can easily spend several hundred dollars a month. A few spend several thousands of dollars a year for biologic therapies (in addition to other medications). Like Rosa's family, some families make significant sacrifices to pay for the needed medications, and several informants reported that relatives abroad have provided financial assistance to buy medications or pay for costly procedures and tests. Other patients reported that they do not always take all their medications at the recommended doses so that they may stretch their supply. A few expressed concern about the quality of the medications available in the IESS pharmacy and worried that the products from Brazil and India are inferior to products manufactured in Europe or North America. Because of this skepticism, they purchased their medication elsewhere, out-of-pocket.

Acutely aware of their patient's financial limitations, the doctors I spoke with expressed a good deal of frustration about the options available to them, especially with their poorer patients. They lament that they often must prescribe a medication because a patient can afford it, rather than because it is the best medication for her symptom, and sometimes patient care is compromised. Indeed, one physician reported that one of the hardest aspects of her job is that she has a limited repertoire of medications to prescribe, as many are not covered by insurance and are therefore out of reach for her patients. A patient on *Plaquenil*, steroids, and immunosuppressants (a common combination) can easily spend $300 a month on medications, a sum that far exceeds the average monthly salary of about $200.[8] Similarly, physicians also complain that because of high costs, they feel they can not order all the diagnostic tests that they would like and that they often work with less information than is ideal. Finally, doctors often have privileges at several hospitals and clinics so that they can provide patient care at a variety of cost (and quality) levels. Driving around town between their offices and several clinic sites is simply a part of their long days.

Lupus is almost entirely unknown to the general public in Ecuador and is absent from most public health discussions of disease and wellness. In fact, most of the women with lupus who I interviewed had never heard of the illness until their own diagnoses, and they had much to learn. Even after years of having lupus, some women had only the most basic understanding of what was wrong with them. Furthermore, many women also found it very difficult to explain their condition to friends and co-workers, many of whom also have only the most rudimentary understanding of biomedical terminology. Doctors told me that they try to explain lupus medically to their patients, but they are often unable to understand the "mechanisms" of their condition; one "blamed" himself for his patients' lack of knowledge, saying that he focuses too much on their emotional well-being and often neglects to educate them. Some of the patients I interviewed have very accurate biomedical knowledge, some have limited knowledge, and some, like Rosa, are unable to articulate any real explanation. These women resort to giving only very partial explanations, while others claimed to have a better-known illness such as leukemia or rheumatic fever.

Compounding the problems for the lupus sufferer in Ecuador is that any mention whatsoever of immune system dysfunction instantly conjures up images of HIV/AIDS in the minds of many. In fact, several women reported to me that they purposely did not tell other people about their condition because they were unable to answer awkward questions about its etiology. Others felt shunned by friends and neighbors who saw their condition, because it affects immune function as a "kind of AIDS," rendering the woman morally and physically threatening. AIDS is still very highly stigmatized in Ecuador as an illness that is associated primarily with homosexuality and prostitution, and local understandings of the mechanisms of AIDS transmission are often based on irrational fears of contagion through casual contact. In contrast then to the United States, where lupus is rendered "meaningless" because suffering is not seen, in Ecuador the association of lupus with HIV/AIDS conjures up fear, stigma, and moral judgment. In this case, meaninglessness might, in fact, be preferable.

CHRONIC ILLNESS SUFFERING

I discuss here very briefly some of the central themes that have emerged in the growing body of literature on chronic illness in anthropology and sociology and in popular culture as a means of framing my later discussions of lupus suffering in Ecuador. Much of the social science literature focuses on the lived experiences of individuals and offers provocative arguments for how to understand the meaning of illness. Most of the themes that I discuss only briefly here will be picked up again and described in far greater detail in later chapters.

Chronic illness ruptures everyday life, temporarily or permanently, changing the sufferer's personal expectations and their life trajectories. Chronic illness removes people from the world of the well, placing them into the undesirable world of the "un-well" or as Paul Stoller, an anthropologist who suffered from cancer, terms it, providing them membership in the "Village of the Sick" (Becker 1997; Good 1994; Sontag 1990; Stoller 2004). In this world, the accepted rules and expectations for behavior are different; consequently, meanings of the "self," or of who one "is," shift (Hawkins 1993). In the "Village of the Sick," one has bodily and emotional experiences that are unique to this world and are only vaguely understood by those outside it. Moreover, the "Village of the Sick" is characterized by the limitations placed on its residents rather than the possibilities open to them, yet it is best known for its unsettling unpredictability (Stoller 2004). Long-term plans and lifelong dreams are often abandoned or indefinitely suspended, very often replaced by a preoccupation with the difficulties of making it through the present day. It is impossible to say how long one will reside in the "Village of the Sick" or how arduous one's sojourn within it will be. Time is often suspended for the sick as the usual markers of the passage of time, such as meals and work and school routines fall away; so too can perceptions of time. Days and nights can seem endless when one is in pain, and yet large chunks of time can disappear from memory, lost in a haze of illness.

Sometimes residence in the "Village of the Sick" is openly recognized and legitimized by others who can easily note the visible bodily signs of ill health and suffering. The weight and hair loss that accompanies chemotherapy for cancer, for example, provides one signpost, as it is almost universally understood as an obvious indicator of distress, pain, and suffering. While being "marked" in this way can be frustrating, especially when the sufferer is attempting to live as "normal" a life as possible, there is comfort in having one's experiences, at a minimum, validated by others. Complaints are understandable, disability is explained and ultimately "courage" is made possible when suffering is readily recognized by others. In contrast, for those suffering from less physically obvious conditions such as chronic pain or lupus, distress often goes unrecognized, and therefore it is rendered illegitimate or may even be openly contested. How do you explain an illness that comes and goes seemingly mysteriously and leaves few visible manifestations? Indeed, if friends, co-workers, and family cannot literally "see" the suffering in obvious bodily signs, how can they be sure of its existence?

Because people with chronic conditions often do not have the energy and therefore the ability to do the same activities and fulfill the same social roles they did before they were sick, social and familial expectations are frequently left unfulfilled, and patients come face-to-face with the harsh realization that they no longer are, and perhaps never will be, the same "person" they were before the illness struck (Estroff 2001; Honkasalo 2001). Unable to be the same friend, co-worker, father, or wife that they were before they became ill, the chronically ill experience a "delegitimation" of the self (Ware 1999; see also Cohn 1999). Thrown into new circumstances that redefine and usually limit what is "possible," those who are ill question who they are and what their social roles might be. Although in the United States few would agree that we "are" only what we "do" and there is some understanding of an intrinsic quality to personhood, those with debilitating chronic illnesses do wonder if they are the same "person" if they cannot do the things that they thought defined them.

In an effort to understand how women in the United States think about these questions of illness and self, I interviewed women with lupus in Kalamazoo, Michigan, and explored numerous internet forums where lupus sufferers discuss issues of concern in their lives. What I found is that women curiously and simultaneously both reject and embrace the premise that they "are" their illness. On lupus message boards where a wide range of topics are discussed, women move easily between affectionately calling themselves and others "lupies," effectively defining themselves as their disease and openly denying that the disease does really define them. For example, one participant wrote long paragraphs describing how much lupus had negatively affected her everyday life, from devastating her finances to straining her personal relationships, but then she declared in bold capital letters at the end of her posting that "I AM NOT MY LUPUS." I also noted that women frequently used pseudonyms for their on-line communications and sometimes the names seem carefully chosen to reveal a missing identity ("NoWhere-Girl"), reaffirm a desirable identity (MelissasMom), or assert an identity that now appears threatened by the illness ("Lupieswimmer"; Miles 2009).

For many, chronic illness provokes deep moral reflection and judgment as sufferers, and sometimes their friends and family, attempt to make sense of what is happening (Cohn 1999; Nichter 1981; Throop 2010; Werner 2004). What, if any, is the message to be decoded in the illness experience, and how can meaning be deciphered from something that seems on the surface to be both arbitrary and unfair? The profundity of their bodily, social, and emotional experiences begs for some explanation, some rationalization for why this experience has come to them and what they are to make of it. Patients ask themselves questions such as "Why did this happen to me?" "Is my illness a punishment?" "Am I somehow to blame for what has happened?" Many of these questions may not have good answers, and while some may find comfort in thinking they are an active person who simply wore out, or they find solace in religion or faith that offers a moral explanation, for many others, the only "answer" is to find some way to live with ambiguity (see Morris 1991).

For women with chronic conditions, one of the most difficult adjustments concerns their inability to live up to socially constructed and very powerful moral expectations of women's nurturing and caretaking responsibilities (Miles 2009; Moss and Dyck 2002). Often too tired and too sick to cook, clean, manage a household, or work, women with chronic conditions must come to terms with how to construct a sense of self and a social identity that is not contingent on their abilities to do certain tasks, especially those associated with caring for others. The realization that they can no longer nurture others is often quite painful, and the process of reconstructing a new and different "self" is arduous but expected all the same (Charmaz 1991). Is a woman always incomplete if she cannot bear or care for children (Manderson 2010)? Can she be a good wife and mother if she cannot be counted on to get out of bed, or a good daughter if she seemingly only contributes to her parent's stress and worry?

Models of chronic illness in U.S. popular culture promote one very obvious model of self-reconstruction that is based on the premise that illness and suffering can and should be "transformative" (Morris 1991; Sontag 1990). Writing specifically about chronic pain, Morris argues that western culture has long been inspired by the Christian theme of saintly martyrdom, which depicts bodily pain as an experience that allows the sufferer to transcend the material and the mundane and to find more meaningful and spiritual understandings about the human condition). According to Morris, "We willingly, if grudgingly, accept pain that accompanies growth or achievement" (Morris 1991:20). Indeed, on internet message boards I found that women very frequently discussed how lupus had furthered their personal growth by helping them to appreciate the little things in life, brought them closer to God, or taught them patience and understanding (Miles 2009).

In Ecuador, at least as of yet, cultural models about chronic illness have not been so fully codified and popularized as they have in the United States, and there is still much uncertainty about the meanings of chronic illness. Of course, in this very globalized world there is obviously tremendous sharing between cultures, and better-off Ecuadorians are reading English-language websites to learn about their illnesses. They are no doubt also borrowing key ideas and orientations about the meaning of their experiences. Yet as we also very well know from countless studies of globalization, individuals and cultures are creative in the ways that they adopt ideas and technologies, rejecting some ideas while embracing others and in the end creating hybrid constructs that incorporate diverse and varied ideas (Appadurai 1991; Marcus 1998).

In the next chapter I focus specifically on the Ecuadorian health care system and outline and describe the various private and public options available to lupus patients. Although there is a public health system that offers care to all at variable costs, that system is frequently rejected by Ecuadorians for a variety of good and not-so-good reasons. Much like in the United States, insurance status, payment possibilities, and cost are central to how women make decisions about where and if they are able to seek health care. In Cuenca, having plentiful options, while important in the abstract, is often not that meaningful in practice.[9] Too few have the financial and social wherewithal to shop for the best medical practitioners and to consider all the possible treatment options available. Most find that they are left to make do with what they can afford or what their limited health plans offer them.

CHAPTER THREE

Health Care in Ecuador

*B*Y THE TIME ROSA WAS DIAGNOSED WITH LUPUS, she had been very sick for several months. During her illness she was hospitalized a number of times, and her family had already mistakenly been told that she had a range of serious health problems. She would sometimes get a little better after some medical intervention, a blood transfusion, or a new medication but then fall desperately ill soon after. When she was finally diagnosed with lupus, there was no sense of relief for her or her family, as is sometimes the case, since she and her children had very little idea of whether that diagnosis was, in fact, the right one, and even if it was, they did not really know what that meant. For them, the reality was that Rosa's condition was obviously deteriorating and that up to that point, biomedicine had offered very little that was truly helpful.

Even though they were given the recommendation to consult a rheumatologist who would be most able to provide care, her daughters had exhausted their faith in the medical system, which had so far seemingly failed them. More salient yet, even with Lucho's remittances from the United States, they had run out of money and could not afford to go to yet another doctor. Indeed, I received a desperate email from her daughters, one of whom, Alejandra, was studying medicine at the university, which included this paragraph:

> Today we went to the clinic with Mami again because now she has inflammation around the heart called pericarditis and she suddenly lacks blood to the heart and has tremendous pains with tachycardia. Her body trembles terribly. We give her pills which control this some, but nothing is really helping. We are going to the clinic every fifteen days for more blood. I found out that there is a lupus specialist but now I don't have faith in anyone. Today she left the clinic and she is worse.

The family is crying all the time and they are always asking me if she is going to die. They don't understand the medical terms the doctors are telling me about and what is happening to my mother.... Papi knows that Mami is sick, but he doesn't know how really sick she is. If he knew he would be calling all of the time and desperate to come home, but as he said, if he came home there would be no money and things would be even worse (Miles 2004:191–192).

After receiving this email I called the family in Ecuador and became even more agitated about their emotional and financial states. While Alejandra was calm but clearly frightened, her sister could not control her emotions, and she burst into sobs at the sound of my voice. I realized fairly quickly that they were at the limits of their abilities to cope and had no idea who to trust medically. I then contacted a good friend of mine in Cuenca, Lourdes, who hails from a very important elite family and asked her to visit Rosa and her family, assure them of financial assistance, and find out through her extensive contacts which doctor Rosa should see. Lourdes probably saved Rosa's life. When she went to their home, Lourdes found the family disillusioned and severely stressed with decision-making in the very unsure hands of then twenty-year-old Alejandra. Lourdes described Rosa to me as very deteriorated and "ancient looking." Lourdes contacted a rheumatologist on the family's behalf and took Rosa to him for a consultation. That doctor confirmed that she had lupus but rather than treating her, recommended that she see another rheumatologist known for his success in working with difficult cases. She left it in their hands to make another appointment with the recommended doctor. Yet days and then a week went by, and they did not follow through on the advice they were given. According to Lourdes, they told her that "the doctor is very expensive for people with scarce resources" but also that they had run out of hope that any doctor would really help. Although it took more than a week, Lourdes was finally able to convince both Rosa and her daughters to see the recommended rheumatologist. He was, in fact, able to help, and although it took several years, Rosa's lupus today appears to be in long-term remission.

Rosa's health care "odyssey," as her daughter describes it, is probably more dramatic than most because her lupus became very severe unusually rapidly; it drained both their emotional and financial reserves quite suddenly, and her social support network was stretched too thin with her husband and eldest child so far away in New York. In addition to being very ill, Rosa did not understand much of what doctors were saying to her, so decision-making was in the hands of her still quite young, emotionally drained, and inexperienced daughters. In many other important ways, however, her case reflects elements that are shared more commonly. Lupus can take quite a long time to diagnose, and patients can languish, or, as in Rosa's case, deteriorate, while they search for a correct diagnosis. Once a diagnosis is made, it is rarely greeted with relief, as the news is not especially good. There is no cure for lupus and no way to know for sure how the disease will progress in any given individual. The disillusionment that Rosa's daughters felt is a natural and common outcome of a lengthy and volatile process. Patients have to relearn to trust the medical professionals they encounter.

Moreover, Rosa's case poignantly points to the ways that economic considerations figure into how health care decisions are made. Rosa's daughters made calculated determinations about what to tell to whom and how this would position them vis-à-vis important resources that could be accessed for care (see Crandon-Malamud 1993). So, for example, their father was not told about the complete extent of Rosa's suffering because they figured he would be more helpful working in New York and sending money home than he would be at his ailing wife's bedside in Cuenca. Worrying him too much when there was nothing more that he could do seemed unkind and unwise. They made the opposite decision in my case. They told me every last detail when I called, no doubt in the hopes that I would be compelled by this information to help as I could. The point here, however, is that they struggled, as do so many others, to find a way to pay for the specialized care that they believed was only available in the private sector. Given the poor state of the Ecuadorian economy and its shamefully low level of investment in public health, the private care system is increasingly seen as not just the best system of choice but in some cases the only one. Indeed, despite their financial constraints, Rosa's daughters never seriously considered having Rosa enter the public hospital. To do so would indicate to all that they were either too poor to afford better or, worse, woefully indifferent about the health and care of a loved one.

THE THREE-TIER SYSTEM

There are three main sources of medical care in Cuenca: the Ecuadorian Institute for Social Security (IESS), which provides medical coverage for about 20% of the regional population; the government-funded and -managed public health clinics and hospitals (Ministry of Public Health [MPH]); and an increasingly expansive private medical system for which individuals may or may not have private medical insurance.[1] Vos et al. (2004) estimate that only a small number (around 2%) of Ecuadorians have private medical insurance, and most of these individuals are undoubtedly in the upper strata of society. Each of these three health care systems has a place in the popular consciousness of the local population, which has definite notions, accurate or not, of how these systems measure up to one another. All descriptions given here represent the systems as they were experienced by my interviewees between 2005 and 2007. In 2008 substantial changes were made to both the MPH and IESS systems. I discuss these changes in Chapter Eight.

Slightly more than half (eleven out of twenty) patients whom I interviewed for this book were subscribers to IESS and they received the majority of their medical care through that system. Because of several problems within the system discussed below, many, if not most, patients supplemented their IESS care—perhaps by seeking a test, buying a medication, or visiting a physician in the more expansive, and expensive, private sector. For those without private health insurance, the expenses incurred in the private system are fully their responsibility to pay. From time to time, some patients will also avail themselves of public health services. The remaining nine women whom I interviewed did not belong to the Social Security system; they received all their care from the private sector. Some have reasonably good private insurance, while others, often those least able to do so, pay all their expenses out-of-pocket. One young woman who had neither Social Security benefits nor private insurance complained that the stress of figuring out how to pay for her health care added to her fears and her difficulties in controlling her lupus. Forced to take off from work for illness, she was earning less at the same time that her expenses skyrocketed. She worried that she would not be able to care for her elderly mother either financially or physically. Her first comment to me in her interview was "this is a really expensive disease" and she noted that the cumulative stress she was under was "too much" for her, and it surely contributed to making her feel worse. She is not mistaken to equate inability to pay for good care with poor control of the disease. Demas and Costenbader (2009:102), for example, report that in the United States, poor access to health care may act independently to negatively influence long-term health outcomes.

IESS

The precursor to IESS, a pensioners' fund, was founded in 1928 as a mutual aid society meant to assist public and private workers with retirement and funeral expenses. Over the years the institute has expanded enormously; in 1935 it was renamed the National Institute of Social Security, and health benefits were added to their services; in 1937 employer contributions became mandatory; and in 1937 the institute became an autonomous entity, unaffiliated with any state institution. Throughout the 1960s the institute continued to grow, and it expanded its categories for eligible associates to include domestic workers, artisans, and rural peasants (IESS 2008). Indeed, as the institute has expanded, its autonomy from the state has meant that it is far more financially secure than any state ministry. Over the years IESS has been able to completely control its own growing budget, and it has even from time to time been able to loan the government money, increasing its political clout. It is considered by some to be a powerful political force due to its financial solvency.

Today, IESS provides services primarily to two different segments of the Ecuadorian population: rural *campesinos* (peasants) and urban public and private employees. *Seguro campesino* (Social Security for rural peasants) requires that the individual sign up in his or her local community, which frequently involves attending an occasional meeting on health promotion or community organizing. *Seguro campesino* has one real advantage over its urban counterpart in that it provides coverage for the entire family and not just the single worker. However, IESS does not have a good network of rural clinics such as those of the MPH, and the primary benefits of the coverage are to be found in the hospital facilities, which are usually located in urban centers such as Cuenca. In other words, only rural communities within easy commuting distance to an urban facility have an active *Seguro campesino* constituency. It should come as no surprise then that only about 11% of rural residents nationwide are members of IESS and that rates among indigenous communities, which are usually furthest from a hospital facility, are particularly low (Vos et al. 2004:9).

For more urban residents, Social Security is most often initiated by an employer for the benefit of the employee, as all registered employers are required by law to enroll their employees in *Seguro*. As might be expected, however, the law is not always enforced, and some small employers neglect to enroll and/or inform their employees of their *Seguro* rights. Since employees pay a portion of the fee (employees contribute 9% of their salaries, and employers contribute 10%), they can sometimes be easily convinced that they should remain "off the books" so that they can bring home more of their salary. In addition to medical care, IESS membership offers low-cost housing and business loans to qualifying subscribers and limited unemployment and disability benefits. In 1986 individuals were granted the right to buy into the social security system, and today a "voluntary" subscriber pays a fee ranging from 25–45 dollars a month, depending on their age. An individual can be rejected by IESS if they have a serious preexisting condition. However, doctors at IESS told me that they occasionally work with a chronically ill patient to help them to enroll in the system despite this hurdle.

Compared with private insurance, IESS is significantly less expensive for an individual, and it was never quite clear to me why more women like Rosa did not try to buy into the system as "voluntary" associates. Because Rosa brushed aside my direct questions about IESS membership, from other conversations with her I gathered that she could never quite come round to accepting the idea of "paying forward" for something as insurance requires. Given her financial constraints and consumer desires, paying for something in advance that she was not convinced she needed made little sense to her. IESS coverage pays completely for doctor visits in the clinic, hospitalization, most surgical procedures, and some medications. In general, IESS's list of approved medications is much more expansive than that of the MPH, although problems with supply are very common. In fact, many long-term lupus patients have learned on what day of the month supplies are delivered to the IESS dispensary, and they plan their pharmacy visits for those days. By the end of the month, the supplies of many of the most common medications are frequently exhausted.

According to a local physician, the IESS hospital is significantly understaffed, and in 2006 in the province of Azuay, where Cuenca is located, there were approximately two hundred thousand individuals affiliated with IESS and only sixty physicians to take care of them. Locally, problems mirror those found on the national level and according to Fretes-Ciblis et al., "The IESS provides inadequate, inequitable services," with problems that include a lengthy restructuring process, which has not resulted in greater efficiency, an overreliance on tertiary care and a consequent neglect of preventative care, poor coordination with MPH services, and a complete absence of any mechanisms to monitor and evaluate care (Fretes-Ciblis et al. 2003:309).

In Cuenca, the new *Seguro* hospital (Hospital Regional José Carrasco Arteaga) occupies a large, fairly new campus at the far eastern end of town. The two main hospital structures are imposing, solid buildings that, while not glamorous, still evoke a steady kind of confidence that modern medicine is practiced there. Years ago, when the building was under construction, a Cuencano proudly pointed to it as we drove by remarking to me on its impressive size and what an improvement it would be over its battered and deteriorating predecessor. It is viewed as a bricks-and-mortar symbol of public responsibility and of Cuenca's improving and modernizing infrastructure. The old *Seguro* hospital, a bleak, abandoned cavern that evokes only thoughts of decay and death, still sadly sits behind a rusted fence on a major thoroughfare of downtown Cuenca.

The hallways in the *Seguro* hospital are always poorly lit, casting a gloomy pallor over the morning routine. Whenever I was there, only about half of the fluorescent ceiling lights were illuminated at any given time. The grey hallways are generally noisy in the mornings, when most doctors are attending patients, and filled with activity as patients talk to family members and each other, babies cry, and lottery vendors sell their wares. Each doctor has a small private office where he or she receives patients. The offices I saw were uninvitingly bare- bones, and most have a cramped "outer" office that holds a small desk with a computer, perhaps a light board to examine x-rays, two chairs for patients to sit in, and an equally small examining room with a simple examination table. When three people crowd into the outer office, it is a tight fit. In contrast to American medical offices, where nurses and auxiliary personnel manage the patient flow from waiting room to examination room and prepare the patient to see the physicians by taking vital statistics and filling out complaint forms, in Ecuador, IESS physicians are completely responsible for all patient contact from monitoring waiting room flow, if need be, to final record keeping.

ON MOST DAYS, DAWN HAS YET TO BREAK IN CUENCA when the line starts to lengthen outside the *Seguro* hospital. Bundled up in coats and scarves against the night time chill, tired and anxious patients await the opening of the waiting room and, soon after, the appointment windows. A little before 6 a.m. the doors are opened, and the waiting patients scurry in quickly in hopes of securing a spot in the rows of hard plastic seats. The central waiting room is sparsely furnished with banks of chairs facing the front service windows, which opens at 6 a.m. Those in the front row will be first in line to be served, which means that they will probably get their first choice of physician. Regardless of health status or age, standing in line in the wee hours of the morning is the only way to make an appointment with a physician in the hospital clinic. Those too sick or too old to suffer through the wait may have a healthier family member stand in line for them; it is not unusual to see children of ten or twelve years old holding a place in line for hours. Sometimes someone can be hired to stand in line overnight. Like most queues in Ecuador, this one can be difficult to manage, and those in line must remain ever watchful, lest someone tries to subtly, or not so subtly, insert themselves in the front of the line. Vigilance is key. Some in line are visibly and audibly ill, perhaps coughing, sniffling, and mumbling their way through the wait, while others stoically hold their own counsel and their place in line. From time to time, I am told, someone faints, and the security guards call the ambulance to take them around the building to the emergency entrance.

Once the service window opens, the line moves fairly quickly, as patients make their appointments with their physician of choice. However, standing in line for hours does not guarantee an appointment for that day or any other. Physicians have only a limited number of appointment slots, and the available times for popular doctors can fill up quickly. Some doctors keep only a few morning office hours, and there is little oversight of physicians' work schedules.[2] As individual physician's calendars are filled for the day a shout goes out, "no more appointments for Dr. Gómez," for example, which is followed by audible groans of disappointment from some who remain in line. As schedules fill, the news moves through the crowd; some abandon the waiting and go home, while others persevere in the hopes of sweet-talking the woman behind the glass partition to squeeze one more appointment into a doctor's morning itinerary. It is always worth a try, and there is nothing to lose.

By 6:45 or so, most appointments have been made, and the crowd has dwindled considerably. Those with appointments have moved down the hallways to wait outside their doctor's *consultorio* (office). Others without appointments may try lingering outside the physician's office door in the hopes of grabbing a moment of her time to refill a prescription or ask a quick question. Most patients, however, simply go home to try again the next day, knowing that if they wish to be successful, they must plan to arrive even earlier. If they are really sick and can afford it, a few will bite the bullet and pay the $25 fee to see their doctor when he attends patients in his private office later in the afternoon.

Patients with appointments wait for their physicians in the banks of airport-style chairs that flank the entranceway to each office. They often pass the time talking to one another, reading the newspaper, or resting. Many are carrying large brown envelopes containing tests results and x-rays. Each waiting patient will have her *turno* (turn, appointment time) designated by the front desk; generally, *turnos* are respected, and patients are careful to keep track of who is next. While most of the time patients carefully monitor the doctor's progress through his schedule of *turnos*, sometimes a doctor is late, and the usual system of polite turn-taking breaks down. The mood turns increasingly agitated as time wears on, and a doctor has yet to arrive. The patients begin to worry that the doctor will not be able to see all the waiting patients that day. Because there is little supervision of physicians' hours, some doctors have well-deserved reputations for working just a few hours a day at IESS.

Like every other social encounter in Cuenca, class distinctions figure prominently into how patients treat one another while they negotiate turn-taking, and the freedom they feel in commanding the doctor's attention outside their designated turn. As described in Chapter Two, Cuenca has long been identified as a city with an entrenched social-class system that results in significant everyday privilege for those who are in the middle and upper classes. Social position in Cuenca is often linked to family surname, and the most important families in town have historical connections to one another that can span centuries (Brownrigg 1972; Hirschkind 1980; Miles 2004). In the 1970s, Brownrigg noted that Cuencanos were able to quickly assess and pass judgment on another's class status by such outward characteristics as clothing choice, style of personal presentation, and demeanor (Brownrigg 1972). In more recent decades, with considerable rural to urban migration and transnational migration, the sharp distinctions that were once possible are less clear, but the basic idea that some are privileged over others is as prominent as always. It plays out daily in every social encounter from forming lines at the bank to the IESS waiting room. Today subtle cues that signal social-class standing and therefore social importance can still be found in hairstyle, height, skin tone, and clothing.

While theoretically the IESS system is egalitarian and every patient has her designated turn to see the doctor, in practice the system is far more elastic and chaotic. Patients who cannot or will not stand in line in the early morning often attempt to slip in to see the doctor between legitimate *turnos*. As is to be expected, in my observations, those who attempted to get ahead of the line appear, based on clothing and hair style, to be solidly middle-class patients who have a sense of privilege over those whom they perceive to be poorer or less well connected. Poor women in *polleras*, those wrapped in well-worn shawls, those whose faces reveal a lifetime of labor, and those who are timid in the face of authority generally do not appear to attempt to circumvent the official system of *turnos*. While some privilege-seekers at least acknowledge others in line and try to charm their way into the doctor's inner office "for just a brief little moment," others literally plant themselves in front of the door so their face is the first thing the physician sees when he opens the door to call out to the next patient. I once observed a middle-class *dama* (lady) literally step in front of a woman in a *pollera* as though she simply was not there, just as Dr. Solis' door began its telltale squeak that signaled it was opening. The woman in the *pollera* could not assert herself in that situation, something the more middle-class woman was counting on. Some patients are convinced that doctors reserve some *turnos*, or scarce medications, for favored patients, but I had no direct evidence that this was true.

In addition to fending off those who have no appointments, even those with *turnos* can find themselves occasionally jockeying among themselves for access to the physician, if only for a brief consultation. During the course of the day the doctor is likely to send several patients to other parts of the hospital for tests, x-rays, or simple procedures. Often these patients return from these procedures, tests results clutched in hand, to confer with their physicians before they leave for the day. There is no order to how these returning patients are to be processed or how they should be attended to, and patients sometimes stand four or five deep just outside the physician's door anxious for a quick word. The queues for tests are no better managed, and the most chaotic doorway on the first floor of the hospital is usually the office where EKG's are performed. With no system of turns and no personnel to manage patients on a first-come, first-served basis, patients simply crowd around the door, hoping to eventually work their way to the front and then in the door.

For lupus patients the IESS experience may be more fraught with difficulty than it is for those with other conditions. There are only two doctors who regularly attend to lupus patients, and they are a study of contrasts. One has a reputation for being difficult. This physician was described to me as ill-tempered by numerous patients, and two women reported to me that he made them feel as though it was their fault that they had lupus. The other physician is Dr. Solis, who has a reputation for kindness and was described to me by more than a few patients as an "angel." A few patients told me stories of the considerable lengths that Dr. Solis went to in providing care or helping them get the most out of IESS during a health or financial emergency. Unsurprisingly, she is quite popular with patients, and predictably, they complain constantly about how difficult it is to get an appointment with her. Some regularly plan to be in line at 3 a.m.

Popular perceptions of the IESS health system vary considerably. Most people describe it in terms that place it somewhere between the negative rankings given to the MPH, and the generally accepted idea that the private system is vastly superior. Those who have *Seguro* coverage span a fairly wide swath of the population, from rural farmers and manual laborers who are at the bottom of the working classes, and in some cases are fairly impoverished, to those who work in offices and whom I would describe as more than comfortably middle class. While patients had a range of complaints about *Seguro*, including the dreadful appointment system, the sporadic availability of medications, the limited range of doctors, and their unpleasant hospital experiences, most were grateful that they had coverage and used their benefits frequently. The wealthier, however, were more likely to supplement *Seguro* benefits with private care because they had the resources to do so. All the same, better-off patients often find *Seguro* easier to navigate, as their social standing affords them a measure of privilege wherever they go. But in general, Cuencanos who have no health insurance, either private or through IESS, look upon the *Seguro* system with some envy, especially those who have chronic illnesses that require continual medical monitoring. At $25 a visit, private medical care is difficult to manage for many.

For most working-class women, even those in administrative office positions, keeping their jobs is essential not just for the income it provides but also because their employers help to pay for their medical insurance. Losing their jobs because of illness is a terrifying thought for these women, as they would lose their retirement benefits and they would have to pay their own premiums, presuming they were accepted by *Seguro* or they would be forced to seek medical care exclusively in the costly private sector. Yet the *Seguro* system often made it difficult for them to take care of their health and remain as full-time employees. Most had to ask for time off to see their doctors, and they found that working a full day after standing in the predawn lines to be terribly taxing physically and emotionally. Moreover, most working women found it impossible to time the pharmacy deliveries to be sure supplies were on hand, and they often expressed frustration and anger at having to return to the pharmacy multiple times to fill a prescription. Some women described their employers as "understanding" or at least tolerant of their needs, while other women speculated that their jobs were hanging by a thread because their employers were losing confidence in their abilities and their commitment to their jobs. More than a few women worried that the forgetfulness that often comes with lupus made them less than ideal workers anyway and that their employers had a right to be concerned about them. Most women felt that it was hard enough to keep one's job while suffering from lupus and that the *Seguro* system unnecessarily added to their stress.

THE PUBLIC HEALTH SYSTEM

Although rich in resources, including oil, as a nation Ecuador has historically been plagued by political and economic instability, high foreign-debt burdens, corruption, and poor governance, which has negatively affected its overall economic development (Fretes-Ciblis et al. 2003). More recently, in the 1980s and 1990s, when oil production faltered, the country experienced four severe recessions and two periods of serious hyperinflation, provoking dollarization in 2000. While economists seem to agree that dollarization stabilized the monetary system, locals found it also created higher prices for goods and services and attenuated their buying power. As is often the case, the economically marginal were most harshly affected by the economic fluctuations, and between 1995 and 1999, poverty in Ecuador increased from 34% to 56% (Fretes-Ciblis et al. 2003:xxxiv).

Similar to many Latin American countries, in the 1990s Ecuador embarked upon a neoliberal agenda for economic growth that, for all intents and purposes, primarily served to increase the well-documented division between the rich and the poor (Larrea 2004; Portes and Hoffman 2003). Under neoliberal ideologies, often promoted by international lending institutions such as the World Bank, attempts are made to reduce public expenditures in health care, education, and social services as they are thought to drain government coffers, limit the state's ability to pay back foreign loans and stay solvent and they reinforce state-dependent economies over "free market" options. Neoliberalism presumes that economies are stronger when there is limited market regulation, taxation, and tariffs and the government unburdened by weighty social-service obligations. In reality, however, neoliberalism has exacerbated income inequality throughout Latin America as the top income earners increased their share of the wealth while those at the bottom were left to make ends meet with a smaller share of the pie, often in the informal sector (Portes and Hoffman 2003).

To those of us who work in the Andes, neoliberalism may call forth images of the folkloric Andean phantom or *pishtaco*, a demon figure that roams the countryside late at night sucking the fat out of unwitting victims who have strayed too far from home (see Crandon-Malamud 1993; Weismantel 2001). Just like the *pishtaco*, neoliberalism attempts to drain the "fat" out of state institutions that were already too lean to begin with. While the *pishtaco* is often portrayed as "white" and therefore interpreted as representing capitalist "outsiders" ransacking the Andes of its riches, neoliberalism represents a state-sponsored project to cut its own fat. It does so quite literally, and the results are manifest first in the reduction in government investment in the public health care system and then in the bodies of its citizens.

The public health system, which in Cuenca includes a number of small clinics and a large regional hospital, is viewed by most working-class Cuencanos as the medical system of last resort. Popular opinion is that the public health system is fine for vaccinations and minor conditions, or even for emergencies that just need a quick suture, but for serious or chronic illness, one is much better off going elsewhere. Most people quite rightly believe that the MPH is overburdened and underfunded and that care is simply inadequate. For some, there is the perception that the system is really only for the very poorest, and therefore the services rendered must necessarily represent the very poorest available. For others, they simply believe that if it is government run and funded, it logically cannot be any good.

This popular perception, unfortunately, is not without some grounding in reality. Two national-level reports document the failures of the public health system to keep pace with demand and the increasing costs of providing services under generally declining economic conditions (see PAHO 2007; Vos et al. 2004). The effects of reduced government investment in health are most significant for the poor, who spend a far greater portion of their income on out-of-pocket medical expenses than do the wealthier. According to Fretes-Ciblis et al. (2003:305), citing a 1998 report, "Among the decile with the least income, health expenses represent 40 percent of income, while among the decile with the highest income, they barely surpass 5 percent of income."

Since the 1990s, the health budget of Ecuador has declined in real terms, making public health spending in that country by the early 2000s "among the lowest in Latin America" (Vos et al. 2004:1; see also Fretes-Ciblis et al. 2003). Throughout the 1990s the country faced a series of fiscal crises; not only was providing health services more difficult for the national government overall, but expenditures in health care fell in relation to other national priorities. Typical of the neoliberal policies implemented throughout Latin America in the 1990s, the Ecuadorian government reduced its commitment to health spending from 1.43% of GDP in 1985 to .55% of GDP in 1999 (PAHO 2007:4). As a result, the Ministry of Public Health (MPH) began to charge user fees for physician examinations and medications, and it has been plagued by numerous strikes by underpaid and sometimes unpaid health workers, crippling clinics and hospitals and leaving the population skeptical and wary. While hospitals remained open during strikes, clinic schedules and office visits were often disrupted for lengthy periods of time. Moreover, the Pan American Health Organization (PAHO) reported that close to 80% of the medical equipment in Ecuadorian MPH hospitals was "obsolete, only partially functional and inadequately maintained" (PAHO 2007:10). Rising drug costs have made it impossible for the MPH to keep a steady supply of medications in its hospitals and clinics and the list of available drugs is quite limited. For lupus patients, among the most commonly prescribed medications, only corticosteroids are regularly available in the MPH pharmacy.

By law the MPH provides free maternal and child health care, but other services such as physician visits and medications have sliding-scale user fees attached to them.[3] However, the system of fee collection is poorly managed and irregularly enforced, creating confusion and distrust among users who do not know when and how they will be charged (Vos et al. 2004). In Cuenca, doctor's consultations are "officially" five dollars per visit at the Vicente Moscoso Hospital; medications are usually generic and either gratis or offered at significantly lower costs than for-profit pharmacies; and hospitalization is free. However, only the most rudimentary diagnostic tests are available in the public hospital and fees for them vary widely. By 2000 there was an increase in the national budget allocation for health care but, according to one researcher, most of that increase has gone towards increasing health workers salaries and not towards improving obsolete equipment and services (Vos et al. 2004).[4]

Doctors who work with poor lupus patients in the Vicente Moscoso hospital often have to make difficult therapeutic concessions because of the patient's poverty and the inability of the public system to shoulder the excess costs for tests and medications. The most sophisticated and effective medications for lupus are simply not available from the MPH, and poor patients usually cannot afford them out-of-pocket, limiting considerably the therapeutic choices. Physicians frequently try to waive their fees for service for indigent patients or cajole labs into running tests at lower costs. They very often save the free samples that drug representatives give them to distribute to the most needy. But these are all just stop-gap measures, and they rarely work well for very long. Physicians consider none of these actions effective strategies for the long-term care required for lupus, and they cannot do any of these all the time and for all who may need it.

In an effort to address a general need for low-cost medications in the city, in 2007 the municipal government opened a network of pharmacies called *Farmasol* to supply a wider array of medications at lower costs. *Farmasol* is meant to supplement the supply of drugs available to poor residents by providing discounts of 25% to 30% and to make it easier for patients to purchase medications by locating the pharmacies in convenient commercial locations, usually near municipal markets where residents go daily to purchase food and other necessities. Customers of *Farmasol* must be able to prove their indigent status before they can avail themselves of the reduced prices (*El Mercurio* 2007b). To increase patient confidence, *Farmasol* outlets are staffed by biochemists and pharmacologists from the University of Cuenca. While theoretically a sound idea, it is unclear to me whether this service will be of much benefit to lupus patients, as none of the costlier medications for lupus, including the heavily prescribed *Plaquenal* were available in the two *Farmasol* branches that I surveyed.

Of course, not everyone has a completely negative view of the public health system, and I interviewed several doctors who work for the MPH who argue that their ability to provide care, if not medications, is often better than the capacities of IESS. According to these physicians, appointments for chronic illness patients can be made a day in advance by telephone and often, perhaps because of the poor reputation or the open wards, there is no waiting for a hospital bed should one be needed quickly. The doctors working for the MPH claim that they are as well trained as any in the city, and many of them teach at one of the local medical schools. Moreover, just like the IESS physicians, many of the doctors who work in the MPH hospital hold advanced, clinical specialty degrees, often from universities outside of Ecuador. They argue that a doctor's visit in the MPH hospital is, relatively speaking, a bargain, but they admit that there is little that they can do to defray the costs of tests and medications.

THE PRIVATE SECTOR

The private health care sector has been present in Cuenca since the founding of the city, but it has obviously flourished and significantly expanded in the last 50 years. The private options can be separated into the nonprofit sector, which includes local, national, and international foundations and institutes,[5] and the for-profit sector, including doctors' offices, clinics, and hospitals. This is by far the more prominent dimension of the private care sector, and some of the most impressive buildings in town are private hospitals and medical office suites. While estimates of the percentage of the population seeking private health services are admittedly poor, what is known is that by far the greatest financial investment occurs in the private sector. Fretes-Ciblis et al. report that private sector health care spending in Ecuador probably accounts for an astonishing 80% of "total health care expenditures," including public expenditures in the MPH (2003:303). But determining who is accessing the private system is not a simple matter, as the different health care options in Cuenca are in no way exclusive. A patient may easily meet a physician in the MPH or Social Security hospitals and then choose to continue follow-up care from time to time in that physician's private office. There is no official means of tracking what percentage of the population accesses private care exclusively, but it seems very likely that most urban residents have accessed private care of one kind or another at least on occasion.

Popular perception is that the private sector is far superior to the public system and that if the option is available (meaning, if there is any way that someone can pay for private services), it is always considered to be a better choice. Many patients choose private hospitals or clinics, especially for inpatient services and procedures, since patient rooms are private, in contrast to the crowded wards in the MPH and IESS facilities. Over the past years, several new hospitals have been built in the region, and the range of medical procedures available in the larger hospitals is now comparable to regional hospitals in the United States. For example, in the Mount Sinai Hospital in Cuenca, currently one of the two most prestigious local hospitals, organ transplants and facelifts are both readily available.

In 2006, ground was broken for a new private hospital, the first of its kind in Cuenca that is directly linked to a medical school. Affiliated with the private University of Azuay, this hospital, which has financial backing from Cuenca's largest commercial family, claims it will provide a "state-of-the-art" teaching and research facility for the region. By 2007 the Hospital Universitario del Río was still not up and running, but they were placing obviously expensive full-color glossy ads in newspapers and at the airport advertising their own private health insurance called "RíoGold." Ecuadorians often use English words in advertising (such as *Gold*) as a device to signal cosmopolitanness and technological superiority (Miles 1998a). In 2007, the photographs in the print and web ads for the hospital prominently featured blond European-looking models in well-appointed settings, leading me to believe that the ads are targeted at a primarily wealthy clientele. According to my local contacts, the hospital continues to actively seek physicians to become *socios*, or affiliated members, which includes access to a private *consultorio* in the hospital complex as well as hospital attending privileges. Becoming a *socio* of the Hospital Universitario del Río costs around $60,000, and this does not include supplying and furnishing the private office.[6]

The Hospital Universitario del Río is by no means the first hospital in town to charge physicians a significant fee for becoming officially affiliated; indeed, it is standard practice. It is, however, by far the most expensive. The evocatively named Monte Sinai Hospital, for example, which prior to the Hospital Universitario del Río was the most "advanced" and expensive hospital in town, charges physicians $50,000 to become practicing associates. Similar to Hospital Universitario del Río, the fee covers the purchase of a *consultorio* but not the equipment in it and hospital privileges.

There is some skepticism in both the professional and lay communities about the Hospital Universitario del Río. One physician I spoke to called it a "business venture" and questioned both the demand in the community for another large hospital and what the expense of becoming an associate would do to the physicians practicing medicine there. He worried that doctors burdened by such large debts (standard interest rates from Ecuadorian banks range from 14% to 16.5%) would start to make medical decisions based on billable costs rather than what was best for the patients. Recognizing that medicine has long been "business" in Cuenca, he found the lengths to which del Río had taken the "physician as entrepreneur" model to be excessive. Another Ecuadorian expressed concern to me that the whole idea of building a private teaching hospital was problematic since it represented yet another movement towards validating the private sector over the public. Cuencanos have long been proud of their public university, the University of Cuenca, and most especially of its medical school, which has always ranked above the medical school of the University of Azuay. She worried that the Hospital Universitario del Río would elevate perceptions about the University of Azuay Medical School and make it impossible for the public institution to compete for students and for prestige.

The glitzy Hospital Universitario del Río and the Monte Sinai aside, much of the private sector is not very "state of the art" but carries the singular cache of not being administered by the government. In fact, while the Monte Sinai looks very much like any regional hospital one might visit in the United States, I have also visited private hospitals that are cold, dark, ill-equipped, and altogether rather sorry looking. Patients have also reported to me that they are not always treated well in these hospitals, as, similar to elsewhere in Cuenca, social class often determines the respect one receives, even when paying for a service. Doctors make strategic decisions when consulting with their patients about which hospital to use, and the patient's ability to pay figures significantly in making the final decision about hospitalization. While all private hospitals offer private rooms, aside from this, the quality of care and the services available in the small, less expensive, and less prestigious private hospitals may be no better than one would find in the MPH hospital. Patients in most small hospitals are responsible for procuring even basic medical supplies, including any and all medications administered, syringes and bandages, and any necessary blood transfusions, as well as providing food and other amenities such as soap.

The private offices of individual physicians are as varied as the hospitals described above. Most, but not all, doctors' offices are located in large buildings associated with one or another private hospital where they frequently have privileges. Everyone in town knows the "good" medical office buildings, where it is believed the best-trained physicians practice. Often there is only one receptionist per floor who directs patients to eight or ten different doctors' offices, although sometimes a small group of three or four physicians will share a receptionist's services. There are no nurses to prescreen patients, and doctors are responsible for most of their own record keeping. Some patients come with prearranged appointments while others are attended to on a walk-in basis. Many doctors handle payment directly, accepting a patient's cash at the end of the appointment, while others have the receptionist do that task. Some physicians have private offices that are fairly unadorned—perhaps a desk, a few chairs, a computer, and an examination table, while others attempt to put their personal stamp on their working environment by decorating their offices with books, carpeting, or art work. Many doctors have teaching responsibilities at the universities, or they attend to patients in the MPH or IESS hospitals in the mornings, and they see their private patients only in the late afternoons until 6 or 7 in the evening, making for an exceedingly long day.

I was most likely to visit physicians in their private offices late in the day when they had time to talk with me at greater length. By 6 p.m. the receptionists had usually left for the day, and perhaps only a patient or two remained to be seen. I was never quite sure how to handle gaining access to a doctor, even when I had called ahead and made an appointment. Doctors generally leave their doors shut and it is sometimes difficult to figure out if they are with a patient, on the phone, or working on paperwork. Like me, most patients approach the closed doors somewhat cautiously, obviously not wanting to interrupt another's *consulta* (consultation). Patients usually quiz anyone sitting nearby about whether the doctor is in, whether he is with someone, and who is next in line.

Drug representatives, I noticed, were apparently not burdened by such scruples. Indeed, most of the time I competed for access to the physician's office with drug company representatives who trawled the offices in the late afternoon in hopes of finding physicians more readily available. Flitting from one office to another to minimize waiting times, these salespeople, invariably good-looking women in very high heels, never ask those waiting if they are queued up to see the physician. Rather, with uncanny swiftness, they manage to literally put a foot in the door long before the rest of us even notice that it is opening.

Because of the financial constraints on the public sector systems, most of the truly cutting-edge medicine in Ecuador is most easily found in the private sector. For example, the most important new therapy for lupus, biologics, has been available in private clinics for several years before the public sector was even aware of them. By late 2007 IESS claimed to have biologic therapy (*Rituximab*, FDA-approved for rheumatoid arthritis), but several physicians reported that the number of doses was so limited that only a small handful of patients could avail themselves of the treatment. Since there were no established protocols to determine who would have access to this precious and limited resource, non-IESS doctors speculated that *palanca* no doubt played a role in how biologics are distributed at IESS, infusing that system with yet another layer of privilege and exclusion. In 2007 I met one rather socially well-connected informant who received biologic therapy from IESS, but many more who were very sick who had not even heard of it.

One Cuencan physician, who was trained in Europe and is by all accounts the most technologically sophisticated rheumatologist practicing in Cuenca, is actively engaged in the international research community and has been running trials of Rituximab among his lupus patients. In contrast to trials in the United States, where the results of biologic therapy have not been all that positive on the whole, he and his patients reported excellent results.[7] Most patients require two or more injections of *Rituximab* per year at a cost of about $1,500 per injection (a real bargain compared with costs in the United States, which can run to $8,000). Most patients still continue to take some of the other front-line medications for lupus in addition to the biologics. Given all these costs and the low rates of health insurance coverage, the number of patients who can afford biologic therapy is still very limited.

CONCLUSION

Because it is home to three universities and three well-known medical schools, Cuenca is popularly understood to be a place with a surplus of good physicians who practice in a highly competitive medical marketplace.

There are close to a dozen rheumatologists in Cuenca, and some who collaborated with me on this project are probably among the best trained in the country; one regularly participates in funded research on lupus and publishes in prestigious international journals. There are state-of-the art hospitals in Cuenca, and both the MPH and the IESS hospitals are in better shape than many of their counterparts in other cities. In other words, Cuenca might be about as good as it gets in Ecuador for the average health "consumer." Yet as we have seen, significant problems remain in the delivery of health care, including poor financing on the national level, unequal access to services based on ability to pay and perceived social status, and unnecessary and burdensome bureaucratic and administrative structures that complicate what could be simple procedures. Women shared both success stories of doctors who were kind and knowledgeable and tragic stories about a system that failed them when they were most vulnerable.

In the chapters that follow I probe more deeply into individual women's experiences of lupus and the ways that having a chronic illness affects their lives and the lives of their loved ones. Throughout these chapters we will see how access and quality of care figure into their perceptions of their illness and partially frame their illness experiences. Some women are grateful for the benefits that IESS offers, while others wonder if the system is really providing them with the best of all possible options. Women with *palanca* often have impressive private care experiences (in addition, sometimes, to receiving IESS benefits), while others find IESS cumbersome and inconvenient. Indeed, in the next chapter we meet two young women who have very different experiences with the IESS health care system and see how their economic and social standing has influenced their perceptions of the care they receive.

CHAPTER FOUR

Liminality

ONE OF THE UNEXPECTED OUTCOMES OF ROSA'S LU-
pus is that her husband Lucho and I have become much better friends. He and I met over twenty years ago when I was in Ecuador for
the first time, and at the start we were somewhat wary of one another. I knew
Rosa for several weeks before I met Lucho, since he was a long-distance bus
driver and was often gone for days at a time. Before I met him, Rosa had told
me that I would surely like him because, as she explained, he had a great
sense of humor. As it turned out, he did make plenty of jokes—I just did
not find them very funny, and, worse, I was often offended by them. Lucho's
sense of humor revolved around telling what I considered to be sexist jokes
about his marital infidelity or making pointed barbs about the bad behavior
of the "rich" American tourists that he saw in his job. I was never quite sure if
his remarks were meant to make him look more masculine or me more ridic-
ulous. For the most part, his "jokes" left me very uncomfortable, and I limited my contact with him.

It took many months but eventually I came to a fuller understanding of
what motivated Lucho's verbal jousting, and I came to see that he had no
clue what to make of me in those early days. Indeed, I realized that I probably made him just as uncomfortable as he made me. In Lucho's world there is
no cultural model for how a poor man should interact in his own home with a
young, female representative of a hegemonic global force (the United States).
In his obvious discomfort around me, Lucho attempted to assert what he saw
as a strong male identity. Over the years as I have become integrated into
the family through godparent relationships and have a clearly defined status in the family, our ease with one another has improved. His jokes today
are mostly self-deprecating, and I greatly enjoy my conversations with him.
When he does tease me now, I know it is with *cariño* ("affection"), and I never

take offense. Moreover, I have learned to appreciate Lucho's hard-working nature and his dedication to his family.

When Lucho immigrated to New York we began talking on the phone periodically, and for the first time, he and I developed a relationship that was unmediated by Rosa. Moreover, in recent years as the family has been battered by health crises, Lucho and I have shared a common sense of helplessness because we were both so far away during the worst of it. We called one another more frequently when Rosa was sick to share news and to talk about what was happening, and we now have a relationship that is warm and friendly and based on shared confidences. In contrast to Lucho, however, I have been able to easily travel back and forth to Ecuador from the United States, and he counts on my periodic first-hand reports about his family. I have had to explain countless times to Lucho what I know about lupus, and we return periodically to a discussion of whether Rosa still has the disease. He grew up poor in the countryside where people were more or less healthy until they got sick, or old and sick, and died. The idea that someone could be stricken with illness in mid-life and then continue to live for decades with an illness that waxes and wanes was difficult for Lucho to fully understand.

Rosa too has difficulty with the concept of lifelong chronicity. Once she became symptom-free, she frequently made suggestions that she did not believe that she still had lupus. In fact, when I last visited her, she reported to me that her doctor had told her that since she had done so well for so long, it was likely that she never had lupus in the first place. I was really puzzled by that assertion since it seemed so clearly obvious that she had lupus and that the treatments for lupus had made her better. Why, I wondered, would her doctor say something that was impossible to verify and potentially very dangerous for Rosa, as she might assume that she has no further need for medications or medical follow-up? As it turns out, Rosa had gotten it all wrong. According to her daughter, the doctor had said only that the latest test results indicated that Rosa's lupus was currently dormant, but that she would need to continue to monitor her health. As her daughter explained to me what the doctor had really said, it occurred to me that Rosa's misinterpretation was yet another sign of her inability to really come to terms with the chronic nature of her illness. In her mind, since there is little evidence of lupus now, maybe it never was there in the first place, which, logically, means that she does not really have a chronic illness.

It is certainly understandable that chronic illness sufferers would seek to deny their condition or cling to the belief that their case would prove to be an exception to the general pattern of lifelong illness intrusions. There is a fine line between hope and delusion in chronic illness suffering; a dose of one or the other at times may be psychologically healthy and even adaptive. Obviously, delusion has more inherent risks than hope. But as I listened to Ecuadorian women and their family members speak about lupus, I could not help but notice how frequently they quizzed me about possible new medications that they heard would "cure" lupus, how often they had tried alternative therapies in search of a full and lasting reversal, or how they thought that maybe their case would be the one to defy the odds.

When I discussed the question of whether lupus patients fully accept the chronic nature of their condition, one Ecuadorian physician agreed that they often did not, but he also took some responsibility for that. "So often," he said, "our patients are traumatized by the diagnosis so we often do not discuss the chronic nature of their condition as we work to keep their spirits up." Another physician expressed some frustrations with his patients, explaining that while his poor patients were for the most part fairly compliant and seemed to accept what he told them, his middle-class patients were often difficult to work with because they were empowered just enough to doubt and question, but not enough either to afford the best treatments or to fully educate themselves. Instead, they harbored nagging doubts and worried that there was a "cure" out there somewhere but that they simply did not have access to it because they were not rich or important enough.

While I believe that some of Rosa's and Lucho's misconceptions about the lifelong nature of lupus may be attributed to their low educational levels and inability to process some of the complicated medical discourses, I also think that much more is going on. Because of the ambiguous nature of lupus suffering, the on-again, off-again dynamics of illness burdens, the lack of knowledge and ignorance of the general public about chronic illness broadly and lupus particularly, and the cynicism women feel about their abilities to access good care, Rosa and many others have never fully incorporated into their lives the concept of illness chronicity, that is, "the persistence in time of limitations and suffering" (Estroff 1993:250), and they periodically question or deny their condition. In other cases, the illness itself may not be denied, but the meaning of the illness for their lives, its chronic nature, for example, may be openly and continually questioned and contested. In other words, there may be general agreement that a woman has lupus, but what that means for her and those around her may not be agreed upon at all.

In particular, there are sometimes difficult tensions between what the woman with lupus understands lupus to mean in her life and what her family or friends understand, making the multiple meanings of "chronic" a daily life challenge. Establishing an identity as a chronic illness sufferer generally means working though a wide range of emotional and interpersonal turmoil, but it is not an ordeal that the sick generally undertake alone. The social networks and support that they rely upon on a day-to-day basis play an important role, for better or for worse, in directing the orientation of the sufferer's mind-set and her lived experiences. Sometimes the sick willingly incorporate the visions of those around them and construct their sense of self-identity in relation to the ways those around them understand the "sick" role, while others may be less obviously compliant with the models provided by friends and family.

CHRONICITY AND LIMINALITY

There is a long history in the social sciences of examining the connections between illness and identity, starting with sociologist Talcott Parsons' description of the "sick role" in western cultures (Parsons 1951). Parsons posited that being sick is a patterned social role that has a number of expectations attached to it. Among the most important, he noted, is that the authentically sick are not to blame for their condition and therefore should be exempt from social obligations during the time of illness. But they have a responsibility to seek appropriate medical care so that the illness episode, and the release from social obligations that goes with it, remains only temporary. Parsons argued that the ill may be perceived as potentially deviant when they do not do what they are supposed to do as "sick" individuals, which includes following doctor's orders and getting well in a timely fashion. When this does not happen and illness lingers too long, the sick are then perceived as manipulative or lazy, and they are suspected of using their illness as an excuse to purposely evade their social responsibilities.

According to Parsons, since society functions on the interdependence of actors, the moral question becomes, How long can others be expected to "fill in" for the sick who have left their social responsibilities incomplete? Can a society or group long support a subculture of the sick whose social-role obligations are perennially left to others to fulfill (S.J. Williams 2005)? A functionalist concerned with how societies maintain order over time, Parsons did not probe issues of self-identity directly, but his recognition that social perceptions of the sick can swing wildly from empathy to suspicion sheds light on the ways that being sick carries with it socially constructed judgments about personhood.[1]

Among the first and most important works on illness and identity is Erving Goffman's now classic but still very salient work on stigma and contested identity and the struggles of individuals to regain a sense of self-identity once it has been "spoiled" by illness or disability (Goffman 1963; see Reynolds Whyte 2009). According to Goffman, someone with a stigma, an illness, or disability, for example, can become a "discredited" person whose illness is read by others not simply as a physical malady but as something that reveals negative aspects of their identity or their "abiding characteristics" (Goffman 1963:43). The stigmatized individual then begins the relentless work of attempting to manage information about his or her stigmatizing condition and the perceptions of others. How, for example, does a person who has carefully constructed an identity of competency and self-sufficiency suddenly take on an identity as someone who is disabled and who needs accommodations and assistance from others? Are they still the same person they were before the illness struck, or have they changed in some fundamental (and often negative) way that others can easily discern? Both social identity, including social roles and position and more existential notions of the self, of who one "is," are significantly challenged by the experience of chronic illness.

Robert Murphy, an anthropologist who at age 48 slowly became paralyzed from an inoperable spinal tumor, wrote poignantly not just of how his illness led others to perceive him differently but also of how his own sense of self altered as his disability increased.

> From the time my tumor was first diagnosed through my entry into wheelchair life, I had an increasing apprehension that I had lost much more than the full use of my legs. I had also lost a part of my self. It was not just that people acted differently towards me, which they did, but rather that I felt differently towards myself. I had changed in my own mind, in my self image and in the basic conditions of my existence. It left me feeling alone and isolated ... (Murphy 1990:85).

Murphy goes on to explain that those who are disabled experience a "revolution of consciousness," a "metamorphosis" so that they no longer see themselves or their "external world" in quite the same way (Murphy 1990:87). A radical shift in reality occurs that undermines how one understands the world and his place in it. More recently, anthropologists and others have written about how suffering from a chronic illness often means periodic or continual disruption and volatility in one's life trajectory (Becker 1997; Moss and Dyck 2002) and how this affects understandings of the self. As an illness progresses or waxes and wanes, life plans shift and change along with the illness, forcing individuals to make accommodations not just in what they do or are able to accomplish on a daily basis but in how they think about their lives, their future lives, their "selves," and their social identity. Both one's present and one's future no longer appear really knowable.

Moreover, the illness experience is not uniform, and as I discussed in Chapter Two, ambiguous chronic illnesses like lupus seem to take a different toll on those who suffer from them than do more defined and well-known conditions like diabetes and hypertension (Napier 2003). As Napier writes, for lupus sufferers in the United States, there is "little or no social construction of their illness to work with or respond to, no model of suffering either to find acceptable or to reject as stigmatizing" (Napier 2003:81). Moreover, the public recognition of a condition as valid and "real," and not the sufferer's fault, contributes to the acceptance by sufferers and their loved ones of the illness and the illness label and helps them to incorporate the illness into their long-term understandings of who they are and how others see them.[2] Things may be worse for some lupus patients in Ecuador than the situation outlined by Napier, since as described in Chapter Two, lupus may not be "meaningless" for some, but rather meaningful in ways that are painfully stigmatizing.

Estroff (1993) points out that over time, the identities of sufferers of well-known and accepted medical conditions can integrate their identities with their medical condition. People with diabetes, for example, can become "diabetics," thus fusing their self-identity with their illness in ways that are easily understood by others. In contrast, illnesses that are mysterious or poorly understood or that provoke reflections about moral responsibility can strip sufferers of meaning, or worse, attribute unpleasant or undesirable meanings to them. In Goffman's terms, they move from being "discredited" to be "discreditable" persons (Goffman 1963), indicating a permanent shift in character. For example, chronic fatigue sufferers, whose condition, like lupus, fluctuates unpredictably from one day to next, frequently experience delegitimation or a "systematic disconfirmation of the experience of being ill" (Ware 1999:312). Because the cause of the syndrome remains elusive and is poorly understood, both doctors and the general public often interpret chronic fatigue syndrome as a psychosomatic condition, one that is mostly in the sufferer's head, and they wonder if the person is lazy, morally corrupt, or mentally, rather than physically, infirm (see Barker 2005).

Similarly, Jackson (2005) argues that chronic pain sufferers in the United States whose bodily suffering is invisible to others "confound the codes of morality surrounding sickness and health" (332). While pain is experienced by all of us as part of the human condition, it is generally understood that pain comes and then it goes. Crises, including health crises involving pain, are usually conceived as significant "ruptures in the order of things" that are supposed to be only temporary (Vigh 2008:8). Chronic pain suffers experience a "falling out of culture" (Hillbert 1984:375) because their symptoms defy the common cultural logic about the transient nature of pain and, importantly, most individuals' personal experiences with it. Like chronic fatigue sufferers, and some lupus patients, chronic pain sufferers are often viewed by doctors, friends, and family as possible hypochondriacs who might be making "a mountain out of a molehill" (Jackson 2005:340), as it is deemed inconceivable that someone could be in debilitating pain for no obvious reason for years on end. Again, the character of the person inside the chronically pained body is called into question.

In trying to make sense of the ways that chronic pain invades the individual life course and a person's sense of social and self-identity, Jackson (2005) and Honkasalo (1999, 2001) have both employed Victor Turner's notion of liminality (see also Becker 1997). While the experience of chronic pain certainly differs from lupus is several ways, the examples taken from this body of literature are easily brought to bear on our understandings of lupus. Both lupus and chronic pain are ambiguous conditions whose most debilitating symptoms—pain and (in the case of lupus) fatigue—cannot be seen by others. Chronic pain, argues Honkasalo (2001:325), is itself an "in-between category" since it cannot be objectively verified by physicians and therefore its presence can never truly be legitimized by medical authority. When others, including medical authority, cast doubts on the patient's authenticity as a sufferer, "patients regard themselves as liminal, being neither healthy nor legitimately ill." Harkening back to Parsons and Goffman, chronic pain sufferers and, I would argue, lupus sufferers, are "easily stigmatized," as their ambiguous status as "sick" but "not sick" opens up questions about self and social roles. They become "liminal" subjects, unable to claim a role and status in either the world of the well or the world of the sick. Moreover, even less stigmatizing illnesses like cancer can leave the sufferer in a permanent liminal place. Stoller writes that a medically designated "remission" does not signal an end to the liminality experienced by a cancer survivor. The knowledge that cancer can always come back leaves one forever just outside the borders of the "Village of the Healthy" (Stoller 2004:186).

Turner's work on rituals and liminality stems from Van Gennep's ordering of the ritual process, especially rites of passage, into three distinct stages: separation, transition, and incorporation (V. Turner 1974). Separation involves the severing of initiates from their previous status, transition concerns the transformative rituals that alter the status of the participants, and incorporation is the process of reintegrating the initiates back into the social group in their altered status. Turner labeled the transition stage the liminal period because the participants find themselves "betwixt and between" statuses. Because the ritual process has demarcated them, they are no longer quite the same as they were before the rite began, nor have they yet been fully integrated back into the group in their new identity or status. The liminal period places individuals "outside of or on the peripheries of everyday life" and provides a space and time for thinking, communicating and acting beyond the confines of established social parameters (V. Turner 1974:47).

The liminal period is also one of intense ritual activity, and it can be a moment for significant cultural creativity (Kapferer 2008:6).

Turner's work generally focuses on social (rather than individual) processes, and he describes the liminal period as a time of *communitas*, spontaneous cultural moments "from which new orientations and structures of life emerge" (Kapferer 2008:6; V. Turner 1969). Turner sees *communitas* as "anti-structure" (V. Turner 1974:46), whereby the normal rules, roles, and structures of social life are left aside, and individuals are united in a kind of "existential unity" (Kapferer 2008:6), where the limitations and strictures of established social roles are abandoned and creativity can flourish. That said, Turner also notes that the liminal period can involve rites that are potentially isolating and alienating to the individual.

Sufferers of ambiguous chronic illnesses find themselves "in and out of time" (V. Turner 1969:96) in a place, the "Village of the Sick" as Stoller would call it, that does not "belong to the prevailing social structure" (E. Turner 2008:35). What is different about the liminal experience of chronic illness from the one described for ritual activity is that the liminality of the ill is rarely an experience that is shared with one's social group, nor is it one that society generally recognizes. Hence, no feelings of shared intimacy occur, no culturally mediated experiential relationships between individuals are created, no sense of "endless power" (if only temporary) is generated (V. Turner 1969:139), and no *communitas* is formed. Moreover, the liminality of chronic illness does not easily lend itself to cultural creativity. Rather, to the contrary, ambiguous chronic illness creates a liminality that is heavily oriented towards isolation and alienation and one that sees too little promise of future reincorporation into "normalcy." Whereas ritual activity clearly ends at some point, perhaps heightening the existential and experiential value of the temporary, chronic illness does not. Even when a lupus patient feels well, like Stoller's cancer remission, she knows she is different, susceptible, and vulnerable.

PSYCHOLOGY HAS ALSO PROBED THE MEANING AND SIG-nificance of the "in-between" experience with the concept of transitional objects and spaces (Winnicott 1975). Transitional objects are most often associated with early child development and especially with the phase when a child learns the difference between "me" and "not me." Teddy bears and security blankets are stereotypical transitional objects that soothe the young infant who is coming to the cognitive realization that mother, in particular, is "not me" and therefore not always available.

Transitional objects are the physical representation of the transitional space. More broadly, transitional spaces are metaphoric, and they exist somewhere between the outer world and the inner world, although they are influenced by both. Transitional space refers mostly to temporary psychological states that have many of the same qualities as liminal spaces; they are fluid and without fixed points, and they can potentially be creative as the psychological tools for coping with change are created during them. However, while creative and comforting, transitional spaces are meant to be just that, transitional. Ideally we move progressively in and out of transitional spaces as life offers new challenges, but they are no place to stay for the long haul. The problem for chronic illness sufferers whose sense of social self is continually questioned is that they may find themselves stuck in a kind of permanent transitional space where they are neither "this or that" (healthy or sick) rather than a kind of "this or that" (wife, daughter, worker, etc.).

In Ecuador the unsettling nature of chronic illness suffering means that women often find themselves, like Rosa, grasping at opportunities to deny their conditions or, on the other hand, yearning for ways, both real and symbolic, to reintegrate themselves into a more easily understood or simply more desirable life trajectory, one that attempts to remove or mitigate the liminal status of living betwixt and between. For some, this has meant that they never fully accept the idea that lupus is lifelong, and they may episodically seek a "cure" outside of biomedicine. Several women I spoke with tried alternate therapies for lupus once they understood that biomedicine could not "cure" them. Two women spent several weeks under the care of two different traditional healers, who urged them to abruptly end their use of all pharmaceuticals. Both almost died from their experiences, and one luckily found her way to the hospital before her kidneys were irreversibly damaged. Others sought out a wide range of patent medicines that they hoped would help, if not cure, their lupus. The most common "natural" product purchased is a syrup called "BIRM," which stands for "biological immune modulator," a root extract from the plant *solanum dulcamar*, found in the symbolically potent Ecuadorian and Peruvian Amazon (see Miles 1998a, 1998b) and advertised heavily in Ecuador on television and globally via the internet. No one reported to me that it was noticeably helpful to them.

For a few, the sense of being in a liminal state was unnecessarily exacerbated because they were told by their physicians, nurses, or ill-informed friends that they would probably die within a few years of their diagnosis. Although the five-year survival rate for SLE is historically quite low, for example, in 1955 only 51% of patients survived five years, by the 1990s and the widespread use of steroids, immunosuppressants, and antimalarial drugs, global studies were reporting five-year survival rates exceeding 90% (Gladman and Urowitz 2002:1257). Yet misinformation persists. Many of the women I interviewed believed their grave prognosis early on, and they lived for years wondering if the next flare would be their last. In some cases, women suspended thinking too much about the future, since they assumed that they would not have one. As treatment for lupus improves and as local medical personnel become more familiar with the disease, fortunately it appears that fewer women are given these misguided death sentences by professionals.

Young women often seemed the ones most profoundly affected by their liminal status and most likely to struggle with and against it. Six women in my sample were diagnosed with lupus at quite young ages ranging from fourteen to twenty-one. The diagnosis has meant disruptions in schooling, resulting in one case of the student leaving school permanently before she was sixteen years old, awkward moments of teasing and false concern by classmates, the abandonment of identity-forming extracurricular activities, and sometimes the end of childhood dreams. One young woman had been a competitive swimmer with aspirations to compete internationally. She can no longer swim as it is too exhausting and the pool too cold, and she finds today that she cannot manage even easy hikes that her university classmates in tourism, some of whom were never athletic, do with ease. Her self-identity as an "athlete" was stripped from her, she told me, as she sat panting half-way up the mountainside and watched as her classmates effortlessly made the climb. Moreover, the young women with lupus sometimes described themselves as trapped in a kind of endless childhood as parents fret and worry about their health and, fearing relapses, often limit the activities of their daughters and their future possibilities. Unable to grow up with the sense of possibility that so typifies youth, they find themselves frustrated and unsure about their options.

In the case studies that follow, we meet two young urban women who were diagnosed with lupus at a fairly young age who have had to make serious adjustments to their lifestyles and life options because they have lupus. Young unmarried women are structurally more liminal in Ecuador than their older married counterparts. They usually live at home and are bound by their parents' rules and strictures at the same time that they are studying, working, and socializing in an effort to make themselves independent from their parents in one way or another. These two cases most obviously highlight the various ways that chronic illness creates ambiguities about self, life course, and life options. Can a young woman who is *sometimes* ill really think about a boundless future? Can she establish herself as a professional at work? Can she find an eligible man to marry? Should she have children? Is she free to make her own decisions or must she listen to her family or her doctor?

In their stories we will see how important family connections and relationships are but also how they are enacted in different ways. Parental relationships figure large for both Paula and Jessica as their worried parents provide much needed comfort and support and unwittingly also constrain and confine the lives and aspirations of their daughters. Parents closely monitor their ailing children, but their watchful protectiveness can sometimes feel like a vise. Paula and Jessica have struggled both with and against their parents to define the long-term meanings of chronicity and the limitations of their multiple liminal statuses. Their stories show how they seek to establish an adult identity at work and at home, in the face of the efforts to permanently infantilize them because they have a chronic condition. Like Rosa, both Paula and Jessica and their families struggle with the idea of what "chronic" means. While their families seem fully committed to the possibility of lifelong illness burdens, Jessica and Paula do not always agree with their interpretations of what that means in their day-to-day lives.

PAULA

Paula is a big woman by Ecuadorian standards, and she has a careless and offhand appearance, a clear departure from the buttoned-down, put-together look of so many women, both young and old, of her social and professional class. Paula is a lively conversationalist and comes across as a positive, optimistic, and peppy sort of person. Paula is thirty-five years old and has had lupus since she was twenty-two. In other words, most of her young adulthood, which ideally should have been spent in a relatively carefree manner enjoying friends, completing an education, and perhaps starting a family was instead spent managing a difficult and intractable chronic illness. Today she continues to live with her parents in a block of fairly new homes in an older city neighborhood. Paula's family is well off, and they have household help to cook meals and clean, they own a couple of SUVs, and the walls of their home are filled with eclectic and tasteful example of Cuencan modern art. Her father is a well-known professional, as is her mother. Paula admits that she has been lucky to keep her job in the same agency where her mother works despite some serious health failings. Paula had no complaints about the medical care she accesses through Social Security and elsewhere; she freely admits that *palanca* has surely influenced the quality of care she has received.

Paula describes herself as a fun-loving person. In the years before her diagnosis, she enjoyed parties, smoking cigarettes, going to dance clubs on the weekends, and hanging out with her friends. Before she became ill, she had finished her bachelor's degree and had a steady job and lots of friends. While her parents did not always approve of her gadabout ways, she thoroughly enjoyed herself and did not much care if she troubled her parents some.

The diagnosis of lupus came as a tremendous "blow" to her, especially since she found out about it in a most "traumatic" way. Paula had always been concerned about her weight and had tried numerous popular, quick-weight-loss strategies, none of which really worked. Undaunted, however, right before her first lupus symptoms emerged, she was on a strict diet that included placing cold pads on her back hips to "freeze the fat away." Her first symptoms included urinary tract problems that she, and her doctors, initially blamed on the "fat freezing" regimen. Soon she started experiencing swollen and painful joints, and she went from one doctor to another in an attempt to seek relief and a diagnosis. In Ecuador patients are generally responsible for picking up lab results and hand-carrying medical records from one physician to another. One evening she left a medical appointment and went straight to an art exhibition where she was to meet her friends. She had her medical files with her and placed them on the chair next to her, where they were picked up by a friend who was studying medicine. He had not noticed the name on the records and blurted out, "Who has this terrible illness lupus? People die from this!" Her mostly uninformed friend went on to explain to her that lupus patients frequently do not live beyond a few years after diagnosis. Paula was dumbstruck since neither her parents (whom she knew were talking to her doctors) nor her physicians had explained her diagnosis to her, and no one had mentioned the potentially very serious nature of her illness.

Once she was over the initial shock, her first reaction, she remembers, was a desire to completely "rebel." She plotted running away from home; "I just wanted to get in my little car and drive far away," she told me. She was angry at her parents and mistrustful of her doctors, who clearly knew things they were not telling her. She felt patronized. When it was explained to her that she would have to change her life to accommodate her chronic condition, she continued to "rebel" and refused to listen or accept the diagnosis, the death sentence from her friend, or the lifestyle changes urged by her parents. She soon found, however, that every time she went out in the evening she would become sick for weeks afterwards. Slowly, she said, she came to the realization that her body could no longer support her "rebellious" behaviors. "I was completely like a child again," she told me, "I had to listen to what others told me to do, not what I wanted to do." Paula has the passing thought every now and then that lupus is her just punishment for her rebellious youth, but she does not linger on that thought for very long.

Paula's lupus was difficult to control for almost ten years, and she suffered numerous health "crises" during that time, several of which brought her in a serious condition to the hospital. Not atypically she also experienced debilitating depression, especially when one illness complication was followed quickly by another. Her work "rhythm" became one week of work and one week home in bed. As Paula described it, "Just when one thing started to clear up, I'd get something else. . . . Even juvenile things like chicken pox were terrible for me. I had lesions everywhere!" The physical symptoms, however, also wrought emotional consequences. "First, I'd get sick, then the steroids would make me swollen, my hair would fall out, and my skin roughened. People see you as ugly, fat, and sick and that depressed me." The physical changes brought on by lupus and steroid use, Paula says, "destroyed" her psychologically. "When I looked in the mirror I saw someone ugly."

Paula's relationship with her parents, especially her mother, whom she is closest to, has been strained, as she has chafed against parental desires to control her choices and lifestyle. She fought frequently with her mother, moving between resenting her influence over her life, yet understanding the necessity of her mother's interventions, especially at work, where her good reputation helped to smooth the way for Paula's frequent illness-related absences. Ironically, as Paula herself notes, she wanted her parents to have less influence in her life at the very same time that she counted on their help and sympathy. Nevertheless, she still is not sure that they always comprehended or believed the full extent of her physical suffering, leaving her feeling angry and depressed. Paula's narrative was filled with contradictory emotions. It seemed to me that she resented being treated like a "child," yet at the same time she needed to feel the full measure of her parents' support and empathy. A difficult tightrope, I imagine, for all to walk. She told me that in her more "mature" moments she knew that her illness increased her parents' stress in part because both the illness and her moods were so unpredictable.

Paula's social and work lives also suffered as she found that her physical limitations, depressions, frequent bouts of illness, and altered lifestyle were difficult for others to understand. Since she cannot stand cigarette smoke now and she will not drink, she thinks that some in her old circle of friends now find her difficult and unlikeable. She and her long-term boyfriend separated a few years after her diagnosis because they fought all of the time about her changing needs, habits, and preferences. No longer the fun-loving party girl she once was, their relationship deteriorated. She now thinks she will avoid boyfriends altogether. In a statement that reveals her frustrations with both lupus and men, Paula cynically stated that "having lupus is a lot like having a husband, something you realize you will have to put up with for the rest of your life."

At work she found support from her mostly female co-workers but then sometimes their concern and solicitude drove her crazy. They fussed over her when she was ill and treated her, she said, as though she was a *"guaguita chiquita"* ("tiny baby") rather than an equally capable co-worker. Paula admits that she was also lucky that, for the most part, her superiors at work were kind to her, although her boss once told her that she would never move ahead at work because of her frequent absences. It is a testament to her dogged determination, as well as her privileged social status, that she was able, with the paid sponsorship of her employer, to complete a master's degree within the last few years. Even then she worried that maybe she was wasting their money, or that they would think they were wasting their money, in training her since her illness makes her future so unknowable.

At the time I met with Paula for an extended interview she was, by her own estimation, doing remarkably well. She had recently been placed in a new position at work, one that she actively pursued, which takes her daily to a remote highland region. Both her doctor and her parents worry about the physical strains of the job and cautioned her against it, but her health has improved considerably since she took that position. "I've gotten only one cold this year—which is really, really rare. Usually with a change of climate I get sick, and one thing turns into another. The doctor is always bothering me that I am abusing myself, but I show her that I am well." Whereas she once found it difficult to walk a city block, Paula now finds herself happily traversing the hilly terrain of the country on foot and comes home glowing with rosy pink cheeks. She is not sure what exactly has made the difference in her health; her father thinks her improvement might be because the altitude has increased the production of red blood cells, while her mother wonders if her recently deceased father is sending his grand-daughter his "energy" from heaven.

Paula speculates that her improved condition is due to the notorious healing properties of the mountain ranges where she works. "Everyone who works there knows this is a special place," she says. "There are things that happen there that cannot be explained." She calls it a "mysterious" place filled with "energy" and local people who are well versed in medicinal herbs. "If I feel unwell up there, someone will give me a tea, and I am better." What she does not connect directly to her remission is the biologic therapy that she was lucky enough to be offered at the Social Security Hospital earlier that year. Rather, she focuses on the therapeutic effects of her daily treks to the high country. Downplaying the curative role of this breakthrough therapy, and emphasizing her own contributions to her good health may be one way to assert a sense of personal control over her own destiny. Since her decision to take the new position was controversial in her family, and since her boss once wondered about her professional future, the seeming success of her decision to take the job is all the more sweet.

Paula's illness began at a time when she was fully enjoying her young adulthood. She still lived with her parents, as is expected in Ecuador, but she had a good deal of freedom. She had a job, her own car, good friends, a fairly serious boyfriend, and a wide-open future. Her "rebellious" personality caused plenty of friction at home, but she was young and more than willing to take some heat from her parents while enjoying her life. Her diagnosis of lupus came as a blow to her in no small part because it seemed to turn her "rebelliousness" against her. The very behaviors that she felt distinguished her independence from her parents were now the ones that made her sick and threatened her career and social relationships, thus placing her even more fully under the yoke of her parents' guidance. Moreover, her parents, she recognizes, have been crucial in helping smooth the way at her job and for seeing that she has received excellent medical care. Only her latest independent act to take the job in the country, despite parental protests, has really worked out for the best. The job has given her a real sense of accomplishment and independence as she is outside the office and away from her skeptical boss and potentially cloying co-workers.

For ten years Paula has struggled to move out of a transitional place somewhere between being fully adult and fully "child"-like. She depends on her parents for emotional support, financial security, and access to *palanca*, yet she does not want to be treated like a child who should listen to parental advice. Being ill made it impossible for her not to follow their wishes. Moreover, both she and her mother characterize her personality as "rebellious," which in the end defines her only as she stands in relation to her parents, since, in the end, her rebelliousness is actualized primarily against their rules and values. The young woman who saw herself as fun-loving, independent, capable, and maybe even rash suddenly found herself coddled and "protected," even from important information about herself, and there was little she could do about it. Finding a fully adult identity both at work and at home has proven difficult, all the more so perhaps because at 35 years old she does not imagine she will ever marry, the quintessential step that removes young women from their parents' home and fully confers adult status. It is likely, she told me, that she will stay with her parents for the rest of her life.

JESSICA

Jessica, who is thirty-one, lives in a simple home in working-class neighborhood in Cuenca with her parents and two of her younger siblings. Her mother keeps a small store at the front of the house where she makes very little money. Her father, who is quite a bit older, is now retired but takes in tailoring jobs to add to their income. They struggle financially, and their home is chilly and dark, simply furnished, and a bit worn-looking, but I always felt heartily welcomed in Jessica's home; her whole family saw my visits as something of an occasion. Her mother never let me leave without partaking of an evening snack of warmed milk and coffee, cheese, and bread, and her father always walked down the street to the busy intersection and saw me safely home in a taxi. Jessica has never gone to college but started working as a bookkeeper in the office of a mid-sized local company right out of high school. She has chin-length brown hair and soft brown eyes that reflect her malleable internal states. They quickly fill with tears when she recounts something sad and then glint with obvious pleasure when something amuses her.

Jessica's lupus began when she was twenty years old. Her lupus manifested in aching and sore joints, which came on slowly and which she ignored for a good while, and then in ugly skin lesions that turned the tip of her nose and cheeks first blazing red and then black. The skin lesions were difficult for Jessica to bear, and she felt that people were talking about her when she passed them on the street. Thinking that she had developed an allergy, she first consulted an allergist, who ultimately recommended that she see a dermatologist. The dermatologist diagnosed lupus and sent her to an internist who specialized in the disease. Jessica's lupus is fairly mild, and after five years on corticosteroids, she was slowly weaned off of all medications.

In contrast to many others, she has never been hospitalized with lupus-related complications. Despite this, she has had several other health problems over the years, and both Jessica and her mother complain bitterly about the crowded conditions of *Seguro* and the costs of medications purchased outside of that system. They question, like Rosa, the motivations of doctors. "They ought to be more caring for people with this illness," Jessica argues. "They ought to give more preference to us. Lupus affects the long and short of our lives." "There should be more understanding," adds Jessica's mother and in a stinging rebuke of doctors in general continues by saying, "They pledged to save lives, not make money." Because Jessica works full-time, she finds it "super difficult" to make and keep appointments with her doctor at *Seguro*, "They probably have a thousand people every day lining up for appointments. . . . It's impossible if you don't have *palanca*!" she laments.

From time to time, Jessica speculates about why she has lupus, and although she roughly understands the biomedical explanations for the illness, she also entertains other theories. Both she and her mother consider the possibility that her lupus was caused by the "bad blood" Jessica encountered in utero. Jessica's mother became pregnant with her just three months after giving birth to her first daughter, and she did not have a menstrual period between those pregnancies. According to her mother, the accumulated menstrual blood can be polluting to the developing fetus, and Jessica's exposure in utero may be the cause of her lupus later in life. While they have both accepted the doctor's rejection of this theory, they also both talked about it with me as though the idea still had some legs. I got the sense that Jessica's mother felt badly about becoming pregnant so soon after her previous birth but also that this conjecture serves to tie Jessica and her bodily complaints to her mother for a lifetime. They are inextricably linked to one another. When her mother was out of earshot Jessica also told me that she wondered if her lupus was triggered by the stress she experienced after she was raped by a boy when she was a teenager. Her mother is aware of the rape but does not like Jessica to discuss it.

Today Jessica continues to monitor her health, and she tries to watch her diet and her stress levels. She has chronically low iron and takes a number of different vitamin and mineral supplements. Occasionally she starts to feel achy or overly fatigued, and she will try to rest for a few days. When she and I first met she described her health condition as "delicate." She has had trouble with her gall bladder, which was ultimately removed, then she developed uterine cysts. She has a great deal of pain during her menstrual cycle and bleeds profusely every other month. On occasion she has had to leave work because the flow is too heavy for regular sanitary pads. Her doctors do not think these new symptoms are related to her dormant lupus, but both she and her mother wonder if there is not some connection. In the family, only Jessica has had significant health problems.

Having lupus has framed much of Jessica's young adult life and her relationships. Her family is a close one, and while she appreciates their concern for her welfare, she also laments the lack of privacy and space she has while living in her parents' home. The house is small, and she shares a bedroom with her younger sister. "Everyone keeps an eye on me all the time," she reports. "I don't have the luxury to scream or get mad or cry about anything because everyone is always watching me . . . everything that I do, or don't do, how I walk, how I eat, how I sleep. Everything! Everyone is afraid I'll get sick again." For example, Jessica worries that if she groans or cries at night from menstrual cramps that she will wake her sister and set her to worrying. "She suffers too. The other day I woke screaming with cramps and I frightened her! If I feel bad, everyone feels bad," says Jessica with some resignation.

Since her illness Jessica has had little success with boyfriends, most of whom "run away," she says, as soon as they find out she has long-term health concerns. Jessica would like nothing more than to start her own family, but she has now given up on finding a husband, and, much to her mother's dismay, she has considered having a child on her own. "I know it is selfish," says Jessica, "to want to bring a child into the world who will suffer without a father, . . . but the doctors say they think I could carry a child. And I want a child. I want to be like other women and have the pleasure of holding my own baby." Jessica has also considered adoption, but single women are not eligible to adopt in Ecuador, removing that possibility.

Although Jessica's mother has spoken to the doctors who have assured her that Jessica is healthy enough to have a successful pregnancy, she refuses to believe them and is deeply concerned about the effects a pregnancy will have on her daughter's long-term health as well as her social standing. Unwed pregnancy is seriously frowned upon. Her mother worries that she will be left to care for both a sick daughter and her infant child if Jessica were to become debilitated. She is also deeply troubled by Jessica's stated objective to find a man to impregnate her (Jessica cannot afford artificial insemination) and wonders what kind of man would father a baby so carelessly and then stake no claim to the child. Jessica's talk of babies deeply troubles her mother, who describes her own life, one primarily driven by concern for her children, as one of "constant suffering," and she often has her own health problems, which she asserts are mainly due to all the worrying she has as a mother. Indeed, even though Jessica's lupus is under excellent control and she considers it a minor difficulty, she still has the unwanted ability, simply by living her life the way she wants, to put her mother in her bed sick with worry. While it is very probable that Jessica's mother would have strong objections to her plan to have a child out of wedlock whether she had lupus or not, Jessica believes lupus has made her unmarriageable and also given her mother free reign to comment upon and surveil every aspect of her daughter's life.

In describing her life choices and options, both Jessica and her mother employ a number of terms that reinforce the notion that Jessica is living a liminal sort of life. For example, in explaining why she wants a baby, Jessica argues that she wants to be "a woman" (as though she currently is not fully adult) and to have a "complete life," implying that her current life at home with her parents is somehow "incomplete." Her mother, for her part, understands her daughter's "desperation" to have a child but adds that she "won't be the first failure . . . there are other women who never marry and have children."[3] In this estimation, Jessica emerges as a kind of failed nonwoman with an incomplete life or perhaps as a grown child whom everyone monitors and watches and always has to "keep an eye" on.

While her mother wishes her to simply accept her fate, admit that she is different, and find a peaceful and content life at home without children, Jessica struggles against this idea, even though her resistance causes her mother, whom she calls her best friend, untold sleepless nights. Moreover, she and her mother have varying interpretations of what her lupus chronicity means. Jessica thinks she is strong enough to bear and raise a child, and her mother does not. Jessica also agrees with her physician who advised her that the best thing she could do for her health was alleviate stress, and he recommended that she regularly go out with friends and have fun. Her mother is not so keen on this idea either, as she would prefer Jessica stay home where she can keep an eye on her. Proper young women do not go out at night meeting God knows who.

When I last visited Jessica, her reproductive health problems had improved, but she had given up the idea of having a child. In the end, she could not bring herself to have the casual sexual relationship that her plan required. She had in fact taken her doctor's advice and found a good friend with whom she went out every Friday night. Sometimes they just had coffee and ice cream and talked for hours, and other times they went dancing. While her parents did not approve of her Friday night excursions, she and her girlfriend continued to go regularly and Jessica loved her nights out. She and her friend could "talk about everything," and Jessica felt truly understood by her. Tragically, her friend and one of her two children were killed suddenly from carbon monoxide poisoning from a malfunctioning space heater. Grief stricken, Jessica finds herself right back where she was before, depressed, and with her overly watchful family still acting as the central focus of her social life.

TROUBLING DUALISMS

A concern for liminality appears in multiple ways in Paula's and Jessica's narratives as they struggle with their negotiated statuses of sick/not sick or adult/child, among others. Both find themselves contesting the limited opportunities their in-between statuses confer and the cloying and annoying concern that sometimes seems to come with them. As Paula's story indicates, however, there is an inherent problem with dismissing the label of "sick" entirely. Can one really expect to harness social support when needed—loving concern, time off from work, and badly needed assistance—and then expect it to disappear quietly when the circumstances change and caring looks and feels like a straightjacket? Both women have family members who persist in defining them as "sick," no doubt out of concern but also as a means to control their activities. Both women also insist that they are "not sick" or perhaps "well enough" and therefore should be free to make decisions about their own lives.

What makes Paula's and Jessica's concerns so poignant is that the usual liminality associated with chronic illness is further compounded by the inherent liminality of their life-cycle position. In other words, chronic illness creates its own kind of liminality that is then further exacerbated by the structural liminality of being a young, unmarried woman. Both young women find that aspects of their childhoods have been extended; they are treated like children by their families and co-workers who feel free to claim a kind of paternal authority over them. Without having experienced the obvious markers of adulthood such as marriage or childbearing and having suffered through infantalizing disability while resident in their parents' homes, they find that they are unable to fully shake their childhood roles. For Paula this has meant that she continues, at least to some degree, to fight the designation of "rebellious child," while for Jessica it means that both her personal life and her everyday behaviors are closely monitored by her parents, who have never abandoned their roles as vigilant caretakers. Because she has been sick, Jessica will always be vulnerable in her mother's eyes, and she must be carefully surveilled even after years of relative good health.

Both Jessica and Paula have actively asserted their adult decision-making potential; Paula took a job her parents did not approve of, and Jessica has seriously contemplated having a child. Paula's decision was the only one actualized, since in the end, Jessica was never able to take the steps to fulfill her desire. Mostly, Jessica and Paula aspire to very "everyday" goals, a good job, motherhood, independent decision making, but as chronic illness sufferers embedded in families, they have come face to face with an "everyday" that is framed by their loved ones in very limiting and cautionary ways.

The past decade for Paula and Jessica has been filled with struggles over authority, who has "authoritative knowledge" and who "knows" what about their bodies. Sullivan (1986) argues that because the physician primarily decodes disease in the body, he assumes the role of the "knower" who, with his scientific skills, is able to "see" inside the body. The patient is, in contrast, the "known," whose own knowledge of bodily processes and experiences is devalued in the face of the scientific authority.[4] This idea resonates as well with the literature on women's reproduction, which argues that tensions exist, especially during birth, as to who has "authoritative knowledge" about what is happening, the physician or the birthing woman (see Browner 1996; Davis-Floyd 1996). Medical authority and authoritative knowledge are never monolithic, however, and Emily Martin, for example, describes how some birthing women can covertly and overtly resist it by refusing to go to the hospital too early or choosing a home birth (Martin 2001).

Given their liminal position as not-quite-fully adult, Paula and Jessica have had to wrestle not only with medical authority and knowledge claims but also with parental ones. Paula's parents withheld information from her about lupus; no doubt she speculates because they wanted to protect her, but it nonetheless rankled, and she rebelled both against them and the medical authority she saw them embodying. Their "knowledge" and their collusion in withholding it from her became a source of confusion and ultimately betrayal. Resisting them, and their knowledge, has become an integral part of Paula's expression of self-identity. Recall too that Paula nearly forgets to mention the biologic therapy she received, and instead she credits her significant health improvements to the "magical" and natural environment of the high mountains. She believes that the fresh air and exercise have helped, but she also points out the far less tangible "mysteries of the mountains" and the wisdom of the country people who live there, for her altered state. She is more than happy to point out that the defiant decision to work there, in spite of her parents' strong objections, was wholly her own.

In Jessica's case, medical authority and maternal authority are in conflict with one another, and Jessica and her mother argue about who has authoritative knowledge of her body. Jessica has in fact tried to harness the authority of medicine in her efforts to convince her mother that she is healthy enough to have a baby without serious consequences. She has visited physicians, they have run tests, and she has brought her mother to the doctor's office, where she was declared healthy enough to carry a child to term. Her mother is unmoved by the medical evidence. She claims a different kind of knowledge, one born of intimacy and motherly concern, and no test result will change her understanding that a pregnancy would debilitate her daughter and create untold burdens on both of them. In the end, Jessica lost the contest, and despite the backing of medical authority and knowledge, she could not get past the obstacles presented by her mother. Where she did succeed, at least for a while, was in filling the doctor's "prescription" that she have more fun. Armed with her doctor's explicit recommendation, Jessica happily medicalized her stress, confronted her mother's displeasure, and went out with her friend.

What Paula's, Jessica's, and Rosa's cases show us is that in the face of liminality, the authority of biomedicine to be the "knower" is not at all universally accepted and that women and their family members sometimes accept medical authority and sometimes reject it, usually in consonance with their own agendas and motivations. Paula's parents call on biomedical knowledge to reign in Paula's behavior, pushing her to contest it by crediting ancient wisdom for her remission. In her case, only she, and not her doctors or her parents, knew what was best for her. In contrast, Jessica's mother relies on her own knowledge of Jessica's body to steer her decision making. She watches her daughter closely, knows her everyday bodily distresses, and she assesses Jessica's social and emotional life. She has come to her own decision about whether Jessica is "healthy" enough to have a child and whether the social and physical consequences of it will be bearable. For her part, Jessica weighs both sets of knowledge very carefully. While she seeks medical authority to counter her mother's protestations, in the end, her mother's knowledge prevailed.

Although Jessica's and Paula's structural liminality makes their knowledge contestations more obvious, their cases should not be read as implying that only youthful sufferers of lupus experience liminality or contest authority. I think that would not be a very accurate understanding of the effects of chronic illness. The sick/not-sick "village," borrowing from Stoller's terminology, is a place where all lupus patients regularly find themselves. It is a place that is, for most, disturbing and insecure. Rosa, as I have argued, has most certainly struggled with accepting chronicity. She so dislikes the liminality created by being chronically ill that she has now claimed the "not sick" identity wholly and completely. She would much rather spend her husband's remittances on something for her new house than on health insurance. For his part, her husband is consistently confused about whether, if Rosa feels healthy, she can in fact be "sick." Both he and Rosa look to Cecilia's case and the evidence is confusing. If lupus can kill a young person, how can Rosa continue to live with it?

In the next chapter, which focuses on loss, I consider the ways that women talk about the losses that have occurred in their lives since they fell ill. As we have seen in this chapter, however, there is a fine line between liminality and loss, and I urge the reader to see how these themes are connected rather than to view them as distinct sequelae. The liminal status of Paula and Jessica as adults, but incomplete ones, has led to a series of losses, including work opportunities, boyfriends, marriage, and motherhood. Similarly, the losses that we see expressed in the next chapter by married women have elements of liminality in them as well. One woman, for example, finds that her fragmented memory and intractable illness has put her in a liminal space where she has no past and no obvious future, while the other, who wants to do so much more than she is physically able, finds living in the interstices of sick and well to be incredibly frustrating. She yearns for a cure that will transport her out of her current betwixt-and-between status.

A view of Cuenca's historical architecture from the Central Plaza

The Social Security (IESS) Hospital in Cuenca (Hospital Regional José Carrasco Arteaga)

The Ministry of Health Hospital in Cuenca (Hospital Regional Vicente Corral Moscoso)

The upscale private hospital and office pavilion Consultorios Monte Sinai

Ongoing construction of the private Hospital Universitario del Río (photo from 2007)

The affordable private clinic Centro Quirúrgico Metropolitano, where Rosa was a patient

A main walkway in the municipal cemetery of Cuenca

The crypts where bodies are housed for up to five years

The glass-fronted entranceway of the Centro Reumatólogo Andar in Ibarra, Ecuador

The water-therapy baths installed in the Centro Reumatólogo Andar

CHAPTER FIVE

Loss

*B*Y 2004 ROSA'S HEALTH HAD STABILIZED, AND SHE was feeling better physically and psychologically. She was no longer "afraid of everything" and "living inside her own head." She was also relieved to be spending less money on doctor's visits and medications. Finally, she could begin saving for other things. Her family life had returned to normal as well: Lucho was still in New York working; her son and two youngest daughters were back in school full time; and her eldest daughter, who was so crucial to navigating the medical system, had moved to Quito where she was completing a medical internship. In early August when school resumed after vacations, Rosa returned to spending her days tending her small store. The store was a few blocks from their rented home, and she sold basic food items, treats for school children, and beer for the workers who congregated at the nearby bus station. The store was located on a very busy street, and there was a great deal of competition, including a new, full-service gas station with a small minimarket. While the store was not very profitable, it did get her out of the house for the day, which everyone thought was a good idea. She talked to neighbors who wandered by, chatted with customers, and watched the traffic on the busy street.

After years of appearing withdrawn, Rosa's personality was reemerging and she started to take pleasure in her family again. She was especially proud of her youngest daughter, Cecilia, who was sixteen and in high school. Despite the family's humble background and "Indian" surname, Cecilia had matriculated into the premier public high school, and she was popular with students and teachers (see Miles 2004). Rosa indulged her by buying her fashionable clothes so that she would continue to fit in. A few weeks after school started, however, Cecilia began to feel tired much of the time; her feet and ankles swelled; and a rash emerged on her legs, arms, and face. She was very quickly diagnosed with lupus. The doctor started her on an aggressive treatment regimen, including a high dose of prednisone, a corticosteroid, and *Plaquenil*, and she was advised to watch her diet. The family was shocked that someone so young could have lupus, but Rosa's continued good health buoyed their hopes that Cecilia too would do well in the long run.

Unfortunately over the next months Cecilia's lupus proved difficult to control, and she continued to have major problems with inflammation, tenderness, and rashes on her legs, hands, and face. She also developed the "moon-faced" swelling of her lower jawline that is typical of steroid use. Although she was popular and had good friends, she felt uncomfortable at school where her classmates continually asked questions about why her face suddenly was red, splotchy, and distorted or how she had gained so much undesirable weight. Some of these questions were not altogether well-meaning. At sixteen years old, these kinds of comments can be devastating to an adolescent's self-esteem, and Cecilia, who suddenly felt ugly and awkward, became depressed.

Her biology teacher, who had some training in medicine, took an interest in her case and consulted with her periodically about how she was doing. One day he suggested to her that perhaps she had developed Cushing's Syndrome, an endocrine disorder caused by high doses of corticoid steroids. He showed her some pictures in a textbook of Cushing's Syndrome, which included faces horrifically distorted by swelling around the jaw and neck, unsightly facial hair, and ugly purple spotting. According to her sister, Cecilia was devastated by the suggestion that she might have Cushing's Syndrome and, worse yet, confused about what she should do about it. She was in a terrible predicament. If her teacher was right, the life-saving treatment for her lupus created a condition that she found impossible to live with: The very thing that made her lupus better, prednisone, made her social life miserable.

Whether her teacher provided her with a solution to her problem or only presented the probable cause as he saw it, is not clear, but what Cecilia took away from their conversation was that if she did indeed have Cushing's Syndrome, she could control it herself by reducing her use of steroids. Moreover, her teacher also mistakenly suggested to her that the swelling was a kind of edema, which was affected by how much she drank. The more liquids she consumed, the worse the swelling would be. The solution to this was, obviously, to drink less. With this bad advice in hand, unbeknownst to her family, Cecilia quietly stopped taking the steroids and started limiting the fluids she drank. No one is exactly sure how long she went without taking her medications.

In early November, Cuenca celebrates the founding of the city with several festive days of parades, fireworks, and concerts. Children have a few days off from school, many businesses close, and there are numerous civic events.

Like most young people, Cecilia spent the holiday with a group of her friends outdoors in the sunny city center, watching parades and performances and eating street foods. That night when she came home she felt quite ill. By the next evening, she had the first of a series of frightening convulsions. She was rushed to the hospital, where they determined that her kidneys were failing. She was put on dialysis and given steroids and multiple chemotherapies. But the damage was done. Cecilia never got better, and she never went home again. In early January she died from lupus nephritis. Years later her physician told me privately that he had never seen a case of lupus become so life-threatening so quickly. I do not think he knew that Cecilia had, on her own, altered her treatment regimen.

Rosa was devastated by Cecilia's death, and the family was haunted by grief and guilt. Cecilia's death seriously disrupted the well-understood continuities of life, as mothers are not supposed to outlive their daughters, especially when they both suffer from the same illness. How could this family, which understood lupus so personally, have suffered such a devastating blow? When I visited the family six months after Cecilia's death, Rosa was still deeply in mourning. Her tearful and rambling conversations with me wandered freely over the events of Cecilia's death and the various actors whom she imagined were somehow to blame for what happened, or whose behavior contributed to, rather than alleviated, her grief. In addition to the schoolteacher, who was singled out for blame, Rosa was unhappy with her physician, and she wondered if he had really tried hard enough to save Cecilia. Years later, when she still could not find a physician she liked as much as him, she recanted this opinion. Rosa complained bitterly about the hospital where Cecilia spent her last weeks and how the staff hounded her for payment of bills even as her daughter lay dying, and she denounced friends and relatives for not being more forthcoming with financial assistance.

While Rosa's life had never been easy as she grew up poor in the countryside, certainly in the twenty years that I have known her, she and her family have made steady economic progress, much of that due to the migration of her son and husband to the United States. When I first met the family, they lived in a tenement in the center of town; five children and two adults shared a two-room "apartment" with a communal sink and toilet in the courtyard and a paid shower down the street. By the time Cecilia was in high school, they were renting the bottom floor of a house with three large bedrooms, a private bath, and a small garden and patio to hang laundry. Rosa had spent freely in the early years of Lucho's migration, and her kitchen was now well equipped with a new stove, refrigerator, and microwave; the kids had a computer to do schoolwork; and they had a new Chevy SUV parked outside.[1] The children were all doing well in school, and the oldest ones were even pursuing college degrees. Not bad for a woman with only a third-grade education and minimal literacy. Cecilia's death suddenly turned their sense of progress and improvement upside down.

In the previous chapter I explored how young women understand their lupus experience and the effect that a chronic illness has on their understanding of their life course. Because of lupus, neither Jessica nor Paula married, and both women therefore found themselves desperately trying to establish an identity that is fully and completely adult, without assuming the roles of wife and mother that are most associated with Ecuadorian womanhood. Both women find themselves in an uneasy place where "sick/not sick" means the prolongation of parental dependency, making them also "not-quite-adult." We learned from Jessica's story that motherhood is a central component of Ecuadorian conceptions of adult femininity and that women who never achieve marriage and motherhood (and preferably in that order) risk being seen as a kind of "failure."

In this chapter I explore the ideas of contemporary feminine identity even more closely and consider the multiple ways that chronic illness further challenges gender-role fulfillment and identity. While the loss that Rosa experienced because of lupus is tragic and obvious, the losses experienced by most women are sometimes less obvious and more a matter of degree. So, for example, for some women lupus has meant that they cannot be the kind of mother or wife they wish they could be, as illness stripped them of their abilities to fulfill these roles as completely as they would like. Women describe losing their jobs because of lupus, their good looks, their ability to parent fully, their established respectability and reputation among friends and family, their independence from their parents and, sometimes, their husbands and homes.

Like women everywhere, the middle- and working-class Ecuadorian women in my predominantly urban sample live complicated lives filled with contradictions and frustrations. Although young women are taught that marriage and a family signify adult "womanly" fulfillment, they are also increasingly encouraged by their families to become educated so that they may be better qualified for more lucrative and stable employment in the formal sector (Miles 2000). In fact, I found that families who migrated from rural to urban areas sometimes privileged their daughters' educations over their sons' since they assumed their sons could always find a job while their daughters needed professional training so that they could "defend themselves" in life (Miles 2004). When parents say they want their daughters to be able to "defend themselves," they mean that they want them to be well enough prepared to enter the workforce so that they can, if need be, support themselves.

Yet even though many women spend much of their adult lives working, most Ecuadorian women are rarely fully independent.[2] As a rule, they continue to live with their parents until marriage, often giving their parents a significant part of their paychecks for household expenses and living under parental rules and expectations. Most often this is a relatively agreeable arrangement, and neither the daughter nor the parents would have it any other way. However, sometimes, as we saw with Paula, the relationship can be more contentious, because daughters and their parents have competing visions of the young woman's freedom of choice. It is not uncommon for parents and grown daughters to squabble over curfews, time spent away from home, and the suitability of friends and, more to the point, boyfriends. Once women are married, they usually establish their own home. If they continue to work, their incomes generally go to help maintain the household and save for their children's futures. Depending on the marriage partner, women have varying degrees of financial and personal freedom and responsibility after marriage, but in general, the focus turns squarely on working for the family unit.

The women in my sample for the most part represent this movement towards greater female urban employment. They were in school preparing for a career, currently working at a job, or very unhappy that their illness would not allow them to do either. Only one woman of the twenty I interviewed had never seriously contemplated working outside the home. Indeed, while the cultural "ideal" Ecuadorian family might still aspire to have the wife and mother stay home to raise children, the economic reality is that it increasingly takes two incomes just to make ends meet. Many urban women in Cuenca today expect that they will work outside the home for much of their lives, sometimes moving in and out of the workforce during their peak childbearing years, and they have added contributing to (or in some cases maintaining) the family's finances to the long list of their care-taking responsibilities. So, while there is much expected of women in Ecuador's modernizing urban contexts, there is, equally, much to lose when chronic illness strikes. Women ought to be good daughters, excellent mothers and wives, and steady employees, and while they need not make it look effortless, they ideally should perform their numerous responsibilities with a measure of self-sacrifice.

LOSS

There is a rich literature in Latin America on the connections between women's social roles and their subjective experiences of illness and distress and much of it centers on the concept of "loss" as central to understanding both women's psychological states and their physical complaints. Most of the time, however, that literature examines the *loss-illness* connection in a singular direction, focusing on the ways that social stress is exacerbated by poverty and patriarchy and how this creates personal, financial, and emotional loss that leads to women's experiences of illness (see Houghton and Boersma 1988; Schoenfeld and Juarbe 2005).

For example, Finkler writes that poor women in Mexico City, a rapidly modernizing and changing megalopolis, frequently suffer from complaints that she attributes to "life's lesions." Life's lesions describes the cumulative health effects on the individual of poverty and economic and social exclusion. Finkler writes that "life's lesions" happen when "the cracks that occur in the broader social system resonate with our daily experience and the fault lines in our lives . . ." (Finkler 1994: 17). Poor and working-class women in particular often cannot control the circumstances of their hardscrabble lives, creating "unreconcilable contradictions" between what life is, including their relationships with others, and what they believe life ought to be. In short, the disappointments of a life unfulfilled lead to physical and emotional suffering (Finkler 1994). Finkler is careful to describe life's lesions as historically and culturally situated, which means that what causes them and how they are expressed will vary, but they are the result of stressful social conditions that shift established economic and moral relationships between individuals, often leaving poor migrant women more, rather than less, vulnerable. When women's expectations for their lives are torn asunder by economic and personal disappointments beyond their control, when they are good women in an increasingly harsh world, they often experience diffuse but debilitating bodily pain and sickness.

Similarly, anthropologists working in the Andes have noted that women are deeply embedded in family and social relationships and that fissures and stresses in those relationships, especially under conditions of economic hardship, contribute to the subjective experience of illness. For example, Tousignant reports that among rural Ecuadorian women, unsatisfactory social relationships can lead to the illness *pena* characterized by depression, tiredness and weakness (Tousignant 1984 and 1989). In the Andes, satisfactory interpersonal relationships are often based on ideas of mutual reciprocity where individuals, especially within families, share responsibilities as well as resources. When a husband profligately spends money in drink, a daughter-in-law refuses to help out at home, or a son will not share his earnings, women's disappointments in their social relationships can create emotional and physical distress. In this case, disappointment in others literally makes women sick. In contrast, *nervios* (nerves), another diffuse physical condition affecting women, often occurs in those who find themselves unable to fulfill their own gender-role expectations fully (Finerman 1989). When women are no longer needed as caretakers or when their social worlds diminish and their connections to others erode, women's disappointment in the loss of social integration can lead to physical infirmity. Here, disappointment in one-self and one's inability to care for and protect others becomes the "patholog-ical" agent.

In both cases, a direct connection is made between women's social and emotional fulfillment, expressed through the performance of reciprocal ties with others, and their physical complaints. In other words, "loss" experienced in interpersonal relationships can lead to emotional disruption, which can trigger physical distress. Darghouth et al. (2006) and Anderson (2000) have noted the connections between physical well-being and a perceived sense of order and control among the poor in urban and semiurban Peru. Family conflicts, for example, are frequently provoked and exacerbated by larger social inequalities (of class, gender, or ethnicity), and they contribute to a woman's sense of a loss of control over her life. As urban families are stressed by economic hardship, reciprocity diminishes, social ties are weakened, and the losses caused by "social dislocations" and unequal social relationships become inscribed on women's bodies in multiple ways. They create a "loss-illness" connection that is manifest in a wide range of culturally salient "stress-related" illnesses (see also Houghton and Boersma 1988; Tapias 2006).

While these arguments are quite compelling, especially in their power to lay bare the precarious lives of poor women, in discussing the somaticization of women's psychological conditions in this fashion we run the risk of interpreting them in a fundamentally dichotomous way that sees mind and body as distinct entities. Despite clearly influencing one another, as long as they are juxtaposed and ordered in a causal lineal fashion (e.g., that loss creates illness), mind and body remain conceptually discrete (see Ots 1990). This distinction, however, may be more apparent than real. Indeed, biomedical research reveals that the influences of the mind and the body are complex and multidirectional; the boundaries between the emotional and the physical are difficult to parse (see Webster Marketon and Glaser 2008).[3] Stress can be simultaneously physical and emotional, confounding how we think about causality. We know that stress changes the way the immune system functions; we know that chronic illness causes stress. What is not at all clear, however, is where one (illness) begins and the other (stress) ends. Moreover, as the cases presented in this chapter will demonstrate, the lived experience of chronic illness reveals that women express the loss-illness connection in a more synthesized way. Women's narratives move seamlessly from loss to illness to loss again; separating one from another, and assigning absolute directionality, is nearly impossible.

For chronically ill women, the losses they experience around their illnesses can be financial and material, such as the loss of a job or standard of living, but they can also be less tangible. Women frequently mention the loss of a sense of "normalcy" in various aspects of their lives. For example, as we have seen, women like Jessica, whose bodily complaints render it difficult or impossible to have or care for children, grieve the loss of "normal" femininity and may consider themselves "incomplete women" because of their reproductive difficulties (Becker 1997; Manderson 2010). Contemporary women's understandings of a "complete" life vary in the small details from woman to woman, but they are also infused with larger urban Ecuadorian cultural understandings of femininity, family, and morality that unite them in vital ways.

Women also struggle over the loss of a sense of control over their life-course as illness renders the future unpredictable and insecure (Moss and Dyck 2002). On a day-to-day basis, women cannot be sure how much energy they will have from one moment to the next. Over time, women usually learn to monitor and prioritize their activities and mete out their energy so that they can accomplish at least some of what they want to do. Because of the multiple challenges to carrying on a "normal" life, many seriously chronically ill patients also find it hard to keep up their relationships with others, including friends and family. Over time, friendships diminish as both common interests and energy fade, further isolating the sick woman (see Charmaz 1991).

In writing about the "social course" of chronic fatigue syndrome in the United States, Ware describes the inability of many chronic illness sufferers to complete their myriad social functions as workers, parents, and spouses and the sense of "role constriction" that accompanies the loss of these vital social roles (Ware 1999). Unable to participate fully in social life, the chronic illness sufferer finds herself increasingly marginalized at work and at home; her sense of identity becomes threatened as her ability to perform social roles diminishes. Sometimes, because it is all they have energy for, women will intentionally focus on an increasingly limited number of relationships (Moss and Dyck 2002). The "shrinking" of their social worlds leaves women increasingly dependent on a smaller set of relationships, often stressing those in multiple ways (Moss and Dyck 2002:153). In particular for women whose lives and sense of self is so often defined by their caretaking relationships to others, chronic illness can devastate a woman's self-concept as she becomes a receiver and no longer a giver of care (Charmaz 1991; Johansson et al. 1999; Moss and Dyck 2002).[4]

For most of the women I interviewed, their social roles and networks did contract over the course of their illnesses, sometimes permanently and sometimes temporarily, and the effects of this loss were deeply felt. Family relationships take on even more significance as nuclear family members are especially called upon to navigate the medical system for the sick woman, take care of her when she is bedridden with a flare, assume her household and child care responsibilities when she cannot perform them, and provide solace and comfort to her as she grapples with her physical limitations and emotional struggles. Families can become closer because of these experiences, and they also can become seriously stressed. For example, some patients and their family members reported that they all happily embraced dietary restrictions or willingly changed leisure activities to accommodate the needs of the sick woman. One young woman admitted that her parents concern also meant that sometimes she was afforded privileges never allowed her siblings.

In other cases, the serious and extended nature of the illness stretched the family's resources to its limits. Financially, the burdens of providing lupus care can leave a family indebted, as it did the Quitasacas, and hard choices have to be made about what treatments they can afford and where other savings can be made. Sometimes the stresses can be emotional rather than economic. Paula's mother, for example, found herself exhausted by her daughter's illness; she had to deal with one health crisis after another for years, her daughter's moodiness and depression, and her husband's seeming withdrawal. "Men," she told me, were "weak" in the face of a family health crisis, and she was the one who had to handle all the emotional as well as logistical details of Paula's care.

The mother of an eighteen-year-old rural woman with lupus revealed to me that she often gets very angry with her daughter because she is withdrawn and doesn't help out at home. Then the mother feels guilty and depressed not just for expressing her frustrations, but even for thinking them. She swings regrettably between being angry at her daughter and angry at herself, feeling sad for her daughter and sad for herself. She is often on the edge of exhaustion as she might have stayed up half the night to get her daughter an appointment at IESS and then returned home to take care of the farm and cook. Her daughter's relentless lethargy simply aggravates her. She quit school and lost her job, so she spends her days in her bedroom and engages very little with her family.

In the following pages I explore how loss and illness mutually reinforce one another in the narratives of Valentina and Leonor. Both women were married with children when their lupus was diagnosed, and they have struggled with enormous losses while navigating their illness trajectories. As they describe how fundamentally their lives have been altered, we hear of their struggles to come to terms with the changing set of expectations about "who" they are. Unable to take care of even themselves for some periods of time, they were forced to relinquish, or seriously rewrite, their roles as wives and mothers but also as members of a larger community.

VALENTINA

Valentina is thirty-nine years old with wide-set, soft green eyes, delicate features, and a light dusting of freckles across her nose. She is tall by Ecuadorian standards, and while she is quite pretty, her most distinguishing characteristic is her soft, lilting voice. She comes across as a very gentle, but also very sad, person. When we first met, Valentina was able to speak to me at length, but the next year when she was clearly very ill, we spoke only briefly, as I feared a long conversation might tire her. I confess that I was shocked at the deterioration of her condition in one year. Her hands were stiff and inflamed, she had difficulty holding the pen to sign the IRB consent form, and her fingernails were black and flaking away. Her hair was cut quite short, mostly because, as she told me, it was falling out anyway. She seemed terribly uncomfortable in her swollen body; she walked slowly and stiffly, and once she sat, she became very still. Her pain was so great that even the slightest movements hurt. During the first interview she shared much about her illness and life before and after it struck, while in the second interview we mainly discussed her current health crisis. Both times we met she worked very hard at maintaining a positive attitude, but the second time it was far less convincing. She could barely hold back the tears as she unconvincingly repeated several times, "Oh well, one must continue on" (*hay que seguir adelante*).

Valentina's symptoms of lupus began in 2000. At the time, she was living with her husband and her two younger children (aged then five and three) and working as a secretary. Her first manifestation of lupus was a sensitive spot on her scalp that slowly grew into a scabby sore that would not heal. She went to dermatologists, changed shampoos, and applied creams, but nothing seemed to help. Then she started to get similar patches on her hands, face, and legs. She also noticed that she was horribly forgetful and could never seem to verbalize what she wanted to say: "It was impossible to find the words," she recounts. Valentina also suffered from increasing pain as time went on, accompanied by overwhelming exhaustion. It took two years from the time of the first symptoms to get a diagnosis of lupus, and she said she felt like an "experimental rabbit" because she had so many medical tests. Each doctor, she said, urged her to see someone else and "insist on a diagnosis." But, she asks, "How was I to insist? I was so sick I couldn't insist anyone do anything!"

In the two years it took to get a diagnosis of lupus, Valentina's personal life was shattered. Her husband, whom she describes as a "brute," never really believed that she was ill. Rather, he thought that she was trying to get out of work, that she was exaggerating her health problems because she was looking for attention, and that she was using a trumped-up illness to manipulate him. He castigated her about household chores left undone, accused her of being a lazy and inadequate mother, and became incensed when her illness forced her to quit her job. Their already tenuous marriage seemed even rockier. Valentina is convinced that through much of her marriage, her husband had been maintaining a mistress and a second household, and he used her illness as an excuse to abandon her and the children and move in with the other woman. Indeed, for awhile she wondered if her philandering husband was to blame for her illness as she, like many Ecuadorians, assumed that lupus, with its immune system dysfunction, was, as she put it, a kind of "cousin illness" to AIDS.

Without a job and with only minimal child support from her husband, Valentina was forced to move back into her parents' home. Her parents, who are fairly well off and live in a lovely home, had already begun to assume many child care responsibilities for Valentina as she became less and less able to care for her children or herself. The move made practical as well as financial sense. Valentina's case of lupus was very severe, and she spent nearly the first two years she was in her parents' home very sick and confined to her bed. She describes herself as being "like a child" during this time, incapable of doing even the smallest things for herself. Lost in a haze of illness, today she remembers very little from that time except for the overwhelming sense that she had lost everything that mattered: her marriage, her job, her home, her health, and her independence from her parents.[5]

Throughout her childhood, Valentina's parents were very strict with her. She says that they monitored her so closely that she grew up thinking that she must somehow be an inherently "untrustworthy" person. When she reached her teenage years, her parents increased their vigilance over her, and she was forbidden to attend social functions at school or go to parties at friends' homes. She could attend parties only when they were held by relatives and she was accompanied by her parents or other family members. Even after she left school, she felt like a "prisoner" in her own home as her parents surveilled her every move and insisted that she come home directly after work. "My parents were too strict with me," Valentina says. "They made me believe that I was a bad person." In spite of their vigilance, however, in her early twenties, Valentina, while still living in her parents' home, became pregnant out of wedlock. She reports that she was openly scorned by her family, both nuclear and extended, and by the families of her friends. Young women of her social circumstances simply should not find themselves in this position. Out-of-wedlock pregnancies are interpreted as a sign of moral laxity in the woman, but they are also viewed as a sign that something is amiss in the entire family. Perhaps the parents were not vigilant enough, perhaps they did not raise their daughter properly, or perhaps a streak of carelessness and licentiousness runs in the family.

Valentina did not want to discuss the father of her child with me, and so I do not know why marriage to him was seemingly not an option. She gave birth and began what she calls her "daily trial" of raising her son under her parents' roof and ever-vigilant gaze. Then, when her son was seven years old, she married the man described above who left her when she became ill, a marriage she now calls a "disaster." Her husband was a "cold" man who never treated her very well and who, much to Valentina's sorrow, never allowed her son to live with them. He remained with his grandparents, something that Valentina did not want but was powerless to change. Just as it was under her parents' roof, in her new, marriage home, Valentina was unable to assert her wishes. The one consolation she has—the one bright spot of having lupus—is that now that she is back in her parents' home, she is closer to her first born son.

Not surprisingly, Valentina has very mixed feelings about living in her parents' house today. On the one hand, she recognizes that without them, she would have no place to go and that they have dropped everything to care for her and her children. She is deeply grateful for that. Her mother, she notes, is "devoted" to her grandchildren, and she is also the one who stays up nights with Valentina when she cannot sleep. Caring for Valentina has not been easy, as her lupus has, at times, made her unable to walk and even sit up, and several times she has had difficulty breathing, began to hyperventilate, and then fainted. When these episodes were recounted to me, it was obvious that they seriously frightened both Valentina and her mother. "What if I hadn't been here?" Valentina's mother asked. "She could have died!" For months at a time Valentina's mother slept on an uncomfortable sofa at her daughter's bedside should she need help during the night.

At the same time that she recognizes the sacrifices that her parents have made for her, Valentina laments the loss of her independence and worries that her own children will be raised in the same overly strict environment that she found so disagreeable and oppressive. She is now, she regrets, unable to control how her own children are being raised. But there is nothing she can do about that; she has no other options. Compounding her sense of distance from her children's lives is that lupus has left her with only dim and groggy memories of their early years. Losing these memories, she says, is akin to losing a piece of her life, as "memories are all we have of who we are."

Her speculation about her husband's infidelity and AIDS aside, Valentina understands that lupus is a disease of the autoimmune system. She also understands that a tendency for lupus might run in her family. She has a cousin in New York who also has lupus and another relative who has rheumatoid arthritis. She believes that everyone in her mother's family carries the potential for lupus in their "blood" but that it "exploded" in her because of the cumulative effects of her life's difficulties. According to Valentina, the multiple problems she has faced throughout her lifetime have each taken a toll on her mind and body and weakened her body's defenses, thus allowing lupus to develop and flourish. In explaining this to me, she made reference to her strict upbringing, the difficulties of being a single mother and living in her parents' home, the separation from her son when she married, and finally her disastrous marriage. As she describes it, her body reached a "breaking" point where it could no longer stand all the pressures in her life. Yet despite her difficult life before lupus, Valentina describes her life with lupus as "one of continuous loss." First, she lost her job and with it any semblance of financial independence from her husband and parents.

Valentina also lost her IESS benefits when she left her job, and she now does not have any health insurance. She pays for doctors' visits and medications completely out-of-pocket. Since she no longer works, she depends on her parents for financial support, although she also receives some child support from her ex-husband, and her brothers in New York often send her money for medications. While her marriage was never good, along with it she also lost having her own home and the opportunity to raise her two children as she sees fit. Now she depends on her parents completely and is in no position to comment on their child-rearing style. Valentina has also found it impossible to maintain a social life outside her family, and she thinks that her friends find her condition difficult to comprehend and frightening. One by one they drifted away. She speculates that like herself, some of her friends probably wonder if there is some connection between AIDS and lupus. Finally, Valentina lost her beauty with lupus. Once quite lovely, as her pictures attest, she now simply refuses to look in the mirror since she does not recognize who she sees there. "I was so pretty, and look at me now!" Valentina explains, pointing out her thinning hair, chafed and raw cheeks, puffy face, and bruised fingernails. In summing up her changed life Valentina said, "It was as though I went to the moon and came back to find everything changed." Yet despite all these difficulties, Valentina tries valiantly to keep a positive attitude. She continually tells herself that "tomorrow, I will wake up a little better" and she prays daily to God to "help her do what she needs to do."

LEONOR

Leonor is a small and compact woman with a naturally hoarse voice, short salt-and-pepper hair, and a firm and penetrating gaze. She lives in a comfortable, but understated, two-story house in a middle-class residential neighborhood in Cuenca. At fifty-five years old, she was one of the older

women I interviewed, and she has had lupus for twelve years. Her lupus began with small, intensely red skin eruptions all over her body that itched tre-
mendously—so much so that at times she said that she wanted to "tear her
skin off." The itching was so relentless that she could not sleep at night, and
she found herself in a constant state of anxiety because she was so uncomfortable in her own skin. Although she was never one to fuss over her appearance, for the first time in her life she was embarrassed by the way she looked.
"I looked so ugly, like a monster. I hated to look at myself!" she said, because
of the welts and lesions on her face. She also suffered from intense joint pain.
She spent a year undergoing tests for allergies and fungal infections and had
multiple skin biopsies before she received a diagnosis of lupus. She calls that
year the "the worst year" of her life because, like Valentina, she just kept getting worse, and no one seemed to know what to do. As her health spiraled
downward, her fear spiraled upwards.

That year was followed by three more years of grave health difficulties, including intense pain and exhaustion and serious uterine and kidney complications. "I had three or four years of intense stress and pain. In reality I
spent more time interned in the clinic than I did at home. Everything was affected, they operated on my uterus, my tonsils, and my gall bladder. I can't remember how many times I was in the hospital." Much has changed in medical understandings of lupus since she was first diagnosed, but at that time,
the conventional wisdom among many practitioners in Ecuador was that lupus patients did not live very long, and she was told by one doctor and several nurses that she probably would not survive past a few years. Adding to
her stress was Leonor's initial misunderstanding about lupus, and she worried a great deal that she had contracted something contagious that she could
pass on to her children. She tried to keep her laundry separate from the rest
of the family, used a separate bathroom, and resisted hugging and kissing her
children to limit the possibilities for contagion. She was forced to quit her
job in an office, and she could no longer take care of her three children, aged
between ten and sixteen. While her husband tried to help out as much as he
could at home, he had a full-time job, and they badly needed his income. He
just did not have the time, without jeopardizing his own job, to take on all
the household duties and provide the care and attention Leonor needed. In
the end, Leonor's elderly aunt, a Catholic nun, came to live with her and take
care of her and her family. Her own mother was ill with diabetes and was unable to offer much assistance.

Before she became sick with lupus, Leonor prided herself on being a very
active person. She enjoyed working outside the home, she hosted and enter-
tained foreign exchange students for months at a time, she took an active part
in her children's lives and schools, and she gladly rolled up her sleeves to take

on household chores and repairs. Before her illness, she did not hire house-hold help, and she was happy to cook and clean for her family while holding down an almost full-time job. On the weekends she and her husband painted and repaired their house together or ferried their international guests and children on weekend excursions to the countryside. "My mother," her daugh-ter told me, "was the kind of person who did everything herself. There are people who always ask others to do things for them, but not my mother. If a light bulb blew out," she said as she pointed to a bulb placed at the apex of their high-pitched living-room ceiling, "Mami would just get a ladder and change it herself."

Leonor enjoyed keeping herself busy, and she thought of herself as an en-ergetic, competent, and capable person. "I always had so much energy and gusto to do things. . . . I hated sitting around." As Leonor described it, she ob-tained a great deal of satisfaction from getting things done and being engaged in the world. In fact, Leonor saw her active lifestyle as having a moral dimen-sion to it: to work hard is to do good. "I was never one to let things go. . . . I think about all the problems we have in the world and I think of our obliga-tions as humans. I do what I can." Today, she pauses to wonder whether the chemicals at the copy shop where she worked triggered her lupus, or whether it could it have been an excess of relentless hard work.

Since her diagnosis of lupus, Leonor has tried to keep up her previous level of activity, but she has found it impossible to do so. Her lupus is very unpredictable, and she can feel *"super bien"* ("super well") one day and then, in an instant, feel completely "fallen" and debilitated. She still tries to do as much as she can on her good days, but she finds too often that when she does she pays for it the next. In fact, often in the midst of an activity now, she will strain something and flashes of intense pain shoot through her legs and hips, leaving her temporarily "paralyzed." "Countless times my muscles have just stopped functioning," she says, and "no matter how much I try, I just can't move." Sometimes the pain she feels radiates all the way to her face and even her cheekbones become sensitive.

The unpredictability of her symptoms and the insecurity she feels about her body and its ability to change dramatically "in an instant" are among the most difficult aspects of her illness. She always thought of herself as physi-cally and emotionally strong and competent, and she expressed that under-standing in her active and busy lifestyle. Now she can no longer count on her-self to accomplish the things she wants to do; she can no longer throw herself into her myriad tasks or lose herself in a project. A few years ago she started a home business and hired workers to help prepare and deliver hot lunches to working families, a job her daughter complains is just too physically demand-ing and stressful. "This is not the kind of job you can put off until tomorrow if you don't feel well," says Leonor. "You have to deliver those lunches!" Her daughter worries that the job is too much for Leonor, pointing out that once in a while something happens in the kitchen, a dish gets burned beyond salvation for example, and they rush around at the last minute trying to come up with some other meal to have ready. Indeed, pacing herself remains a challenge for Leonor. Even after all these years, she still will frequently do too much one day, setting herself back for several days afterwards.

Her children are now fully grown, and all are married, but Leonor continues to worry about the long-term effects that her illness had on them and the formation of their adult characters and personalities. She worries that their childhoods were marred by her illness and that growing up with a mother whose day-to-day health often swung wildly surely took its toll on them. Although she is confident that she was able to give her children enough love and affection, even through her illness, she was not able to set the example of commitment to hard work that she wished, and the up-and-down nature of her illness left everyone in the family feeling insecure and unsure. She worries that her son, for instance, is not as forceful as a man "ought" to be because of the constant stress and worry he was under while growing up.

To make matters worse, early on in her illness her children overheard conversations about the possibility that she could die. Leonor worries that living under the constant threat of this has affected their personalities. Their childhoods were not as carefree as they should have been, and her daughter's reserve and her son's sensitivity are the outcome, she thinks, of living under the dark cloud of their mother's possible imminent death. Leonor's daughter, who sat in on the interview, confirmed that she was constantly afraid that her mother would die and that she felt so "impotent" to help her. Her mother, she noted, sacrificed everything to give her children a little bit more than she had. Leonor cannot help wondering what her life, and their lives, might have been like had she never had lupus.

Leonor has used *Seguro* throughout her illness. At first, she had coverage through her employer. Later, when she lost her job, she was able to enroll as an individual, paying $45 a month. While she expresses a great deal of trust and faith in her IESS doctor, she is also quite dissatisfied with their supplies of medications. She questions whether more could be done for her condition. Too often, the medications she needs are not in stock when she goes to fill her prescriptions, and she wonders whether she has access to the best therapies for lupus in IESS. Despite having lupus for quite a long time, Leonor was not at all sanguine about the current standard treatment options, and she was among the most interested in hearing about whether I knew of any new breakthrough therapies for lupus. I make it very clear to all of my interviewees that I am not a physician and have no training in lupus education, but only Leonor seemed to have a hard time grasping the idea that I had no breaking medical news to report and no new therapies to recommend. She continued to probe me throughout our interview about what I knew about state-of-the-art lupus research. I had the sense that Leonor had no intention of ever "accepting" lupus and the limitations of lupus in her life. The series of "highs and lows" that she continues to experience and the pain and weakness she feels every evening have circumscribed her life in ways that she does not and will not accept. The thought that there might be a cure on the horizon (and that I might know about it) seemed especially salient for Leonor.

REVERBERATIONS

On any given day in Cuenca there are three "rush hours": one on the morning; one at the midday lunch hour; and the last at 6 p.m., at the close of the business day. While the morning rush is hurried and disperses quickly, at 1:00 and 6:00 the streets of Cuenca are filled with workers making last-minute purchases of bread and milk, waiting for buses to take them home, and lingering on the street corners, chatting with co-workers and friends. Over the years I often found myself gazing admiringly at the groups of younger women who filled the streets at these hours, and I was not alone in my assessment. When Alejandra, Rosa's eldest daughter, was a preteen, she pointed to a group of office workers one day and told me that her dream was to grow up and have a nice office job like them. The appeal is obvious. Wearing the uniforms required by most employers in Cuenca, which usually consist of short, tight skirts, and colorful blouses or scarves, the women appear perfectly groomed from hair to nails, and they exude an obvious kind of feminine confidence. To me they were the closest thing I saw in Cuenca to the women portrayed in *telenovelas* (soap operas) that everyone in Cuenca watches. They are young and pretty, and their presence on the city streets declares a modern kind of femininity; they are both beautiful and capable. While these women are but a small percentage of women who work in Cuenca, and formal-sector jobs are hard to get, they are, nonetheless, the most visible symbols of the successful working urban woman and, no doubt, a source of inspiration for some and envy for others.

While these semiprofessional female office workers in Cuenca most certainly occupy the upper levels of women's employment participation in terms of security and salary, they are part of a larger trend that can be seen among women across classes throughout the region. Indeed, the second half of the twentieth century in Latin America is marked by the slow but gradual shift from very patriarchal gender relations, where men control most of the productive labor, to somewhat more egalitarian ones (Arriagada 2006; Chant 2002). As fertility rates have declined and educational opportunities increase, more Latin American women are working throughout their lifetimes (Chant 2002).[6] According to Chant (2002:546),

> While use of the term "crisis" to describe current transitions is open to contestation in feminist circles, the factors deemed to have given rise to contemporary trends in Latin America range from increased access to contraception, demographic aging, the relaxation of social and legislative restrictions on divorce, the growth and consolidation of women's movements and the influences of neoliberal restructuring.

As women's workforce participation becomes vital to their own economic well-being and that of their families, or provides for a level of consumption understood as "modern," employment has become an increasingly important component of how women construct their personal identities (see García and de Oliveira 1997:381). Especially for younger women who have grown up being encouraged to finish high school and maybe even college, the idea of having a career, and not just a job, has taken on real resonance (Miles 2004). Moreover, under conditions of economic stress such as those found in Ecuador, to be a good woman and mother may very well mean continuing to work as a means of providing educational and consumption opportunities to others. As Leonor's daughter framed it, part of a mother's "sacrifice" today may mean working outside the home so that her children can have access to better education and more consumer goods. Indeed, as it becomes more difficult for families to make it on one salary, middle-class women's contributions to household income become increasingly important.

Although poor women have long worked to help support their families, their work is mostly in the informal sector, where the divisions between domestic responsibilities, especially child care, and the public responsibilities of work may not be so distinct. For example, maids and market women often bring their children to their workplaces, while other women, like Rosa, spent their children's early years working from home, knitting sweaters, making confections, or selling cooked food in their doorway. Most of the women in my sample, in fact, eleven of the fifteen who ever worked, were employed in more formalized settings, where bringing children to work would not be possible, including one woman who worked as a janitor. Four worked in more informal settings, where child care and work could be accomplished simultaneously. Of the remaining five informants, four were at least part-time university students preparing themselves for "careers," and one never worked outside her home.

Similar to women elsewhere, despite their increased participation in the labor force, Chant notes that in general women in Latin America rarely gain real economic independence from their work, and work generally does not "replace the centrality of domesticity" in women's lives (Chant 2002:552). Rather, women simply incorporate work into an "ever-expanding portfolio of maternal obligations" (Chant 2002:552). Indeed, in popular culture, perceptions of women's roles, as we saw in the preceding chapter, still highlight the importance of children and families for a women's self-fulfillment. Remunerated work does not take the place of domestic roles for a woman's sense of self-fulfillment, but it can act as an important complement, especially when "caring" for one's family includes a concern for their economic well-being. Even these models, however, may be in flux as women's roles continue to evolve. Rosa's daughter Alejandra, for example, is now almost thirty years old and has been married for more than five years. Yet she continues to focus on her career as a physician, working more than forty hours a week, and has no plans to have children in the near future. She may be at the forefront of yet another shift in how gender is enacted in Cuenca as the possibilities for career women to forgo having a family altogether increase. But that is all still to unfold.

Before they became ill, both Leonor and Valentina fully embraced their dual identities as working women and mothers. Work gave both women a sense that they were contributing to their children's well-being and drew them into a larger network of friends, colleagues, and co-workers. Valentina's employment allowed her a small degree of independence from her parents when she was a young woman, helped her support her son, and later gave her economic flexibility in her troubled marital home. Convinced that her husband was spending his money on maintaining a second household, Valentina's salary decreased her dependence on, and her subordination to, her husband. She had some of her own money to spend as she saw fit, and she did not have to answer to her husband. When she lost her job, it began a domino effect of other losses that culminated in her return to her parents' home and a complete loss of her financial, personal, and social independence. Any money she has now comes to her from others. For Leonor, work has a slightly different meaning than it does for Valentina. For her, work is a moral good, something that a person does to contribute to the betterment of herself, her family, and her community. To work hard is to make a contribution to the family's present and future. Thus, Leonor's sense of herself as a moral actor was shaken when she could not contribute her labor, both domestic and extra-domestic, to her household and community.

Similarly, both women were devastated by their inabilities to perform their roles as wives, and especially mothers, and they struggled with establishing a sense of their own self-worth and identity even though they often could not care for their children on a daily basis. Several authors who have examined Latin American *telenovelas* as a window onto popular culture perceptions of gender point out that good women in *telenovelas* always put their families ahead of their jobs and are perceived as self-sacrificing (Beard 2003; Tate 2007). On television, even a "bad" woman can be redeemed through performing successfully as a mother (Tate 2007). Moreover, we have seen in the previous chapter how the inability to be a mother has left Jessica and Paula in a state of permanent liminality, where they are never able to claim a fully adult female status. Here, the loss of the ability to perform a mother's roles fully and the assignment of those caretaking roles to others has women feeling inadequate and victimized. Valentina had to give up the idea that she could raise her children the way she wants to, and she now must submit to her parents' authority in raising them. Worse yet, she has lost her children's "past" since she has no memories of their young lives. What kind of a woman is she, she wonders, if she cannot even remember the small details of her children's infancy? Leonor, too, was not able to be the kind of mother she thought she could be. She was too tired most of the time to model the behaviors she wanted taught to her children and her illness, she fears, had an impact on their development and personalities. They are fearful when she wanted them to be fearless.

Although the losses are numerous and easy to list, nevertheless, the ways in which loss and illness intersect in these narratives makes it difficult to really disentangle the two. While Valentina does see her life with lupus as "one of continuous" loss, and this obviously depresses her, she also describes terrible losses that occurred before the illness struck and that, moreover, she believes may have in fact provoked her latent lupus to "explode." Her story is one of continuous illness and loss and loss and illness rather than one punctuated with a clear before-and-after shift in psychological, social, and even physical dimensions. Her lupus was always there; it is just manifest now. Leonor's narrative more clearly identifies direct loss from lupus, but she does not separate her physical pain from the emotional stress that comes from it. "I had three or four years of intense stress and pain," and "I spent more time interned in the clinic than I did at home," she tells us. Her physical suffering and her mental and social anguish are inseparable here in these two statements, as "stress and pain" are uttered in the same breath and weighted equally and her medical treatments are considered most significant in their relation to her time "at home."

Both Leonor and Valentina have found that having lupus has altered their relationships to, and perspectives of, time and they are now confounded by time in ways they never were before. Whereas their days were once ordered by their work and child-care schedules, and sometimes life felt hectic and rushed, they now find that time slips away from them, sometimes in large chunks, in ways they cannot control, and certainly do not like (see Charmaz 1991). Both women are hazy about long periods of their lives when they were particularly ill. For Valentina, this has meant that she literally has forgotten time and in so doing lost of piece of herself.

Because Leonor refuses to fully accept the changes that lupus has brought to her body, she experiences "temporal incongruence" on a regular basis. Temporal incongruence occurs, writes Charmaz, when there is a disjuncture between what the ill body will permit or allow one to do in a given amount of time and the expectations of structured time (Charmaz 1991:171). When she simply cannot accomplish the things on her "to-do" list, when her efforts to accomplish something are cut short by inexplicable pain, or when the stresses of her catering job becomes too much, Leonor finds herself frustrated and unsure. Even after many years, she has not reconciled the disjuncture between what she wants to do for her family and what she can do. Her use of the term "paralyzed" to describe her physical experiences highlights the sharp contrast between her desired state of activity and accomplishment and its dramatic curtailment by a sudden stopping of that activity by a complete "paralysis" of parts of her body. It was not just that moving was difficult, it was impossible.

While women in modernizing urban Ecuador in general find themselves navigating difficult social and economic terrain as they seek to have a "complete life," women with lupus struggle to hold on to even the barest semblance of a "normal" life. Learning to live with loss is a common challenge, but it is an even bigger one for those suffering with chronic illness (Charmaz 1991). As women with lupus assess their lives, what they once were or what they wanted them to be, they often come face to face with a new reality that prohibits the realization of their expectations for themselves. Dreams for the future, their own and their children's, must be refashioned along very different lines. The ways in which social losses, emotional distresses, and physical health intersect are seemingly commonsensical on the one hand, but they are complicated by women's own understanding of their lives. While illness undoubtedly and perhaps obviously provokes losses, it is not really as simple as this. As Valentina and Leonor show us, stress, illness, and loss are inseparable, and each has the power to catalyze the other.

CHAPTER SIX

Suffering

WHEN I VISITED WITH ROSA EIGHTEEN MONTHS after she was diagnosed with lupus, I thought she looked terrible. Her face was swollen and distorted by the steroid use, and it had a distinctively ruddy color. She moved very slowly and cautiously, shuffling her feet as she walked, and she seemed to lack interest in, and have difficulty following, conversations. She now wore pants regularly to stay warm, something she told me once she could never do. She grew up in the countryside wearing the *pollera* skirt, and while she had shifted to more modern skirts a few years earlier, pants heretofore were out of the question. I could not help but notice that Rosa had stopped doing many of the things she had previously enjoyed and excelled at doing, including cooking and knitting. Her hands, she told me, were now awkward and stiff and she found it too difficult to move her fingers in the right way to knit and to focus her mind for long enough to count the stitches. I described her at the time as a "shadow of her former self" as her usual vitality, good humor, and interest in others were completely missing. She was seeing her rheumatologist fairly regularly as her lupus at this point was far from controlled, and she was still taking several different medications. Her children had taken over cooking meals and tending their small store whenever possible, and Rosa spent most her days at home watching television.

While we talked repeatedly about her illness at the time, one experience in particular brought home to me the real difficulties of her condition. I accompanied Rosa to a routine appointment with her rheumatologist that spiraled into a three-day hospital stay and gave me the clearest indication I had yet of how unpredictable lupus could be and how difficult the medical system is to navigate. In the days before the appointment, Rosa had been having regular headaches, worrying everyone. The day of the *consulta* dawned cloudy, cold, and rainy and Rosa and her daughter were out first thing in the morning to have blood work done prior to her afternoon consultation. They had to take two buses to the lab in the center of town since their twenty-year-old Datsun taxi that Lucho had left behind would not start that morning. At one o'clock Rosa and her daughter Alejandra, who was in medical school, picked me up to retrieve the lab results and head to the doctor's office. In the taxi, Alejandra became quiet as she studied the various computer printouts from the lab. By now she knew good numbers when she saw them, and she did not see them. At a minimum, Alejandra whispered to me, she figured that the doctor would order a blood transfusion, which he had done the last time her blood counts looked like they did that day. On the other side of me, Rosa was taciturn and seemed uninterested in what her daughter and I were discussing, and she quietly gazed out the window. Alejandra's interpretation of what the lab results would mean for Rosa turned out to be on the conservative side.

The rheumatologist we visited is a small, compact man with a quiet voice and an authoritative demeanor. He did not examine Rosa that day but knew from her lab results that her condition had deteriorated. He was concerned that she could have a dangerous flare that might set her back for weeks or even months. He quietly told Rosa that she would need two rounds of a powerful immunosuppressant and perhaps several blood transfusions and that this could best be done in the hospital. To my left Rosa said nothing but "*Sí, doctor*," as tears filled her eyes. The doctor then turned to Alejandra, whom by this time he had identified as the person most likely to understand what he was saying, and who made many of her mother's medical decisions. He treated Alejandra with considerable respect, given their multiple status differences (age, gender, class), and he spent the next 15 minutes negotiating with her how, both logistically and financially, this treatment plan would unfold. They discussed hospitals (which one was affordable to the family yet met the doctor's care standards?), buying medications (where could Alejandra reliably purchase the needed drugs at the best cost?), and procuring blood. Alejandra would have to go to the Red Cross office downtown to purchase blood, which turned out to provide one of the most vexing complications of all. When we left the office, the bad news finally resonated with Rosa, and she collapsed with disappointment on the stairs and wept. She did not want to go again to the hospital, and she was frightened that her health would spiral out of control. Alejandra and I tried to console her by repeating the doctor's words that this was not too very serious but simply had to be done so that things did not get worse. The rest of the afternoon was consumed with preparing Rosa for her stay in the hospital.

Settling Rosa into her hospital bed was no easy affair; the flurry of activity that occurred that afternoon was enough to exhaust anyone. When we left the doctor's office, we were given a prescription to fill at a pharmacy, one of the few in town that would be sure to carry the specialized medication. The hospital where she was to go was too small to have its own pharmacy and nearby ones were poorly stocked and did not carry the medications that Rosa needed. We purchased the pricey medication from the pharmacy in one of the best hospitals in town, one that Rosa could not afford to stay in. We also went back to Rosa's home to pick up the personal items she would need and to feed her. Like most others, her hospital does not provide food for patients and all meals are brought in by family members.

Her other children also had to be told about the medical setback and comforted. Marisol, the middle daughter, is extremely devoted to her mother and, predictably, she burst into tears at hearing the news. Rosa packed her personal belongings in a bit of a daze, putting a few small items in a shopping bag and forgetting her undergarments until her daughters reminded her. In the end, she could not eat anything. Once we had Rosa comfortably settled in the hospital, we hurried into the center of town to the offices of the Red Cross to purchase several pints of blood. However, as it turned out, the supply of blood at the Red Cross was too low that week, and they could only release blood for a dire emergency or if blood donors were brought in to replace the units taken. We had a hurried discussion about who might be able to give blood the following day. When I left them that evening, we had decided that the children would go home that night and work on finding a donor. None of them could donate blood for a variety of reasons, including that one had done so very recently. Logically, they could ask Rosa's siblings and in-laws, but Rosa did not want them to know about her latest hospital stay. She knew that most of her relatives did not really understand what was the matter with her and she worried they would blame her for not taking proper care of herself. She did want to be lectured by them.

The next afternoon I found Rosa alone and pensive in her hospital room. Her children had found a blood donor, and she was hooked up to an IV and had already received one transfusion that morning. The room was gloomy and cold, and her IV continually malfunctioned, but Rosa seemed to be feeling better; she was far more sanguine than she was the day before, and she seemed to want to talk as we slowly worked our way through the bag of chocolates that I brought. While she was grateful that her children had found a blood donor that morning, she was deeply uncomfortable with the person who gave the blood. Alejandra was a very good student but she also had wild tastes in boys, something that had long troubled her parents. Much to her mother's displeasure she was hanging out with a young man in the neighborhood who was thought to be a bit of a playboy and who was believed to be involved in illegal activities. It was this young man that Alejandra turned to for the favor of making a blood donation. Rosa hated that she felt helpless to object and that she was put in the horribly uncomfortable position of having to accept this gesture from a young man she would not even allow in her home. What would be the price for this in the future she wondered? How could she face being indebted to such a young man? As the afternoon passed, Rosa talked about the loneliness she felt with her husband in New York, her worries about her children, and the lack of support she felt from her extended family. At one point she looked right at me with tears in her eyes and asked me if I knew why God was punishing her like this. "What have I done?" she asked me plaintively. "I'm a good person. What did I do to deserve this suffering?" I interpreted her question as primarily rhetorical but I nonetheless assured her that I knew she was a good person.

Rosa's "Why me" question is one that chronic illness sufferers often ask themselves and others as they struggle to make sense of what is happening to them. Surely there is some rational explanation for what seems completely capricious and wholly undeserved. As a Catholic, Rosa has been taught that sooner or later we all must pay for our sins, yet her own suffering strikes her as out of proportion to her rather trivial transgressions. Rosa's attempt at making meaning from her illness has left her more than vaguely dissatisfied with what she understands about suffering and human agency. Yet I know that long before she became ill, Rosa described her life in terms of her personal suffering. She grew up poor and, she thinks, unfavored by her parents; her husband was frequently insensitive and sometimes crass and offensive; her favored eldest son has abandoned her for New York City; and she often feels misunderstood by her sisters and brothers. Her life has been difficult, and she has suffered, and that is before lupus struck.

The idiom of suffering that Rosa uses to describe so much of her life is one that typifies much of Ecuadorian women's understandings about their lives, and it gives particular resonance to their illness experiences. In this chapter I explore the notion of female suffering in Ecuador, often expressed in the term *sufrimiento*, and discuss how this term acts as a means by which larger culturally relevant conceptual schema are referenced, articulated, and negotiated. When Ecuadorian women discuss suffering or *sufrimiento*, they are moving beyond their individual circumstances and are calling upon a complex set of cultural meanings and indexing a host of institutional structures, many of which act to constrain their lives. In particular, *sufrimiento* evokes very specific Ecuadorian understandings of women's gendered experiences. It finds its roots, I argue, in Catholic teachings about the roles of women and the nature of sacrifice and morality. While *sufrimiento* is not the only important "idiom of distress" (Nichter 1981) that women use to interpret their experiences, it is one that speaks very clearly of both the immediate physical and emotional pain of an ambiguous condition *and* the existential and structural experiences of being an Ecuadorian woman.

SUFFERING AND *SUFRIMIENTO*

In the past two decades or so, medical anthropology has been elaborating on the ways that suffering is experienced (see Kleinman et al. 1992). Suffering is now understood to be a "social experience" and not solely a physiological or psychological one (Kleinman et al. 1997:ix). Social suffering, which includes bodily distress, is thought to be linked to unequal social relations, both local and global, that are most likely to afflict the poor and the marginalized. Studies in medical anthropology have focused on understanding the meanings, causes, and processes of suffering in an effort to link quite explicitly the structural (i.e., social) and the experiential dimensions of it (Kleinman et al. 1997). When women suffering from lupus in Ecuador speak of *sufrimiento*, they are simultaneously referencing both a deeply felt, personal affliction and speaking in a kind of shorthand for the structural position of women. Pain and suffering are historically, structurally, cognitively, and emotionally created.

In the Andes there is a long and complex historical discourse on the meanings of suffering, much of it infused with deeply religious, especially Catholic, overtones, and not all of it is very consistent. After the colonial period, which saw the Catholic Church dominating public and economic life, in the nineteenth century many Latin American countries began to restrict the political and economic influence of the church. Ecuador, on the other hand, took a different approach, and the authority of the Catholic Church intensified during this time. According to one historian, despite efforts by liberals to "modernize" Ecuador, "the Catholic Church was considerably more powerful in the 1880s than it was in the 1780s" (Lane 2003:94). At one point, from 1869 to 1875, Ecuador was virtually a "theocracy" as Ecuador's president, the devoutly Catholic Gabriel García Moreno, officially charged the Ecuadorian state with the duty of protecting the church, made Catholicism a requirement for citizenship, and declared Ecuador as a nation of adherents to the Catholic devotion to the Sacred Heart of Jesus (Lane 2003; B. Williams and Healy 2001). Explanations of the Sacred Heart of Jesus reveal a concern for devotion, quite literally, to the wounded "heart" of Jesus, which symbolizes life, love, morality, and pain. The visible wound in Jesus' heart, so often displayed quite graphically in bloody church iconography, reveals Jesus' heart's "vulnerability, its unprotectedness, its human love" (von Hildebrand 2007:98).

A nation that declares its devotion to the Sacred Heart of Jesus submits to the idea that Jesus is the ultimate Lord and Master but also seeks to make amends to others for the suffering of Christ on the cross. President García Moreno was flamboyant in his Catholic practice and in a public display of devotion in 1873, he carried a cross through the streets of Quito during a Good Friday passion play to highlight Christ's bodily suffering (Lane 2003). Solidifying his reputation as a Catholic martyr, in 1875 as he left morning mass, García Moreno was assassinated by liberal opponents brandishing machetes. In a biography of his life, written in 1914, García Moreno's last words—spoken after his bloody body was laid at the feet of the statue of the *Virgen de los Dolores* (Virgin of Pity/Pains)—were reputedly "God never dies!" (Maxwell-Scott 1914).

Although generally associated with medieval Catholicism and monasticism, self-punishment as a means of moving closer to the divine was still practiced widely in nineteenth-century Ecuador. Indeed, Ecuadorians appear to have been very much taken with the idea of inflicting pain on themselves. Women, whose sexuality is associated with Original Sin and the casting of humans from the Garden of Eden, were viewed as especially in need of penitential practice (see Stølen 1991). In the 1860s Friedrich Hassaurek, a German American journalist and traveler, described the following women's mass, which he claims to have witnessed in a Quito church.

> Towards sundown the curate preaches a short sermon, and then leaves the church in utter darkness. The organist then plays a Miserere, the women bare their backs and lash them with cowhides, to which sometimes small pieces of iron or other hard substances are attached. When this discipline is over, they depart in silence. The blood sprinkled over the stone floor and on the walls betokens the eager earnestness of their devotion (Hassaurek 1967:76).

Hassaurek goes on to report that during Lent, both men and women from the finest families in Quito engaged in similar activities when they confined themselves to church grounds for nine days, while observing daily deprivations and nightly episodes of self-flagellation. On leaving the church after the required time, the participants were publicly greeted by friends and family, making their ordeal both a private and a public symbol of devotion and sacrifice. While Hassaurek does not tell us what was in the minds of the penitents he observed, most often self-punishment is linked to the notions that pain brings one closer to God through its associations with Jesus' suffering. Suffering is a morally charged sacrifice (Asad 1993). To inflict pain on oneself is to recognize humankind's existential dilemma of sinfulness and to accept willingly the burdens of suffering that lead ultimately to salvation.

Nineteenth-century Ecuador's practice of Catholicism, as elsewhere, however, was eclectic and seemingly contradictory. At the same time that medieval self-flagellation flourished, there emerged under García Moreno's devotion to the Sacred Heart a call for a more romantic Catholicism, one that saw pain and hardship not as a penitential duty but rather as a source of spiritual inspiration and love and that sought to use Catholicism to defend the common people and create an "Empire of Morality" (D. Williams 2001:149; see also Escalante Gonzalbo 2006). According to Escalante Gonzalbo (2006: 116), who writes generally of the romantic viewpoint, "The people . . . was a collective entity, an abstraction, which was defined precisely because it suffered. It was no longer the masses, the ordinary people, the mob that distinguished itself by its vices: it was not guilty or suspicious; it was not a threat, but a victim." Under García Moreno, Ecuador embarked on public education programs established by the church, as well as campaigns and laws to monitor and regulate public morality (Williams 2001). Even today, Ecuadorians sometimes refer to whole communities, especially indigenous ones, as "suffering" because of their historic marginality. These *pueblos sufridos* ("suffering towns") are often described with a kind inevitability, as though their geographic and social isolation were an outcome of natural rather than social conditions. The appellation seems to refer to existential conditions, which are not amenable to change, rather than to situational ones.

Today, Ecuador is still predominantly a Catholic nation, although the state is no longer officially tied to the church, and Catholic symbolism is ubiquitous in public and private life (Roberts 2006).[1] Most homes have small altars to the Virgin Mary, many shops have portraits of Jesus on their walls, and saints' days are celebrated with impassioned reverence, even in urban areas. Holy Week events in particular are celebrated with considerable vigor, and processions in Cuenca still reenact "the Passion" (suffering) of Christ as he carried the cross through the streets to his crucifixion on Mount Calvary. Often participants playing Christ flagellate themselves or have others do so as a visible symbol of suffering and devotion.

The most "present" everyday symbolic vehicle in Ecuadorian Catholicism, and one that is particularly important for women, however, is not Jesus but rather the Blessed Virgin Mary. Whereas God, Christ, and the saints enter only occasionally into daily practice for the average Cuencano, the Virgin, who takes a variety of likenesses based on different apparitions, is ubiquitous (see Roberts 2006).[2] Moreover, she is not perceived to be a distant character whose disposition cannot be swayed; rather, she is thought to pay heed to her worshipers' laments and to grant their wishes, at least on occasion. The Virgin Mary is often seen as an intermediary between humans and God, and much communication from the divine comes through her. The Virgin's sympathetic nature, much like the devotion to the Sacred Heart of Jesus, is thought to be an outcome of her own human suffering, which can be traced to her role as the "Mother of God." Indeed, on Good Friday, the most somber day of the Catholic Holy Week, Cuencanos visit seven churches and say the rosary prayers for the "Seven Pains of Mary," the most dramatic of which was watching her son die on the cross. The very human suffering of Mary, as a woman and as a mother, make her an accessible and sympathetic figure to Ecuadorian Catholics and, arguably, a role model even for modern women.

The most controversial academic exegesis directly linking Catholicism to suffering and women's social roles is a once quite polemical and now much ignored article published by Evelyn Stevens in 1973, titled "Marianismo: The Other Face of Machismo in Latin America." In this article, Stevens attempts to provide an historical and contemporary account of the "syndrome" of *marianismo*, which she describes as the tendency of Latin American women to interpret their lives through a lens of suffering and abnegation. Stevens argues that *marianismo*, while based on Catholic veneration of the Virgin, should not be confused with a religious cult but is now fully secular and integrated into contemporary notions of Latin American femininity. In short, *marianismo* is rooted in the idea that the "ideal" woman, like the Blessed Virgin, exhibits moral superiority at all times, has spiritual strength in the face of misfortune, and "has an infinite capacity for humility and sacrifice" (Stevens 1973:94).

Stevens suggests that women's *marianismo* is a counterpoint to men's *machismo*, providing women, many of whom are dreadfully subjugated by *machismo*, with a moral superiority in their relationships to men. While men may be obviously dominant and dominating, perhaps even abusive, women who endure and submit in the end emerge morally and spiritually superior. This frequently results in the strengthening of social support, as family, and even friends, rally around the long-suffering mother figure. Stevens also writes of the sexual prohibitions put upon women through *machismo* and *marianismo* and, among other things, discusses the shame and disgrace that fall upon women who do not carefully guard their virginity and limit their sexual activities to marriage. Unwed motherhood, for example, offers a visible symbol of a woman's troubling sexuality and her moral laxity, and it is highly stigmatized.

Stevens' article was soundly critiqued throughout the 1980s, mainly because it suffered from all the conceits of the time in which it was written (as all published work does). In particular, the kinds of very broad generalizations described above no doubt strike today's reader as deeply problematic. Far more wary of universalizing truths than scholars in the 1970s, feminists writing about Latin America in the late 1980s and 1990s argued that Stevens' generalizations about *marianismo* served to homogenize Latin American women by considering them all of the same ilk, strip them of all agency since they appeared to react rather than act, and legitimize obvious social inequalities by interpreting them as cultural choices (Borque and Warren 1981; Ehlers 1991; Nash 1990). In other words, feminist anthropologists argued that women in Latin America are too diverse to be summed up with a universalizing paradigm and to do so disguises the structural causes of women's oppression.

Keeping in mind these critiques and without disagreeing with them, I would still argue that aspects of Stevens' portrayal of male and female relations resonate in the literature on gender and health in the Andes and in the discourses of the urban Ecuadorian women with whom I have worked for more than twenty years, both those who are ill and those who are not (see Stølen 1991; Anderson 2000; Mitchell 1994). Women in Ecuador from a broad range of social categories of class and ethnicity do speak of female suffering or *sufrimiento* as a distinct condition experienced by women, but one that is also very much "taken for granted." By this I mean that while it is generally recognized and it is often invoked in conversation, it is hardly ever parsed and never discussed outside the contexts of a particular example. Women do not discuss *sufrimiento* as a concept; they discuss only their experiences with suffering. In a general sense, women, much like the *pueblos sufridos*, come to their suffering "naturally" simply because they are women. Moreover, suffering is not a neutral event; much as the suffering induced by self-flagellation practiced centuries earlier, it is both a marker and a declaration of a moral position. Female suffering, often associated with the *dolores* (griefs) of the Virgin Mary who saw her only loving son crucified, is accepted as the fate of the moral woman; life is full of pain and loss and events that she cannot control.[3] Physical, emotional, and social pain is considered to be part of a gendered spiritual inheritance.

In my experience, the range of what qualifies as *sufrimiento* for Ecuadorian women is broad. An Ecuadorian physician with whom I discussed *sufrimiento* told me that he would describe it clinically much as others might describe depression, as it is manifested in sleeplessness, lack of eating, and a withdrawal from communicating with others. But I think it is a far more fluid and culturally framed concept than his austere description would imply. I have heard poor women describe their lives of grueling poverty and hardship through the idiom of *sufrimiento*, and I have listened while elite women use it to describe the difficulties of being a sentimental woman in a seemingly uncaring world. *Sufrimiento* is not an illness, or an illness category, but a kind of "being in the world" (Merleau-Ponty 1962) that is distinctly feminine.

In contrast to Stevens, however, I do not want to overgeneralize the concept or present it as a definitive model or defining principle of Ecuadorian femininity. Indeed, following the tropes of my own times, I argue that gender and religion constitute kinds of "institutions" (in the broad sense that Saris uses the term); they provide the rough outlines through which more individually and discursively relevant interpretations of female suffering are generated. Moreover, consistency is difficult to find. Different women not only think about *sufrimiento* differently, but an individual woman may be wholly inconsistent in how she references the meanings of it from one utterance to the next. As Saris (1995:66) describes it, "Institutional discourses—things to be said and ways of saying them—are produced as discursive objects and then questioned by running them into one another within the narrative."

What will become clear in the following two case studies is that the concept of *sufrimiento* is just a starting point for these women to think about how lupus is to be integrated into their more expansive life stories. Both women, Carmella and Mercedes, discuss *sufrimiento* in similar ways, yet the meaning and outcomes of their individualized *sufrimiento* are quite different. In the first case presented here, Carmella uses the concept to broadly outline, in a rather undefined way, the general nature of her life. She has suffered from a series of painful personal problems that have exacerbated her health problems, leading to further suffering. Carmella is desperately trying to find some meaning in her personal and bodily suffering, but it is difficult. She worries about moral transgressions and questions her own behavior and what she thinks her illness might signify to others, but in the end she comes up with no comforting answers. In contrast, the second case discusses Mercedes, whose personal life is only marginally better than Carmella's; yet she has an entirely different interpretation of her suffering. A member of a conservative Catholic movement, Mercedes sees her illness as an opportunity; it is a "gift from God" that has the potential to bring her everlasting salvation.

CARMELLA

Carmella is a small woman in her late forties, with short, rust-colored hair. It is hard to say what she would look like if she did not have lupus, since her physical appearance today is so marked by the classic side effects of extensive steroid use. Her face is perpetually swollen and puffy, especially around the lower jaw, and her large protruding brown eyes sit in liquid pools. Even worse than the facial swelling, in her mind, is the fine down of blond hairs that cover her chin and cheeks, another side effect of steroid treatment. When sitting down, Carmella appears to be robust, but when she stands up, it is obvious how very small she really is. Like many Andeans, she carries the weight she has gained on steroids almost entirely on her upper body.

Carmella gives the appearance of always rushing, and while sometimes she is, often she just cannot quite seem to fully catch her breath. Her lupus is fairly severe; among other problems, it has impacted her heart and lungs, and she often is out of breath after taking just a few steps. She is a government office worker with some seniority now, and she accesses most of her care through the social security system. Because Carmella lives in a neighboring province, about a 45-minute bus ride to Cuenca, she regularly has to take substantial time off from work to see her doctor. Fortunately, her employer has been fairly understanding, as she cannot afford to lose her job. Carmella's story of lupus is among the most difficult that I heard, not just because of the severity of her condition but because of the ways in which her diagnosis compounded other problems in her family. In summing up her life, she describes it as one of unrelenting *sufrimiento*.

Carmella is from a locally notable family in her town, and her father was once a minor elected official. But the family is not really wealthy, and their social position has not protected Carmella from a harsh life and may have increased the public scrutiny to which she feels subjected. Like Valentina, when she was a young unmarried woman, Carmella became pregnant. Appalled, and fearing social censure, her father sent her to Quito to live with distant relatives. Carmella continued to work in Quito and raise her daughter while she waited out the shame and stigma that comes to unmarried women who have babies. Through his personal connections, her father was able to secure a job for her in Quito in a branch of the government where she still works today. She returned to her hometown and her parents' home when her daughter was four, continued working, and eventually married and had two more children. Her marriage was never a good one, as her husband was temperamental, frequently drunk, and occasionally abusive.

When I first met Carmella she had had lupus for about five years, and it started when she was in the midst of a severe life crisis. Her second daughter, aged fourteen at the time, fell ill with myelodysplastic syndrome, a very serious blood disorder thought to be a precursor to leukemia. Carmella was told by local physicians that her daughter's best chances of survival were to seek treatments in the United States at St. Luke's Children's Research Hospital in Memphis. With little savings and modest incomes, Carmella took it upon herself to earn money so that she could take her daughter to the United States to seek treatment. She appealed to foundations for grants, inquired at banks for loans, and pleaded with friends and family members for gifts and *prestamos* (loans). At one point, she said, she was so desperate for money she even went to the "drug dealers" and "loan sharks" in town and asked them for a loan. To her surprise, there is a certain honor among thieves, and they gave her a gift of $5,000 to, as she quoted them, "help the poor sick child."

Emotionally stressed and physically exhausted, Carmella believes that she wore herself out during her daughter's health crisis, and in addition to everything else she was doing, she often stayed up all night making cakes, party ornaments, and handicrafts to sell. It was during this period of extreme stress and anxiety that her lupus emerged. As she tells it, "I was just like you, completely fine. I went to bed late one night after making cakes and woke up the next day with swollen and weak hands. After that, everything went wrong." Carmella was in and out of hospitals and doctors' offices several times in the next months as they tried to figure out what was wrong and alleviate her pain. At the same time, she was preparing for their departure to Memphis, where her daughter was scheduled to receive care. She was eventually diagnosed with lupus just a few weeks before they left. "The doctor told me I had lupus and said I had to suspend the trip. How can I suspend the trip?" I said. "I have an appointment already, and my daughter is dying! Look, I have to go, and I will go, no matter what!" The doctor gave her a prescription only for low-dose steroids and analgesics since she did not want to prescribe a more effective medication that required close monitoring of the patient. When they arrived at the hospital in Memphis, Carmella's health was fragile; rather than putting her daughter in a wheelchair, she was the one who could not walk. She claims she got through that trip on pure adrenaline.

When they returned to Ecuador, Carmella's daughter was much improved, but Carmella's own health declined rapidly. She spent much of the next six months in the hospital with a number of very serious conditions, including cardiac, kidney, and pulmonary complications. Her personal life deteriorated as well. Soon after she was diagnosed with lupus, her husband started questioning her diagnosis and expressed his suspicions that Carmella's condition and her daughter's illness were somehow related diseases and that the two of them were contagious. He refused to sleep in the same bed with Carmella and separated his eating utensils and plates from theirs. According to Carmella, whenever they disagreed, which was often, he dismissed what she had to say by calling her a "*luposa*," as in "shut up, *luposa*," as though it was some sort of well-understood insult. As Carmella's condition worsened, her husband grew increasingly unpredictable. One night when they argued he knocked her to the floor. When their daughter came to stop their fighting, he hit her as well, breaking her nose. The police were eventually called, Carmella pressed charges against her husband, and he left the house. They are now divorced. While Carmella expressed that she was relieved to have her husband out of the house, she feels sad about the failure of her marriage and the abuse she and her children endured. She worries now about providing for her two younger children. Her husband gives her some money for child support, but it is never enough to cover even their basic school needs.

By the next year, the condition of Carmella's daughter had stabilized, she was doing well in her classes at the university, and Carmella was intensely focused on her own health concerns. Her lupus was difficult to control, she was obviously depressed, and she continued to have difficulties breathing. When I met with her privately the first time, it was clear to me that she was desperate to talk; I barely had time to sit down and had not even asked a question when her story (and tears) poured out of her. The rejection by her husband was a deep psychological blow to her, but at the same time, she was relieved that she no longer had to deal with his fiery temperament. Her sense of rejection, however, extended far beyond her husband. Carmella felt "disguised" rejection from neighbors and friends, who, she noticed, stopped coming to see her, neglected to invite her to parties, or went so far as to make comments about her unfortunate weight gain or facial hair. She claims people were so bold as to ask her, "What happened to you? You used to be so pretty?" "I look in the mirror only twice a day, in the morning and at night, and I don't look other times. I look so fat, so swollen with these horrible hairs, and I say no, no, no, I am not going to look." Lupus, she says, took all of the joy out of her life. Living with lupus is "like being crippled without anyone knowing" and like "having a life without really living." Having worked in a public office for more than twenty years, she knows everyone in town. She is convinced that because of her health and personal problems, she is the topic of a great deal of gossip. Carmella was one of the most garrulous informants I met, and her narratives are filled with contradictions and half-formed thoughts that she seems to be exploring as she is speaking.[4]

In so many ways, lupus is the quintessential "postmodern" illness, flush with ambiguity, conditionality, and subjectivity (see Napier 2003). Carmella's narrative exposes the realities of how individuals come to terms with living with ambiguity. For example, Carmella's conversation doubles back periodically on questions of morality and the relationship between moral behavior and illness. So, in discussing her life prior to having lupus, Carmella makes it clear that she led a "clean life". By a "clean life" she means that she did not smoke, drank only a little at an occasional party, and was never sexually promiscuous. Yet when I asked Carmella directly whether she thought that these activities could cause lupus, she said "of course not," and she gave me a fairly accurate biomedical description of the disease process. Nonetheless, it seemed to matter to her to tell me that she was somehow morally blameless. She pointed out to me that she has a distant cousin who died from lupus in Denmark, but that she thinks she died because she did not take care of herself and drank too much whiskey. Not surprisingly, Carmella also worries considerably that others are making moral judgments about her and her daughter because they are both sick. She supposes that others believe that each person is morally responsible for what happens to them and she assumes that others are wondering whether she does not somehow "deserve what she gets."

Carmella uses *sufrimiento* as a mobile concept that describes her own responses to the hardships of her life. Most often she describes her life as one of "endless" *sufrimiento*, primarily because of the vulnerabilities that come exclusively to women. As an unwed mother two decades ago, she violated strict moral codes and faced both public and private censure. She was effectively exiled to Quito, billeted with distant relatives, where she "suffered" alone until her family decided that she could come home. The father of her child faced no such consequences for his behavior. Today, she seemingly cannot help herself, and though she rejects moral explanations for her illness, like a scab she cannot leave alone, she pauses over and over again to probe them anyway. Then, like so many other women, she married a man who proved to be more than a disappointment. She speculates about whether her *sufrimiento* while living with him was not the cause of her lupus. In a way that is similar to Valentina in the last chapter, she imagines sometimes that a lifetime of *sufrimiento* finally erupted in lupus and she also understands that lupus exacerbated her *sufrimiento*.

Like Leonor, Carmella too worries that her illness has affected how her young son, now aged twelve, understands life. She fears he is "like a traumatized child who knows more than he should know." She tries to hide her pain from him, but it is usually not really possible for her to do that. Indeed, while her physical pain is obvious, she finds what she calls the "psychological" dimensions of the disease harder to accept. She suffers from the cruel rejection by her husband and her friends, the occasional unkindness of strangers, and the indifference she sometimes feels from nurses and doctors. One of her first comments to me was that "the worst part of this illness is how alone you feel. It is the psychological things that hurt the most."

In the end, by employing the idiom of *sufrimiento*, Carmella is attempting to bridge the gap between the known and the unknown, linking her dubious lupus experiences to easily understood discourses about female vulnerability and morality. Because the details of her illness are so difficult to grasp, for her and others, and because the unknowns of lupus are never comforting, *sufrimiento* provides Carmella with an idiom that allows her own moral innocence to be actualized, articulated, and communicated. Like other women and like the Virgin, she suffers with a wounded and vulnerable heart. By placing lupus within a life story that is characterized by *sufrimiento*, her lupus becomes integrated into a narrative plot that not only makes sense to her but becomes a plea to others to find some common ground through which they can relate to her experiences.

MERCEDES

Mercedes is in her early forties, with short, dark hair that frames her lively face. In contrast to Carmella, who is often on the verge of tears, Mercedes is always quick to smile, and she tells her story with a glibness that belies its seriousness. "Looks like I won the prize," she declares ironically when talking about her lupus or her family troubles. The "prize," of course, is one that no one desires. Like Carmella, Mercedes' life has been difficult, but even more financially precarious.

She lives in the central historical district of Cuenca, in a rambling and crumbling *conventillo*. *Conventillos* are large homes often built a century or more ago that have since been carved up into multiple dwellings. They often have two or three floors, with a central courtyard that, most days, is filled with hanging laundry from the many households that rent rooms in the building. There is little privacy in Mercedes' rooms: she has two bedrooms and a small dining room and kitchen, and one can easily hear the noises from her neighbors' radios and televisions through the rickety door and window frames. She has been married for more than twenty years, but for most of that time she has been the sole income earner in the family. Five years after they were married, her husband suffered a cerebral hemorrhage. While he has recovered some functioning, he is unable to work, and, as she tells it, he does nothing but hang out in the street and talk foolishness with his friends. She has two grown daughters; one recently left her husband and returned to her mother's home with her young daughter (another of Mercedes' "prizes"), and the other is recently married. Her own mother lives nearby and is a source of significant support for Mercedes. Mercedes' mother told me that she is a very tough person, and she expects the same from Mercedes.

Mercedes' lupus began in late 2002. "I remember it completely clearly," she says in describing her first hint that something was wrong. It was near Christmas, and she had spent the morning outside in the sun, watching the traditional *Paso del Niño* parades. When she returned to her house, she was terribly hot, and she took a cool shower. "I sensed a smell of burning in the shower. At first I thought it was the shower [she had an electric showerhead, which easily shorted]. I went out to run some errands, and when I came back I took another shower because I was so hot. Again I smelled the odor, like a wet, burnt cloth. That was the smell. When I got out I saw that my face, my chest, my head was completely red." Over the next few days, her hands began to swell, and the skin lesions grew more intense; then her nose blackened, and the pain began. A few days later she could not even comb her hair because of swollen hands and aching joints.

It took almost three months for a diagnosis of lupus to be made, and by that time, she was terribly ill. As the doctors struggled to get her lupus under control, Mercedes was hospitalized. In the hospital she became delirious, and her doctor prepared her family for Mercedes' imminent death. "I lost all notion of time. All! I didn't know who I was. I just dreamed I was walking through a field of flowers. Thank God I have my prayer group. They were behind me the whole time." Mercedes survived that crisis, but her lupus has remained difficult to manage. She has had significantly problems functioning well at work as she is often forgetful; her supervisor gets annoyed at her and calls her a "fool." Because of illness, she was forced in 2006 to take six months of disability pay, which greatly reduced her family's income.

Mercedes' family is far poorer than Carmella's, and she expresses many ideas that are associated with a more rural or "traditional" Andean worldview rather than more urban, cosmopolitan, or biomedical conceptions. Mercedes and her mother speculate on a broad array of theories about the causes of Mercedes' lupus, including contagion, spirit intrusion, and contact with contamination. However, all the theories that they discuss return to the theme of the vulnerability of Mercedes' difficult and precarious life and the *sufrimiento* she has endured as a female head of household. Mercedes is in the unenviable position of being the primary breadwinner for her family and is responsible for doing most of the housework.

In a way that is similar to Carmella's interpretations that *sufrimiento* can wear down the body, Mercedes and her mother believe that Mercedes is physically worn down from her double duties and therefore is at risk from various potential dangers. One speculation is that Mercedes works too hard and was therefore vulnerable to spirit intrusion because, as Mercedes' mother notes, her symptoms began soon after she returned from the cemetery to visit the tombs of family members. Cemeteries are very liminal places in Andean cosmologies, where free-floating spirits wander and play havoc with humans (Allen 2002). Mercedes' mother speculates that Mercedes' everyday exhaustion and the sad nature of her visit weakened her, making her vulnerable to an encounter with *mal aire* ("evil wind"). *Mal aire* is an "Andean" illness linked to the idea that certain places, especially cemeteries, are associated with evil spirits that can enter a body and weaken it.

Mercedes and her mother also consider the possibility that Mercedes' housework routines, especially her household cleanliness standards and practices, are to blame. Because Mercedes works outside the home, she is often short on time and frequently washes her clothes (by hand) first thing in the morning before leaving for work, so they can dry during the day. Many Andean people consider that contact with cold water can potentially induce illness, but the shock to the system that occurs when one throws one's hands into icy cold water first thing in the morning is especially dangerous and debilitating. But Mercedes has no choice, as she must be at work by 8 a.m. According to Mercedes' mother, another possible cause of her illness is Mercedes' penchant for clean and polished wooden floors. Most older houses in the central historical district have aging wooden floors that many people polish with kerosene to keep the wood looking conditioned, which has the added benefit of killing fleas. However, the smell of petroleum is very powerful, and it lingers in the air for days. Mercedes is always overly zealous, and she polishes her floor, according to her mother, several times a week, and she wonders if the exposure to the "chemicals" weakened her body. A further source of contamination that they consider is the possibility that Mercedes' job as a cashier might have given her lupus. At her job Mercedes handles money all day long. That money, they told me, passes through thousands of unknown and possibly germ-contaminated hands. Who knows what illnesses it might be carrying?

Her mother's speculations aside, Mercedes is most convinced that her lupus is linked to something far more exalted. A few years before she was diagnosed with lupus, Mercedes began to participate in a conservative Catholic movement called the Neocatechumenal Way in her local parish, but her participation has become truly significant only since she has been diagnosed with lupus. While Roberts (2006) reports that in Quito, many of her Catholic informants were dismissive of religious "fanaticism," in far more conservative Cuenca, where the Catholic Church reports its highest membership, the Neocatechumenal movement seems to be thriving. Neocatechumenism is an evangelizing movement that emerged in poor neighborhoods in Madrid, Spain, in the 1960s and 1970s and was sanctioned by Pope John Paul II in 1990. According to the official Vatican website, the movement started with a Spanish painter Kiko Argüello, who, in the midst of an existential crisis, "discovered in the suffering of the innocent people the awesome mystery of the crucified Christ which is present in the 'least' of the earth" (Cammino Neocatecumenale 2000).

As explained to me by Ecuadorian participants, the goal of a Neocatechumenal is to achieve salvation through everyday practice by incorporating scriptures in a more integrated way into daily life. The Neocatechumenal movement focuses on "postbaptismal" catechism by creating small learning groups or "communities" within parishes, which meet two to three times a week to discuss Bible passages and their lives with an eye towards finding wisdom in the Bible for contemporary life. Opinions about the Neocatechumenal movement in Cuenca, among those who do not participate, are mixed, with some finding it "way too conservative" (see Roberts 2006). However, several of the women I interviewed participated in the movement and found it crucial to providing meaning for their illness experiences.

Mercedes believes that before she joined the group, she was most certainly "bound for hell." Her sins, as she tells it, were of anger and resentment for her life's sorrows and hardships. She fought often with family, especially her husband and his extended family, which has been of little help to her since his disability. She was filled with "resentment" for "being out in front all alone." Through her participation in the Neocatechumenal movement, however, she came to a new interpretation of her life, and she now believes that her *sufrimiento*, including her husband's incapacity to work, her lupus, and even her daughter's failed marriage, are "gifts" from God. According to Mercedes, God has a "complete plan" for all of us, and "conversion" to a truly Christian way of life "doesn't come free." Suffering is an essential part of learning how to abandon selfishness and sin. She believes that she has been specially chosen by God to suffer because he loves her and wants her "conversion" to be "complete." Her challenge is to recognize the gifts that her lupus and her suffering are and to make her everyday life an acknowledgment of those gifts.

Although Mercedes readily offers up this interpretation (and did so in two different interviews spaced a year apart), when I asked her to explain the concept of a "gift from God" and questioned why a loving God sent her such difficulties, she was surprisingly honest about her own doubts. Nodding her head to my questions, she admitted that she often had trouble understanding the idea that God brings suffering. She pointed to the devastating tsunami that ravaged South Asia in December 2004 and admitted to me that she was having difficulties reconciling why God would allow such horrific destruction and cause so much human suffering. Yet she continues to receive great comfort from her Neocatechumenal participation and credits the group with saving her life and her soul.

THE TRAGIC AND THE MESSIANIC

When analyzing illness narratives, Williams and Healy (2001) suggest that we consider thinking in terms of constructing "explanatory maps," which highlight the myriad directions that narratives can take, rather than focusing on the notion that a coherent pattern ought to emerge either organically or analytically. Similarly, in emphasizing this point for the "banal" condition of headaches among Peruvian women, Darghouth et al. (2006:17) write that women's narratives "come to speak of troubles that cannot be conceptually confined to the boundaries of the body, and, therefore, bring together personal and interpersonal spheres of existence and suffering." Carmella's and Mercedes' narratives and the ways in which they use the concept of *sufrimiento* provide ample evidence for how illness narratives become embedded in dynamic life stories that are "lifelong" and continually produced (see Manderson and Smith-Morris 2010). Both women discuss their suffering not as something that is limited to their lupus or that began with their diagnosis but rather as a further expansion of a series of difficulties that have plagued them throughout their lives. Lupus has forced Mercedes to reexamine how she has reacted to her lifetime of hardship, leading her to embrace the Neocatechumenal interpretation of suffering that teaches that ultimate salvation comes from suffering intensely. For Carmella, *sufrimiento* provides a well-worn idiom through which she can position herself as blameless, making her experiences less strange and more acceptable both to herself and to others.

When Mercedes discusses her lupus, she most often expresses a classic "messianic" interpretation of her suffering. She sees it as linked to a larger body of "knowledge" about the order and meaning in all human experiences (Escalante Gonzalbo 2006). According to Escalante, messianic interpretations seek to uncover a rationale for the human experience of suffering, although, as Mercedes herself hints at when she wonders about the tsunami disaster, sometimes the meaning may be obscure and difficult to understand. From a messianic perspective, human suffering, like all experiences, is part of an irrefutably logical and often divinely inspired system in which punishments, rewards, or reparations are meted out based on some purposeful judgment (Escalante Gonzalbo 2006). Holding fast to any interpretation of illness, however, is difficult, and Mercedes struggles very hard to make her *sufrimiento* serve an obvious purpose. She is an intelligent woman; seeing her lupus as a "gift" from God, while surely a comfort to her, is not always easy. Sometimes she seriously ponders her mother's theories about dirty money or chemical intoxification, and Mercedes makes snide and sarcastic comments about the "prizes" she has "won." I read these comments as a sign of her internal struggles to come to terms with the logic of her very ambivalent "gift" of lupus. Despite being openly troubled by the explanation that a God who loves could also cause so much suffering for her and for countless others, Mercedes persists most often in explaining her own suffering as emanating from a loving God. Her *sufrimiento* is virtuous and it has a distinct purpose: to bring her closer to God (see Throop 2010).

Carmella, on the other hand, is Catholic but not a Neocatechumenal, and she speaks of *sufrimiento* not as a gift but a burden: indeed, an outcome of a lifetime of heavy burdens. Carmella does entertain some messianic interpretations of her condition, but these are far from comforting ones, since they involve interrogating her own moral behavior and questioning whether she is being "punished" rather than rewarded (as Mercedes might see it). But the notion that Carmella's suffering comes as a punishment for her own sins—an idea she cannot abandon—is also one that she will not fully accept. In the end, her *sufrimiento* appears less amenable to obvious messianic interpretations, as it is not a logical outcome of past events, nor does it lead to some higher purpose (Escalante 2006). Carmella's suffering most often sounds fully tragic because she has no obvious explanation for her fate. She never indulges in discussions of how the experience of having lupus may provide her with some practical, spiritual, or existential reward or benefit. She does not think that she has a lesson to learn about life through her illness, nor does she think lupus has made her a better person, a common "messianic" North American trope about chronic illness (Ehrenreich 2001; Miles 2009).

That does not mean, however, that her illness experience is meaningless. By using the idiom of *sufrimiento* to describe her life and her illness experience, Carmella works to connect her ambivalent and stigmatizing experiences to a set of well-understood life conditions and admirable existential qualities that always, or should always, provoke sympathy if not empathy. *Sufrimiento* is something that women, such as the Virgin Mary, experience because they are left vulnerable to punishing social and emotional forces. Carmella's own *sufrimiento* began when she was rejected by her family, endured her difficult married life, and reached almost unbearable levels as her daughter fell ill, followed by her own health collapse. Implicit in evoking *sufrimiento* is the idea that feeling deeply the rejection and disappointments and pains of one's life is, in itself, a description of a moral position. Lupus was not the cause of the *sufrimiento* either for Carmella or Mercedes, and although it may have intensified it, their lupus was integrated into a lifelong story of *sufrimiento*—one that starts in both cases when events took a serious turn that blatantly exposed the raw vulnerabilities of each woman's social, economic, and personal lives.

For better or worse, neither Carmella nor Mercedes can speak of her own illness experiences without making reference to the moral discourses of pain and reward that are inherent in Catholicism and elaborated in the concept of female *sufrimiento*. Both women contemplate their life experiences through a lens of moral reckoning, probing their past and present behaviors, questioning what others might be thinking, and trying to position themselves as worthy, to themselves and to others, of having their suffering recognized as "real" *sufrimiento* and therefore understood and sanctioned. Their suffering becomes "virtuous," if only temporarily (see Throop 2010).[5]

Sufrimiento may be a double-edged sword, as it provides a context through which meaning can be shared and understanding reached, while its associations with a kind of moral righteousness can provoke doubt and insecurity. Carmella and Mercedes struggle emotionally with the moral ramifications of what they think suffering implies. While the struggle for meaning has no simple answer, for who can really explain the "why me?" of something as ambiguous as lupus, the symbolic value of *sufrimiento* as an idiom of distress lies in its ability to partially dispel the emptiness of the tragic and to remind women, and those close to them, that their suffering is not without some moral significance.

Although there have been glimmers of hope in the case studies presented in the last three chapters, Paula's sense of accomplishment in her new job for example or Jessica's improving health, overall these chapters have focused primarily on the difficulties and struggles of women's lives. I have emphasized so far how having lupus puts into sharp relief women's structural vulnerabilities and lays bare the tensions inherent in women's struggles for autonomy, connections with others, and identity. Being sick often strips sufferers of choices about who they are and what they can do, exacerbating for some what are lifelong struggles. In the next chapter I change gears slightly and focus on two women whose experiences with lupus are largely framed in less pessimistic terms. While I am wary of falling into the well-worn narrative trope of ending on an optimistic rather than pessimistic note, and I am concerned about critiques that I might be privileging those who have a "positive" interpretation of illness suffering by having these cases be the last the reader encounters, I do think that they represent a part of the Ecuadorian reality that is as valid and important as any other.

CHAPTER SEVEN

Transformation

 *F*OR THOSE WITH FEW ECONOMIC RESOURCES IN Cuenca, the municipal cemetery is the only place to bury the dead. Although the Catholic Church now officially accepts cremation under some circumstances, the long church history of banning cremation, combined with its continued ambivalence towards the procedure, has made Ecuadorians, in general, loathe to cremate the recently deceased. Burial, though expensive, remains the preferred option. The cemetery in Cuenca is on the outer fringes of the central historical district and its gated landscape mirrors that of the rest of the city. There is a section with some very well-tended marble crypts surrounded by manicured ornamental greenery, which is where Cuenca's wealthier citizens are buried. The rest of the cemetery, however, appears disorganized and overdeveloped.

No doubt once rather elegant, most of the cemetery now looks chaotic and run-down. Multistory, white-washed concrete tombs dominate the landscape, with burial chambers placed one on top of the other, four and five layers high. As the city has grown, the cemetery has expanded in the only direction it could: up. Because of increasing pressure for space, several years ago the city imposed new rules on the internment of bodies in the vaults. For a reasonable fee, bodies can remain in full-sized chambers for up to five years. After five years and without exceptions, the body must be exhumed, with the remains disarticulated and placed in a smaller niche or cremated. Family members consider it their duty to be present when their loved one's vault is opened and to handle the remains themselves. No one wants to hire the kind of person who does this kind of thing for a living. Stories abound in Cuenca about families encountering surprisingly well preserved bodies in the tombs and the tools and techniques required to separate the bones from still-intact tissue.

As they approached the fifth anniversary of Cecilia's death, Rosa and her children began to discuss how they would handle the pending disinternment of her remains. Rosa's children expressed some trepidation to me about the process itself, and there was some disagreement about what should be done with the remains. Rosa wanted nothing but "the best" for Cecilia, and she had asked her adult children to contribute to the purchase of a permanent niche for the bones, at a cost of nearly $2,000. Alejandra, the most vocal on this issue and often the most practical thinker in the family, thought this was an unnecessary expense and that the best thing to do was to cremate the remains for a few hundred dollars. Rosa and Alejandra were at odds with one another over Alejandra's continued refusal to contribute to what she thought was an unnecessary expense. The children all agreed, however, that Rosa should not be present when the vault was opened; she should not have to smell the decomposed remains of her "angel," touch her once-pristine white burial dress, or watch as they clumsily struggled to disarticulate the bones for removal from the vault. Rosa actively grieved for Cecilia for years, and she has just started to emerge from her mourning. Her children feared that the stress induced by this gruesome task, and the memories it would undoubtedly bring flooding back, would reverse the emotional progress she had made.

Cecilia was by all accounts a delightful young girl. The youngest child for the first five years of her life, she experienced the liberty of affection that Ecuadorian parents and siblings bestow primarily on the youngest child. Moreover, she was both her elder sister's and then younger brother's playmate growing up, and her childhood was long and reasonably carefree. In comparison to her older siblings, Cecilia's life was, like most younger siblings, considerably easier, as she had to fight fewer battles with her parents. The family was significantly more financially secure by the time Cecilia was in school, she had few responsibilities to care for younger siblings, and her older siblings had already reworked many of their parents' more conservative attitudes and values.

Whereas Alejandra grew up when the family was very poor, had child care responsibilities from the time she was seven years old, had to plead to be allowed to visit friends or attend a party in high school, and struggled to convince her mother to let her attend the university, Cecilia had no such concerns. As a younger sibling she had few familial responsibilities, she was given a good deal more freedom to attend social events, and her future in higher education was all but assumed. She always did well in school, and her mother was duly proud when she qualified to matriculate at one of the better public high schools in town. This was interpreted as a sign of her potential for upward mobility. After Cecilia's death, her mother made a point of showing me Cecilia's room and all her worldly possessions. In contrast to Alejandra, who had few privileges growing up, it was clear to me that Rosa took some satisfaction that Cecilia could keep up materially with her classmates.

After her death, Rosa began the process of transforming Cecilia from a lovable, yet fully human, youngest daughter into a quasi-divinelike creature, who, in the end, was too good for this earthly plane (see Scheper-Hughes 1992). Rosa speaks of her now only rarely, and when she does she uses only the most reverent tones; she calls Cecilia "her angel." She talks now about how helpful Cecilia was at home; how so many people were touched by her suffering in life and her untimely death; and the exceptional nature of her friends, both boys and girls, who still come by to see Rosa now and again. While Rosa does not understand why God would take Cecilia from her, she does understand fully why God might want to have her with him. It is certainly an understandable, if not a natural human tendency, to revere the dead in ways we often do not revere the living, and Rosa's discourse of transformation is not all that surprising or uncommon. "Don't speak ill of the dead" is a time-worn aphorism that has meaning across place and time as the deceased is transformed from a flawed, living person into a memory. Often those memories romanticize the dead, making them into the person the grieving wish they had been, rather than who they really were. Most of us, I imagine, hope that we too will be remembered for our very best qualities.

While Cecilia's "transformation" from girl to angel was made by others after her death, discourses of transformation are also a part of the illness, not only the death, experience. This chapter will expand on the idea of transformation as a means of interpreting the chronic illness experience and explore the ways that discourses of transformation, which are so very common in American thinking about illness, are elaborated upon by Ecuadorian women. I have already touched upon this theme in Mercedes' story in the preceding chapter as she struggled with rationalizing her religious faith in a loving God with her life experiences of suffering. In her way of thinking, God has given her, in the form of lupus, an opportunity to transform her afterlife by using her suffering in this life to bring her closer to God. Here I explore the idea of transformation more explicitly, and in particular I consider how women think about transformations of their "selves" in this life, and not just their souls in the next one. I will link the concept of transformation to American ideas about the role of the individual and the importance of self-actualization and discuss the ways that this idea, which may still be emerging as a salient cultural model, is shaped and given meaning in Ecuador.

TRANSFORMATIONS

The metaphor of the transformative nature of illness and suffering is one that has a long history, especially in Western thought[1] (Escalante 2006; Morris 1991). In *The Culture of Pain*, David B. Morris argues that western culture, starting with ancient Greeks and Romans, building with Christian martyrdom, and culminating with Romantic art and poetry, has consistently been inspired by the idea that bodily pain is an experience that allows the sufferer to transcend the material and the mundane and to find more meaningful and spiritual understandings about the human condition. "Pain," writes Morris, "whatever else philosophy or biomedical sciences can tell us about it, is almost always the occasion for an encounter with meaning. It not only invites interpretation; like an insult or an outrageous act, it seems to *require* an explanation" (Morris 1991:34, emphasis in the original). Given this, the experience of chronic pain can be revelatory and visionary, and "it ennobles even as it destroys" (Morris 1991:199).

Morris argues that the multiple "unknowns" associated with chronic illness and especially chronic pain expressed in questions such as, "What is this? What caused it? When will it go away?" provoke the ill to ponder the even more elusive "Why me?" question, for which there are usually only unsatisfactory answers. The quest for meaning, he argues, extends well beyond the answers that biomedical science can usually provide, since knowing about the workings of synapses, for example, does not fulfill our need for understanding why one person suffers with dreadful pain and another does not.

The theme of the transformative power of chronic illness is expressed often in art, literature, and popular culture.[2] Susan Sontag, for example, describes how in the nineteenth century, tuberculosis (TB) sufferers were frequently described as more spiritually attuned than others, implying that suffering from "consumption" quickened the mind and spirit in desirable ways (Sontag 1990). Ignoring the less poetic aspects of TB, including fetid breath and bloody phlegm, nineteenth-century artists and writers focused on the romantic notion that suffering from TB was linked to a kind of moral quest. In this period we find descriptions of ethereal, flushed, fictional characters such as Helen in *Jane Eyre* or Mimi from *La Bohème*, both of whom are portrayed as wiser, more philosophical, and spiritually superior than their healthy counterparts. Illness somehow metaphorically transported these individuals out of their squalid environments and petty concerns, elevating their perceptions, feelings, and thoughts.

In Thomas Mann's *Magic Mountain*, published in 1924 before the development of penicillin, which quickly cured TB, the main character Hans passes seven years in a TB sanitarium on a Swiss mountainside. There he finds a host of afflicted characters who engage in erudite debates about the meaning of life. In one discussion the "humanist" argues that "therefore, the dignity and nobility of man was based in the Spirit, in illness. In a word, the more ill a man was the more highly human he was, and the genius of illness was more human than that of health" (Mann 1996:456). In *The Magic Mountain* all that is worthy in the human spirit is linked to the experience of illness, which allows humans to be better than they might otherwise be.

More recently, medical anthropologist Jean Jackson writes that chronic pain sufferers today engage in transformative discourses as they look to find some "silver lining" for their otherwise inexplicable and undesirable experiences. Jackson, who worked in a pain clinic, quotes one informant as saying that even though she had no significant reduction in symptoms, the pain program she entered brought her "tremendous things I probably would never have gained if I had not injured myself," including a greater understanding of "deficiencies in my own self…" (Jackson 2000:127). The experience of illness and the treatment regimen encouraged her towards self-exploration and ultimately transformation. Becker, writing specifically about affliction in late twentieth-century United States, links the metaphor of transformation to what she terms "core American values" (Becker 1997). These values, which include perseverance, personal responsibility, and personal transcendence, are understood by the chronically ill to be desirable characteristics that lead to, and can be achieved by, sickness and healing (Becker 1997:164).

Becker writes that the kinds of transformative metaphors used by patients will vary by many factors, including the level of disruption the condition causes in their lives. In some cases, disruption is permanent, and individuals speak of learning to "rise above" existential loss, while for others, hope for recovery or improvement may provoke alternative narratives about the quality or meaning of life or the importance of appreciating the moment (Becker 1997). Becker notes that "hope" becomes the basis for thinking about the impact of illness in one's life. "Hope is essential to efforts to create continuity: without hope there is no future. When hope is lost or absent, people introduce images of death or nothingness, or emptiness in their narratives. People must have hope to live out the cultural notion of transformation" (Becker 1997:177).

The idea that personal transformation can, and perhaps should, be achieved by those suffering from chronic illness is widely touted in popular American self-help rhetoric of illness management, where pink ribbons, "live-strong" bracelets, and "races for the cure" dominate public attention about chronic conditions. The standard trope is that personal transformation can be achieved when those stricken with illness adopt a positive attitude, embrace the lessons to be learned from suffering, and openly and actively seek self-betterment. Cancer patients, ideally, should become "cancer survivors" who understand and celebrate life with a renewed enthusiasm and meaning (Sulick 2010). At "Race for the Cure" events, breast cancer "survivors" are often singled out in the race to do their own "victory" lap or given special t-shirts or sashes that declare to all their hard-won status. The

LIVESTRONG Foundation, formerly headed by Tour de France bicyclist Lance Armstrong, a cancer "survivor," is typical in its orientation that promotes the ideas that cancer is the start of a new orientation to life and that the individual does indeed have "agency" over disease (see Jain 2010). As the first verse of the LIVESTRONG Manifesto states,

> We believe in life.
> Your life.
> We believe in living every minute of it with every ounce of your being.
> And that you must not let cancer take control of it.
> We believe in energy: channeled and fierce.
> We believe in focus: getting smart and living strong.
> Unity is strength. Knowledge is power. Attitude is everything.
> This is LIVESTRONG.[3]

For lupus patients in the United States, one venue for enacting the "self" work crucial to the illness transformation is the internet, where "lupies" can ask questions, post stories and comments, and interact with one another. Many of the web venues have walls where individuals can post their own stories of lupus suffering; many of these contain obvious references to how the illness experience fundamentally changed them (Miles 2009). The personal stories of lupus sufferers are usually emplotted in similar ways, and they frequently highlight the happy life the patient had before lupus struck, the confusing onset of illness symptoms, the often difficult process of obtaining a diagnosis of lupus, the losses experienced as the illness progressed, and, most important for our discussion here, the ways that the illness experience has altered the narrator's perceptions of life.[4] In particular, these narratives often focus on how the woman attained personal inspiration through learning how to "stop and smell the roses," by taking "one day at a time," or by forming a closer relationship with God. One woman included these words in her online story:

> I believe every experience offers fortitude, endurance and strength of character if I am willing to learn from it. Today I will welcome this teacher into my life, looking for what I can learn rather than fighting or fearing it, thereby freeing my mind to enjoy as much as possible.... Every now and then when my arms are too weak and painful to brush my hair or when one leg refuses to support my weight, the thought of being crippled still settles like a rock in my stomach.... Yet, I adamantly refuse to entertain "what if's." As with anything in life acceptance and a sense of purpose are the keys to a peaceful, fulfill-

ing life. . . . Acceptance and a peaceful co-existence with your disease awaits you if you will move towards it (Pledger 1998).

Indeed, the most ubiquitous symbol of lupus is the butterfly, a creature whose very beauty is the result of a dramatic transformation from an ugly caterpillar, and there are countless references to it in popular literature about lupus. Butterfly motifs frequently serve as borders for web pages and on some sites, the butterfly can be found floating across the computer screen in various shades of purple, pink, and orange. On one site, the user's cursor turns into a butterfly, and so every move of the hand produces a sweep of butterflies that flit across the screen. The meaning of the butterfly is generically positive, and it is meant to convey inspiration and hope for transformation and renewal. The butterfly serves to remind women that chronic illness is a process that should, ideally, fundamentally transform them in a good way. Often women note the processes that transform a caterpillar into a butterfly, and they refer to the complex, mysterious, and unknowable ways that beautiful changes can occur. Through the butterfly motif, lupus patients are encouraged to see their illness, or their current negative state of mind about their illness, as a necessary stage in their not yet fully accomplished transformation.

The other very potent symbol of lupus, the wolf, has more mixed metaphoric uses. Most often, the wolf is portrayed as attacking the lupus sufferer, who is forced into a lifelong and unrelenting "dance with the wolf." The "crafty" wolf is seen as poised to strike at any moment, and it must be "tamed" if the sufferer is to live a decent life. On one website, a participant wrote the following about the wolf:

> Wolf—within me
> Dark, and hidden in my blood
> Waiting, stalking to destroy me
> We alone do battle
> And you so easily overcome me (Jean a.k.a. Wolflady 1997).

Yet at some point, as Becker's work would indicate, eventually accommodations to the disease have to be made, and the wolf begins to take on a less threatening visage. For example, at the end of her book titled *Travels with the Wolf*, which chronicles one woman's experiences with lupus and medical mismanagement, Melissa Anne Goldstein writes, "In celebration I lift my head to the rising sun whose rays caress the desert flower, the river and me. Then once again, I set my feet on the road east, the wolf beside me" (Goldstein 2000:264).

Finally, taking accommodation one step further, one website reverses all the negative metaphoric connotations usually assigned to the wolf and, portraying it as a symbol of strength and power, urges sufferers to "embrace" rather than reject the wolf (i.e., lupus). The wolf is characterized on this website as a creature whose own struggles, which include those against insensitive humanity, have given it special gifts that can enlighten and guide women with lupus. Wolves are brave and loyal and have a deep inner strength. The author of the website urges readers to take a "mind journey," reject the negative images of the wolf, and embrace the idea that the wolf represents the strength and beauty of nature and intuition. "Look into the eyes of the wolf, into the animal soul. There is haunting there. I see intelligence, loyalty, strength and spirituality. . . . Walk with the spirit of the wolf, he will be your companion and protector." After multiple pages of verse and prose, much of which is focused on the traits of wolves that humans would no doubt admire in other humans, the author's own transformation is complete so that in the end, she writes, "I am the wolf, and the wolf is me," completing her "mind journey" transformation.[5]

It is no doubt true that cultural storytelling about self-transformation is helpful to some (see Frank 1991), giving them a sense of hope and of common struggle. For others suffering from chronic conditions, however, the pressure to "transform" oneself and to see illness as an uplifting experience may be onerous and a source of anger or even disillusionment (see Hawkins 1993). What happens when transformation does not happen? Has the person who does not transform properly somehow failed some unspecified test of character? Cultural critic Barbara Ehrenreich, who is best known for her book *Nickel and Dimed* about poverty in America, has also written critically about her own experiences with breast cancer support groups and the ubiquitous upbeat orientations of these groups. In a scathing 2001 commentary in *Harper's* magazine, Ehrenreich discusses how the popular cultural discourses about the transformative potential of cancer and the redemptive nature of suffering also serve to silence other voices and interpretations of the illness experience. There is no place, it seems, in much of "Cancerland" for anger or for critiques that shift the focus away from the individual (Ehrenreich 2001).

Thus, when Ehrenreich posted a message to an online breast cancer support group expressing her anger at having cancer, her distrust of corporate polluters, her disgust with the "sappy pink ribbons," and her difficulties with insurance companies, she was roundly rebuked by other members who felt her negative attitude was far from helpful to herself or others (see also Lochmann Jain 2010).[6] "You need to run, not walk, to some counseling. . . . Please get yourself some help and I ask everyone on this site to pray for you so you can enjoy life to the fullest," wrote one indignant participant (Ehrenreich 2001:50). Most problematic to Ehrenreich is the concern that cancer patients are encouraged to "suspend critical judgment" while they focus exclusively on bettering the self, thus leaving unexamined the social contributions to illness, including the lack of access to good health care or poor government oversight of polluters. Moreover, as Lochmann Jain points out, these discourses assume that a cancer patient is able to access needed care and has the time that such self-work requires (Lochmann Jain 2010).

To be sure, most of my informants in Ecuador, and particularly the ones whose lupus is difficult to manage, did not discuss transformation, use metaphors of transformation in their conversation, or obviously seek to communicate to me some redeeming quality in, or outcome of, their illness. Many, like Rosa and Carmella, wondered why they were being punished or, like Ehrenreich, really could not see a "silver lining" to having a serious illness. Most saw their illness as something they had to endure ("like men," as Paula says) for a variety of reasons, but they put little pressure upon themselves to turn their experience into something generally positive or uplifting. They mostly wished it would go away and their lives regain a sense of normalcy, or they employed the idea of "suffering" as a culturally appropriate mode of expressing a moral identity. That said, however, discourses of transformation were not completely absent, as we saw from Mercedes' narrative, and a few women did make passing comments about wanting to learn something from the experience so that they might help others. Some thought their participation in this project might improve general knowledge about the illness and in that way help others. Others made vague comments that they might one day want to share what they have learned with other patients.

The two women highlighted in this chapter, however, have much more explicit discourses of transformation than most, but very different orientations to it. Sonia, who has had lupus for thirty years interprets her illness as catalyst for greater self-discipline, which has helped her follow more closely the guidelines of her faith as a Seventh Day Adventist. Now and then she shares what she has learned about discipline and diet with others in her family or church. Monica, who is much younger and lived for a time in the United States, is determined to make her lupus experience meaningful both for her and for others. A university student, she has taken on the goal of establishing a lupus foundation in Cuenca, which she hopes will provide basic services and education to those not as fortunate, insistent, or savvy as her.

SONIA

Sonia is in her late fifties, but you would not know that from looking at her. She is an animated character with a lively face and only a few soft wrinkles around her lips and eyes. She wears just a trace of lipstick, but her cheeks have a natural healthy pink glow to them. Her hair is cut short and frames her face attractively, and she wears colorful, yet tasteful clothing, typical of women of the established middle class. Sonia is thin and energetic looking, and her conversation is fast paced. She was among the most cheerful woman I interviewed. Sonia has worked her entire life in her father's retail store in the central historical district of Cuenca. The shop has had some ups and downs over the years, but it is a solid business well located on a busy corner. Sonia's father no longer runs the store, and today Sonia manages the recently renovated shop along with one of her cousins. She has several employees who work the counter, and she enjoys the daily interactions with them and her customers. She keeps up with the latest trends and works hard to keep her store up-to-date. I interviewed Sonia at her store in a cozy back room, where she goes to finish paperwork at the end of the day and meets with sales representatives. She works until 7 p.m. most nights, when she closes the shop, and her husband picks her up to return home.

Sonia's lupus began when she was twenty-six years old, when she first noted some minor swelling and pain in some of her joints. This lasted for more than a year, but she did not think too much about it. She assumed she had some kind of arthritis, but since it did not slow her down too much, she just tried to ignore it. That changed dramatically one afternoon following a day-long Sunday visit with relatives, which was spent outdoors playing volleyball and sitting in the sun. In the afternoon they all piled into a car and went to Baños, a nearby town with natural hot springs. There they lounged in the Turkish baths and sat in the sun around the temperate pools until the evening came. She recalls that day very clearly and notes it as the last day she ever spent frolicking freely in the sun.

The following day she literally could not get out of bed, as she found her legs "completely paralyzed." It was "impossible," she said, to move them. They called the doctor immediately, and a number of tests and exams were conducted, but they could not find the "cause" of her condition. The best the doctors could say was that it was probably some kind of arthritis. After a few days she was able to walk again, but her legs and especially her ankles remained stiff and swollen. She continued to have tests for rheumatoid arthritis, but as she understood it, they "never encountered the cells" for it, and so they really did not know what she had.[7] Despite the lack of a confirming diagnosis, she was given steroids, which helped to reduce the inflammation. She continued to have swelling, however, especially in her ankles, and had a hard time walking. Work became difficult for her as she could not stand for long periods of time behind the counter.

In 1980 one of Sonia's nephews planned to travel to the United States to study. On the urging of her father, Sonia accompanied him so that she could go to the Cleveland Clinic for a consultation. She was told nothing about her diagnosis while she was still there, but when she returned to Ecuador, she received a letter from the clinic telling her that she was diagnosed with Hashimoto's thyroiditis, an autoimmune disorder that primarily affects the thyroid gland and creates a state of hypothyroidism. The clinic urged her to return to the United States for treatment but she could not afford a second trip. She chose instead to take the diagnosis to her local doctor who began thyroid hormone replacement therapy. However, she continued to suffer from pain and swelling, despite the treatment. Finally, two years after her first bout with paralysis, her doctor found the "lupus cells" in a blood test and diagnosed lupus.[8] Sonia described receiving the diagnoses as a difficult experience. "It was traumatic for me to learn I had lupus because everyone said it was terribly serious and that it would get progressively worse." Scared, and unconvinced (for several reasons) that biomedicine could really help her, Sonia went to Quito in search of an alternative medicine "cure."

Several years before her symptoms began, Sonia had converted from Catholicism to Seventh Day Adventism, a Christian denomination that advocates a healthy natural lifestyle, including vegetarianism and abstinence from drugs and alcohol. Seventh Day Adventists believe that God wants people to be healthy and the way to achieve that is through self-discipline, especially in diet and exercise. In Quito, Sonia consulted a "naturalist" who put her on a restricted diet and prescribed numerous herbs, and she saw a homeopath who prescribed "little balls" made from "who knows what?" She also stopped all her pharmaceuticals, including corticosteroids. She traveled back and forth from Cuenca to Quito to see the naturalist, but little by little she became worse. Each day her legs and fingers became more swollen, and the pain became harder to bear. A rash emerged on her legs and buttocks; her hair fell out in handfuls, leaving her with bald spots, followed by vomiting and diarrhea and then pleurisy and difficulty breathing. By the time she decided to return to the care of her doctor, she was very sick, yet, oddly, she was convinced that the natural "cure" had been effective. Her latest blood test, she reported, found no more "lupus cells." She continued,

> I believe the naturalist had cured me of these cells, even though everyone was telling me that I was much worse. . . . I must have lost 50 pounds under this treatment. I was a real skeleton, and my nerves were shot. I couldn't sleep, and I remember once that I went 15 days without sleeping. I started hallucinating. Whenever I saw anyone I was

terrified because I always saw double. One time the doctor came to the house, and I screamed like a crazy person because he had shaved off his mustache, and I thought he looked like a monster.

Sonia's physician was not optimistic. Worried that too much damage had been done to her heart and kidneys, he gave her corticosteroids, blood transfusions, and "a million other things." He also announced, however, that the prognosis was not good, and "there was nothing more to be done." At that point, according to Sonia, everyone believed that she would die, and "they despaired completely" for her life, yet that was not to be. One night as the family gathered outside her sick-room door, she saw a light in the middle distance, which she immediately interpreted as a sign from God. "I am a believer!" says Sonia, "and I believe it was a complete miracle." The light came closer to her, and she felt something touch her abdomen. She wanted to tell her husband, and the nun watching over her what was happening, but she could not speak. Then she heard a voice say a very simple message: "Sonia, you are going to get better." That night she dreamed about delicious foods, and the next morning she woke up hungry and asked her husband to bring her "milk, grapes, whatever there was. . . . I ate like a crazy person for days. My husband was frightened to give me anything because he thought I would vomit, but I didn't." Little by little, day by day, she gained weight, and her health improved. It took several years for her to regain all her strength and health. Today she is in good health but remains continually on a low dose of steroids.

While she was ill, Sonia tried to learn as much as she could about lupus, and most of what she read really frightened her. "I wondered if I should have read so much because it just terrified me," she said. But she always believed she would get better, and her illness has been "a tremendous challenge" to her faith. Sonia believes that she defied the odds and did not die because of the strength of her faith and the knowledge that she has not completed her "labor" here on earth. Sonia explains that Seventh Day Adventists believe that "it is our responsibility to take care of what God gives us," which includes our physical bodies. Since her illness, she has followed the Adventist diet even more closely than before; she eats no meat, drinks no alcohol, and she has "disciplined" herself so that she may enjoy the health that God has given her and that He wants her to have.[9] She is also very careful about being in the sun. "There are always consequences for what we do," Sonia explains, "and we must avoid all excess. I am very disciplined now in diet and in how much sun I take. I have learned so much about how to care for my health, but naturally. No one thought I could live even two years, and here I am thirty years later!" While Sonia admits that at first it was difficult to change so many of her habits, she so much enjoyed outdoor sports and feeling the warmth of the sun on her back, discipline is so routine to her now that it no longer feels like a "sacrifice."

When discussing her recovery from the brink of death and how she has maintained her health for so long, Sonia's narrative focuses almost exclusively on the things that she has done or that she can control, and she mentioned biomedical interventions only when I specifically asked her about them. In fact, her narrative is filled with statements that would lead one to believe that recovery came about without the use of medications but rather through diet, fortitude, faith, or strength of character. For example, when Sonia began to feel better physically but was not yet ready to return to work, she looked for ways to make a contribution and to continue her fruitful "labors." She enjoys working with older people, and so she started volunteering in a home for retired nuns. She credits this experience with helping her to get better physically and emotionally because it forced her to get her mind off her own problems, at the same time that she was able to serve others. "The nuns were my cure!" Sonia says laughing, "And without pills!" When asked, she freely admits that she has taken steroids continually for the last thirty years, albeit at lesser and lesser dosages as time went by.

Yet the steroids seem to be an afterthought, a trifling intervention, in comparison to the self-work that Sonia has undertaken. In her mind, God created a "miracle" when she was at death's door so that she could continue her "labors" on earth, and it is her responsibility to be dutiful in maintaining her current good health. "I have had a tremendous experience with this illness, pain long and terrible, in the end I had all, all, all the bad things that one can have. My nervous state debilitated me completely; it's very frightening. I endured so much and for so long. I don't ever want to return to this again, so it's important that I discipline myself. God does not want me to return to this again."

Sonia has worked hard to transform herself into a person who accepts what has come her way and who has learned to overcome disappointment and disability and embrace "sacrifice." She has reached, she says, a certain *tranquilidad* ("tranquility") about her life and how to live contentedly. After a miscarriage, she was never able to get pregnant again, and while she admits that "a child complements a home," one never came to her. She was not, compared with others, she notes, "traumatized" by that absence. Her husband, she reports, accepts her and loves her as she is. He is Catholic but respects her faith, and he has never made her feel bad that she could not have children. Sonia admits that when she was younger, she often worried about the future and what further health problems might come her way and she had trouble with depression. Over the years, however, she has accepted fully the teachings of the Bible and the Adventist faith and has learned that she cannot continue to worry about tomorrow since no can know what it will bring. "I have learned to live for today," Sonia says, "and not worry too much." Sonia occasionally counsels members of her church who are ill and provides explicit testimony about the power of self-discipline and faith in overcoming chronic illness.

MONICA

Monica is a very stylish, expertly made up, and charming twenty-five-year old woman with long dark brown hair that glints with golden highlights. Monica clearly cares very much about her appearance, and she always dresses with a great deal of care. Even her casual blue jeans are pressed and accented with towering high heels. She is quite small but seems to fill up a room with her perfume, her easy bright smile, and her infectious giggle. I noticed that sometimes she smiles even when the conversation turns bleak and painful. Her tendency to smile and laugh, even when she is troubled, she told me, is both a blessing and a curse. People, she says, often congratulate and admire her for appearing to be so optimistic in the face of her frightening illness, which can be nice, but then, they do not look or ask beyond her smile to see that, in fact, she is sometimes very scared and depressed. Monica often feels pressure to appear cheerful since that is what is expected from her, especially at home where her parents worry too much about her.

In our interviews she smiled and moved glibly away from possibly painful topics. For example, because she is an organ transplant recipient, she will never bear children of her own. Her response to my questions about how she felt about this was to say that she is now used to the idea and that her plan is to be "everyone's favorite aunt!" Like Sonia, Monica's family owns a successful retail business in town, and she has a comfortable middle-class lifestyle. When she was in high school, she spent a year abroad in the United States and even though she is hesitant to speak, her English is still quite good.

Monica was fifteen years old when she started to experience some pain in her joints, especially in her feet. She noticed that sometimes if she stayed in one position too long, she would not be able to move her feet well enough to walk. The pain in her joints seemed to move around quite a bit: one day her elbow hurt, and then the next day, it was her knee. But, for the most part, she was not overly troubled by the pain. Monica describes herself as a *"chica deportista"* (sports girl), and she assumed that her pain was related to her practice of Taekwondo or another of her numerous athletic endeavors. Then, one day she awoke to find that she could not get up. She was in a great deal of pain, and her joints were so inflamed and swollen that she could not move her ankles or her elbow. The severity of the inflammation frightened her, especially since she had done no exercise the day before, which might have accounted for the pain. She found herself "prostrate" in bed for close to three months, leaving it only to go to the doctor until she was diagnosed with lupus and began steroid treatments.

Over the course of the next several years, Monica was treated for lupus by a rheumatologist, but she, like Sonia, also explored different therapies and treatment options. At one point her father, who refused to believe that she could not be cured, accompanied Monica to Peru to meet with a renowned traditional healer. That healer performed several ritual cleansings with herbs and prayers, but in the end, he said that he could not cure her and that she should go home to return to the care of her physician. In contrast to Sonia, however, Monica did not suspend taking her medications while under the alternative healer's care and she suffered no ill effects. Her father explained that they tried the healer because, "I just didn't want to accept that my daughter could not get better. You'll try anything to help your child."

Monica too says that from the time she was a small child, she was interested in the ideas of alternative or as she calls it "oriental" medicine. When I asked Monica if "oriental" to her meant Asia or the other *oriente*, the Amazonian region of Ecuador, where nature and indigenous groups are synonymous with mysterious and sacred healing knowledge, she said they were "equal," and that there was no real difference between them. "Occidental" medicine, according to Monica, is based on taking medications that act on the physical body. "Oriental" medicine (from the "orient" or *oriente*), on the other hand, locates illness primarily in the mind. "All illness is based in the mind, and if one doesn't cure the mind, one can't cure the illness," says Monica. "There's a masochistic side to all of us. Wherever one goes . . . home, school, work we have interactions and emotions that make us sad or angry and then this can cause us harm. Illness comes from deep inside one, and one must investigate oneself deeply."

In Monica's case, she hints that social problems at school created emotional difficulties for her. Because she was an outstanding athlete who much preferred hanging out with boys than with girls, other girls were jealous of her accomplishments, her independence, and her easy rapport with boys. They gossiped about her behind her back and harassed her to her face, creating tension and stress that she thinks manifest itself in lupus. Her goal now is to maintain a peaceful and positive outlook so that her health remains stable. However, despite her thoughts that illness is largely located in the mind, Monica is extremely careful about taking her medications and following through on all her physician's recommendations.

When her condition stabilized, Monica continued with the plans she had made much earlier to study in the United States during her last year of high school. Although her doctor and her parents were not completely comfortable with her decision, she left Ecuador for nine months, taking with her all the medications she would need. Her time in the United States went well; she lived with a hospitable and caring family, and she returned home in good health. She then began classes at the university and flew through her coursework in tourism in record time. She was nominally employed at her father's store, mostly so that she could be enrolled in *Seguro* and receive the health benefits. Soon, however, for reasons she was not able or willing to fully describe, she began to have numerous complications, including problems with her kidneys. She continued to be monitored regularly, but her kidneys continued to decline until they failed completely.

The first time I spoke with Monica, she hesitated to assign blame for her kidney failure, but at our second meeting, both she and her father hinted that they believe that she received inadequate care from her private-sector physician. Monica was placed in the hospital for over a month where she received "mechanical" dialysis, then she continued with dialysis for several months afterwards, going to the clinic several times a week for lengthy sessions. Eventually she was given a catheter and taught how to perform peritoneal dialysis at home. She remained on dialysis for many months while her parents sought the money to pay for a kidney transplant, which was now the only long-term solution. The donated organ would come from her older brother.

While Monica's family is middle class, the expenses of Monica's illness, and certainly the transplant costs, around $25,000, were well beyond their means, and transplants were not then available through the IESS system. Their family began to seek help wherever they could find it, and in the process, they broke some important social customs. Monica's father describes middle- and upper-class Cuencan society as "closed" and says that personal troubles, like serious illness, are best hidden from public view. "No one wants anyone to know when there is a problem in a family, and so we stay quiet and don't ask for help. It was very difficult for me to have our family problems known." Yet despite their hesitations to go public with their inabilities to pay for needed medical care, Monica's family did seek assistance outside the family circle. They contacted local and national level charitable organizations and foundations in their search for funds.

Eventually they were given a great deal of assistance from a local Protestant foundation that agreed to help fund Monica's surgery, but with some strings attached. Monica and her family had to submit to a number of "conversations" about the Protestant faith, which made them uncomfortable. In the end, they sat through the proselytizing lectures and took the financial assistance, but they were not forced to convert from Catholicism. All the same, the experience did not sit well with Monica's father. He was grateful for the money but quite unhappy that his own faith was challenged in the process. Monica also received a significant cash donation from her U.S. study-abroad host family, which organized a fund-raiser at their church. The experience of learning how to ask for help and how to manage resources has stayed with Monica and transformed her thinking about what her lupus might mean for herself and others. Moreover, while she is extremely grateful for the assistance she received from the foundation, she and her father both believe that there should be help for others that is not tied to accepting attempts at religious conversion.

To that end, Monica has spent the last few years trying to find ways to turn her personal experiences with lupus into something that can help others very directly. "I want to be able to help others with what I know," Monica says. "I was given lupus for a reason." Working with a local physician, she and her father approached drug companies to find ways to reduce some of the out-of-pocket costs for medications. To date, they have succeeded in convincing a European-owned pharmaceutical company to offer a very expensive immunosuppressant at greatly reduced costs. Patients have to purchase the medication in some quantity, which is difficult for the poorest patients to do, but, as Monica says, it is, at least, "something." Monica also talks a great deal about wanting to start a support group for lupus patients in Cuenca, one that is focused more on providing information and financial assistance for health care services, rather than on interpersonal support, as is most common in the United States. Her goal is based directly on her own experiences, and she envisions establishing a foundation that would support lupus patients by funding treatment, including organ transplants.

Monica began talking with other local foundations about how to raise money locally, nationally, and internationally and how to organize, register, and administer a foundation. Until 2007 when several tax laws were changed, many foundations in Ecuador received substantial financial support from taxpayers, who were allowed to designate up to 25% of their income taxes to registered foundations. This changed when President Rafael Correa overhauled the Ecuadorian tax system, including eliminating the provision that citizens can donate to a foundation in lieu of paying the government. The reasoning behind this change was to avoid tax fraud and the administrative oversight over what constitutes a legitimate "foundation." Too many foundations, it seems, were mere paper foundations and had been established primarily to avert paying taxes and to funnel money back to the wealthy taxpayer. Since the new tax laws took effect, foundations have found it much more difficult to meet their financial demands; many small foundations have closed or significantly curtailed their operations. Monica's initiatives too have been put on hold as she considers other means of financing her plans. Monica's father insists that she will figure something out sooner or later and that she will succeed in establishing a foundation one day, because as he describes it, "Monica doesn't really like to take 'no' for an answer."

METAPHOR AND ILLNESS

In discussing metaphors of illness in the United States, Susan Di-Giacomo stresses the importance that American "individualism" plays in framing discussions about the transformative nature of illness (DiGiacomo 1992; see also Young 1980). Focusing mostly on popular culture models of illness, DiGiacomo also hints at the long historical roots of individualism as both a social and humanitarian good in U.S. society, and she shows how that lays the framework for the idea that the illness experience can result in individual transformation. Indeed, while individualism is something of an American myth, it also has very deep historical and cultural relevance. Benjamin Franklin, for example, wrote of the rugged individualist who is free to question and relies on his own judgment and discernment in the pursuit of moral perfection. This theme was elaborated on by de Tocqueville in his mid-nineteenth-century analysis of America democracy, which argued that in America, every man is a self-made man. This stands in contrast, of course, to European monarchies of the day, where patron-client relationships linked individuals who depended hierarchically on one another and limited opportunity and potential for many. Reinforced publicly through popular culture references (think of the lone cowboy here), politically through democratic practices and ideologies, and religiously through Protestantism, which concerns itself mostly with personal salvation, both the myth and the reality of individualism and an individual's potential to transform have become guiding metaphors for Americans.

In U.S. medicine, notions of individualism come to the fore in a variety of ways, from how we assign "risk" to how we understand treatment (DiGiacomo 1992). For example, cancer risk is almost always posed as consisting of individual risk factors such as genetics, smoking behavior, diet, exercise, and, in the case of breast cancer, age of first menarche and the number of children a woman has birthed and not social risk factors such as poverty, environmental contamination, or chemical exposures (see Balshem 1993). This notion of individual risk is so pervasive in American thinking that even in neighborhoods where obvious cancer clusters have been noted, the discourse from public health personnel is largely centered on how an individual can beat the odds by personal decisions such as avoiding smoking and getting screened regularly (Balshem 1993). The focus, in other words, is squarely on what the individual can do to care for himself or herself (Balshem 1993).

This kind of individualism, in fact, frames the rhetoric of self-help, provoking Ehrenreich's annoyance discussed earlier. She thinks cancer discussions should be focused on our social responsibilities for care and prevention and not on individual attitude and behaviors. DiGiacomo echoes Ehrenreich's concerns, noting that the popular-press books on healing and the mind written by the *New York Times* best-selling author and physician Bernie Siegel, for example, reinforce the notion that we, as individuals, contribute to our own illnesses and healing through our attitudes. "If individual persons are conceptualized as the knowing authors of their personal destinies, and experience is cast in psychologistic terms as 'feelings' it then becomes reasonable for Seigel to ask his patients why they 'needed' their illness" (DiGiacomo 1992:121). In other words, Seigel believes that a person gets sick for a reason, too much stress, for example, and that the experience is meant to teach him something. Moreover, learning that lesson creates important transformations that lead to both healing and to a better life. For Seigel, healing originates in the patient's attitude and there are "no incurable diseases, only incurable people" who have given up and succumbed (Seigel 1986:99). Illness, for Seigel, should be a "motivator" for personal change (1986:111).

Monica's ideas about the cause and cure of illness echo to some extent the very same ideas that DiGiacomo critiques, in particular, that we are somehow each individually responsible for what happens to us, even in illness. In fact, Monica takes full responsibility for having become ill, saying that she believes that illness is located first in the head, that humans have a masochistic tendency that turns social influences against the self and body, and that we become sick as an outcome of how we react to the stresses of our daily lives. Healing too, she adds, comes first from within. While she credits these ideas as coming from "oriental" (and not biomedical) influences, whatever those may be, they are in fact also very closely linked to the general orientations of North American self-help discourses.

Sonia, on the other hand, is slightly more pragmatically oriented. For her, illness is a result mostly of poor physical care and a lack of discipline, which can best be achieved through adherence to a strict Adventist faith. Her church has taught her that she is individually responsible for the care of her body, God's gift to her, by maintaining a proper vegetarian diet, avoiding alcohol and tobacco, and getting enough exercise and rest. While their orientations are different, both Sonia and Monica stress the role that the individual plays in creating health and illness, and they believe that good health can be achieved through individual effort over the mind and the body.

In general, Ecuadorians cannot be described as rugged individualists, and individual self-fulfillment is not, I would argue, obviously valued ahead of family and family obligations and responsibilities. We have seen in previous chapters, for example, that Jessica's plan for starting a family collapsed under the weight of her mother's objections; Carmella was forced into exile by her parents' shame of her; and Valentina is in no position to complain about the way her parents are helping to rear her children. Yet despite the lack of emphasis on the individual, transformational discourses can be found in Ecuador, although they are in no way ubiquitous. It is impossible to describe with any certainty all the influences on Sonia's and Monica's ways of thinking—their ideas, like those of all of us, are no doubt built from varied and various ideas that circulate in our families, communities, and institutions—but it is noteworthy that they were both heavily influenced by American ways of thinking.

While in high school, Monica spent almost a year living with an American family, one that was able to harness resources from their Protestant church to aid her in paying her medical bills. She reveres this family for the help they gave her and showed me a small book they put together to document their church fund-raising efforts on her behalf. Moreover, she speaks English very well and reads it even better, and she has spent countless hours on the internet reading about her illness and immersing herself in the self-help literature provided on various foundation web sites. Her discourse of individual meaning-making sounds very much like what one would find on such sites. While Sonia traveled only briefly to the United States, as an Adventist (a religion that originated in the United States) she is continually exposed to Protestant teachings that stress individual effort in taking care of oneself physically and spiritually. God wants all of us to enjoy good health, she believes, but that comes with personal responsibility to care for the body and soul. She credits her own good health to her individual transformation into a truly disciplined person.

Despite their embrace of American discourses about chronic illness and the potential for personal transformation that comes with it, both Monica and Sonia reject the unquestioned hegemony of western biomedicine, if not in principle, then in theory. So, even though she would never dream of stopping her steroid regimen, Sonia blatantly refuses to credit biomedicine with her recovery from lupus. Rather, natural medicine and personal self-care, endorsed by Adventist teaching, is her source of inspiration and hope. Similarly, Monica's life as a transplant recipient is measured by medications and biomedical monitoring, yet she too sees wellness as located in "oriental" teachings that stress the powers of her own mind to heal. Biomedicine cures the symptoms, not the cause, she tells us, and true health comes from within.

Hope for both of them resides within their own selves, in their discipline and attitudes and their abilities to overcome their conditions.

It is impossible for me truly to know the extent of the influence of American models of individualism and transformation in Ecuador or to determine whether Americanized transformational discourses will become more prevalent as access to the internet and support-group philosophies increase there. Indeed, Catholicism, as we have seen in the last chapter, certainly has its own long history of seeking meaning in suffering and the value of suffering for the elevation of the soul, if not the living person. Mercedes will suffer through her "prizes" in this life in the hopes of achieving complete salvation in the next.

Moreover, as I discussed in Chapter Two and in Paula's case (Chapter Four), there is a robust discourse about the curative properties of nature in Ecuador. This discourse includes a belief, or perhaps only a hope, that a different kind of knowledge—one older, native, and natural—exists. Indeed, a radio advertisement for a popular Ecuadorian nationwide chain of natural health products claims that we all might be healthier if, like our indigenous neighbors, we lived "closer to nature" (Miles 1998a). Both Monica and Sonia embrace a certain kind of self-awareness and self-discipline as a key to healing that reflects American notions of individualism, at the same time that their verbal (if not actual) rejection of biomedicine seems to represent an effort to create a more locally salient interpretation of their individualism. Monica does not see her discourse as modern or western but rather as ancient and from the *oriente*, while Sonia invokes the language of Godly "miracles" and faithful following of natural practices to describe her recovery.

CHAPTER EIGHT

Living with Lupus

WHEN I LAST SAW ROSA, SHE WAS DOING REMARK-ably well. She had moved to the new two-story home that she was still in the process of building, and she enjoyed cooking in her well-equipped kitchen and gardening in the yard. She planted several fruits trees, has a small patch of herbs for cooking and making teas, and has seemingly commandeered every planter and tin can she could find to house a flowering plant. For the first time in her adult life she now lives in a place that is her own. Rosa lives with only two of her children now, her youngest son, who is still in high school, and her middle daughter, Marisol, who graduated from college and works as an accountant. Marisol is completely devoted to her mother and does all she can to ease her burdens. She shares her small paychecks with Rosa, consults with her mother about house-construction decisions, and helps around the house as much as she can.

While the upstairs of the house is finished and boasts wooden floors and a tiled kitchen, the downstairs remains a bare shell of a house. Their goal is to live in the bright, sun-warmed rooms upstairs and rent the downstairs as a steady source of income. Lucho remains in New York, for the most part pretty unhappily, so that he can send money home to finish the construction. He is starting to feel trapped in New York. He is getting older and day-labor jobs are becoming harder for him to get, yet he knows that once he returns to Cuenca, he will never be able to earn enough money to complete the work on the house. He becomes frustrated when he sees that his meager earnings do not go much beyond paying the monthly rent in New York.

Rosa's health is so stable now that the sun does not seem to bother her, she no longer limits her diet, and she often fails to see her physician and take her medication. As I described earlier, she even believes on some level that she never really had lupus. While complete remission from lupus is rare, Rosa has been symptom free for several years now. The devastation that the disease brought to her family has receded and it now seems more a part of a very sad past, rather than her daily experience. Rosa's daughters are somewhat concerned about her cavalier attitude about her health. They chide her into seeing her doctor from time to time and quiz her about whether she takes her medications. Alejandra also worries about whether, like Cecilia, she or Marisol will develop lupus one day. Alejandra is always quick to laugh and make fun of herself, and she jokes about her own occasionally overwrought reactions to the smallest ache or fatigue she may experience. She "panics," she says, immediately thinking that her exhaustion might be the first symptom of lupus. For now, both young women are quite healthy and very busy.

Even though lupus no longer plays an obvious role in Rosa's day-to-day life, her years of illness and her daughter's death from lupus have permanently altered the ways that she and her children think about and live their lives. Who they are as individuals and as a family has, I believe, been permanently altered by their experiences with lupus. Most obviously, Lucho remains in the United States much longer than he anticipated; they could have saved far more money if they did not have all the medical expenses that Rosa's and Cecilia's illnesses brought. Marisol's education was prolonged, as she took time off to help care for her mother, and the family had to reduce its level of consumption, selling their car, for example, in the wake of Cecilia's death and the debts her illness created.

What is less obvious and much harder to pin down are the ways that Lucho's absence has combined with Rosa's and Cecilia's illnesses to impact family roles and obligations and the subjectivities and identities of the various family members. The experience of watching their mother's health crisis years ago and of having to find ways to cope with it while their father was away has no doubt shaped the children's personalities and the relations between them, perhaps in ways that can never really be isolated or known. Marisol has always been devoted to her mother, but how has Rosa's illness and Cecilia's death strengthened and altered that bond? The second eldest son, Beto, is married with a child of his own, but as the eldest male in the family who has not migrated, he feels obligated to step in at important junctures when a male presence is desirable. During Cecilia's illness he lost his job when he took time from work to be with his family, and he calls or stops by to visit his mother nearly every day. He has tried to be a strong male figure in his younger brother's life.

Billy, at sixteen, is by far the most reticent Quitasaca, and he seems to me to be without the confidence and enthusiasms that I saw displayed by his older siblings when they were growing up. Billy's personality today is in part shaped by his early life experiences, which include his eldest brother's migration to the United States when he was just two, his father's departure when he was six years old, his mother's protracted illness beginning when he was seven, and his sister's death when he was twelve. Billy's cautious and reserved demeanor is nothing like any of his siblings, but neither are his early life experiences. Surely his life has been shaped in part by lupus, a force that has caused illness and death among his loved ones and extended his father's absence from home.

SUBJECTIVITIES

The idea of "subjectivities" has had something of a reawakening in anthropology as we attempt to understand the various forces that shape the way individuals understand their worlds and behave in ways that make both personal and cultural sense. As an orientation to understanding why someone thinks or acts the way she does, examining subjectivities necessarily incorporates a broad analysis of historically situated social and cultural meanings that contribute to shaping people (Ortner 2005). For Ortner, the focus on subjectivities includes a concern for inner feelings and affect but also for the ways that cultural formations, including local and global configurations of power, frame and constrain individual agency (Ortner 2005).

What makes revealing subjectivities so difficult, however, is that "culture" is not something that can be demarcated easily or framed absolutely (Biehl, Good, and Kleinman 2007). Culture does not "exist" as something to be captured by critical analysis; rather, it is always evolving and "constantly remade through social encounters, ethical deliberations, political processes and writing" (Biehl et al. 2007). In other words, uncovering what culture says and does exactly, and then writing about it, is no simple trick, as nothing can be taken at "face value," and rational consistency is neither real nor likely (Fischer 2007:424). "Subjectivities," writes the provocative Michael Fischer, "are raucous *terra incognito*, landscapes of explosion, noise, alienating silences, disconnects and dissociations, fears, terror machineries, pleasure principles, illusions, fantasies, displacements, and secondary revisions, mixed with reason, rationalizations, and paralogics—all of which have sociopolitical dimensions and effects" (Fischer 2007:424).

In this book I have attempted to explore the ways that a bodily experience, being sick with lupus, intersects with Ecuadorian women's lives and selves as they are lived within particular historical and political circumstances. Similar to Parish, I do think that suffering puts subjectivities into sharper relief than we might otherwise find them, as the unexpected, the unwarranted, and the undesirable provoke us to be become "questions to ourselves" (Parish 2008:9). I have argued here that women's illness interpretations are constructed partially from their personal experiences with lupus, how severe it is, the level of disruption it creates, when in the life trajectory it began, partially from their personal life experiences with family, schoolmates, and even strangers, partly from their exposure and commitment to social institutions and configurations of power, including religion, class, and the medical system and partly from their culturally constructed understandings of femininity. The focus of the book has been to demonstrate the creative interplay between the personal and the social, the emotional and the cultural, the private and the institutional, with the goal to highlight the intersubjectivity of life experiences.

Similar to what is described in the literature on culture-bound syndromes among women in Latin America, I am drawn to the idea that configurations of power do matter a great deal in the options, interpretations, and subjectivities that are described here. Indeed, the case studies outlined point to a range of powerful influences that seem to affect women's experiences in important ways; separating these influences from one another has proven difficult. For example, gender matters considerably in how women understand their lives, selves, and social roles, but gender understandings are also framed by ideas about religion, morality, and class. Rosa's reticence in her doctor's office and Cecilia's tenuous understanding of her social position are gendered responses at the same time that they are influenced by the intersections of class and gender. When Rosa interacts with her physicians, she is as much a woman as she is a woman of "humble" origins, someone whose class standing places her in a double bind of subservience. Afraid to ask questions but also suspicious of the motives of her physicians, as is Jessica's mother, Rosa now denies her condition—and in doing so strips her physicians of any real authority over her health.

Cecilia's fragile social self that was brutally tested by changes in her appearance, and her life-course position as an unsure adolescent girl navigating a difficult life stage from a marginalized social-class position, contributed to her tragic end. Finding herself the object of prying and possibly ill-intentioned curiosity brought a kind of negative social attention to her that she did not have the wherewithal, or social savvy, to combat. We have also seen how middle-class Leonor and working-class Jessica never stop wondering if their lack of social leverage means that they are somehow getting less care in IESS than others who have *palanca* and are more powerfully situated.

We have seen here how a woman's ability or inability to fulfill the multiple gender-role obligations and expectations is a central preoccupation that frames how she understands her illness and her conceptions of her self. Lupus alters, either temporarily or permanently, a woman's ability to perform the expected behaviors inherent in the roles of daughter, wife, or mother, threatening her sense of identity and her connection to others. Yet, as we have seen, how this plays out in individual lives varies considerably. For many, the unattainable gender-role expectations placed on them create a powerful and sometimes oppressive sense of loss and even failure. The association of lupus with HIV/AIDS by some exacerbates women's feelings of alienation and isolation. Moreover, because of facial lesions or the side effects of steroids, many women felt "ugly" and "monstrous," further destabilizing their claim to femininity, and their own sense of self-worth, resulting in shame, avoidance of others and, in Cecilia's case, ultimately death.

Almost every woman reported serious feelings of depression surrounding her illness. Sometimes their reports of depression were about the past when they were first diagnosed or before their symptoms were controlled, but for others, especially those whose lupus proved resistant to improvement, depression and loss are constant companions. The doctors I spoke with easily recognized this dimension of their patients' suffering, but I was not always sure they understood the deeper roots of it. It is not just that women are afraid that they may die, or that their expectations for their lives have to be temporarily or permanently altered because of illness, but their very status as "complete" and worthy women is threatened.

For Jessica and Paula, whose lupus came when they were young, chronic illness has meant that both women awkwardly remain simultaneously adults with jobs and responsibilities, and not-quite-adults under their parents' ever-watchful eyes. Living in their parents' homes well into their thirties, both women can no longer imagine a future as a wife and mother. Jessica faces the knowledge, reinforced by her mother, that she is a permanently "failed" woman because she will not have children, while Paula still inhabits the role of the rebellious child even though she is now a bit long in the tooth for that one.

Valentina and Leonor, both wives and mothers when they became ill with lupus, saw their abilities to fulfill those roles in the ways that they wanted to attenuated, resulting for both in a sense of inadequacy and loss. Valentina's and Carmella's marriages fell apart under the strain of their illnesses, forcing Valentina to rely on her parents once again, and Carmella to ultimately sell her home and move to a much smaller apartment. Leonor was not able to be the mother and wife that she wanted to be and could not teach her children the life lessons she found most meaningful, shaking her own sense of herself as a moral actor.

Carmella and Mercedes, along with Valentina, activated culturally understood Catholic notions of female suffering as a way to stake some moral ground for an experience that is otherwise difficult to explain and therefore potentially morally suspect. Carmella and Valentina both reference their lives prior to lupus as extraordinarily difficult ones; both had children out of wedlock in families that were intolerant of that kind of transgression; both followed that experience with unhappy and violent marriages. For these two women the cumulative effects of being vulnerable women, judged negatively by others, their intrinsic goodness ignored, and then seemingly trapped in unhappy marriages led to a build up of stresses that "exploded" in lupus. Their understandings of cause and effect compel us to reconsider the multiple implications of the loss-illness-illness-loss connection.

Despite the multiple hardships recounted here, few women saw their lives before lupus as truly disconnected from their lives after lupus. Rather, most women had worked through a process of meaning-making that aimed to synthesize their understandings about their lives in some significant, albeit not necessarily comprehensive, way. Estroff argues that chronic illness creates a disruption in the life course and that over time the patient learns to accept the chronic condition as a part of his or her self-identity (Estroff 1993). Lupus most certainly created "disruption" in the lives of sufferers, but this disruption was resolved for many women by reworking their life narratives and creating logical connections between life before and life after the onset of lupus. For example, women considered whether they were too rebellious, too active, had too much exposure to harmful chemicals or circulating germs, or if they suffered too much emotional pain, among many other possibilities. In these scenarios, lupus is woven into a complete life history rather than being seen as a rupturing event that defines two distinct life stages. From this perspective, loss, illness, mind, and body intermingle in inseparable ways and are not necessarily lineally or uniformly causally related.

The social and emotional suffering referenced by women, suffering that is linked to their very womanly virtues of caring too much, allowed them a discourse to frame their own subjectivities in alignment with well-understood cultural narratives about the existential fate of women. While Carmella's and Valentina's suffering seems wholly tragic, Mercedes, the Catechumenal, interpreted her suffering, which included a severely disabled spouse and sole economic responsibility for her family, in more messianic ways, that is, as a means towards long-term salvation of her soul. In all these cases, female suffering became an idiom through which social negotiations of the self could be referenced in ways that recognize the structural and cultural vulnerabilities of all good women and the especially egregious personal conditions of these particular women.

Ecuadorian women are enmeshed in dense family networks that they rely on for care much of the time, and solace some of the time. These relationships thoroughly aggravate them on occasion, but their centrality in making life meaningful and in easing burdens is not usually seriously questioned by anyone. Paula and Jessica, for example, both chafe at the surveillance of their parents but also recognize that their parents' vigilance is an expression of their devotion to them, and neither one has considered making different living arrangements. They both spar with their parents from time to time, but they are also highly invested in their relationships with them. Real independence, financial or otherwise, is neither practical, nor, I think, desirable.

Similarly, Valentina's resentment at her parents for their overly strict upbringing is tempered by her gratitude for the ways that they have cared first for her son and then for Valentina and all her children. Her parents provided the only safety net available, and they have been there for each of Valentina's health crises. It is they who take her to the doctor, care for her at home, and stay up nights tending to her. Sonia's and Monica's parents took a similar role with them, Leonor's aunt stepped in to help care for her, and Rosa's children dropped everything when she was ill to care for her. The burdens of care (financial and emotional) for lupus are not insignificant. They resonate throughout a family as children, parents, and sometimes extended family members are called upon for help. Everyone's life is changed in the process.

Indeed, the strength and solidity of family bonds means that lupus is not an illness of the individual in Ecuador, but rather one that reverberates throughout the family, usually for an extended period of time. Women with lupus count on their families for so much at the same time that they try to protect them from the worst of their fears and sorrows. Women discussed how much their parents, their mothers in particular, their husbands, and their children suffered for them and what effects this has on all of them. Jessica and Monica both specifically discussed how they hide their physical and emotional suffering from their families, but a concern for the stresses put on family members reverberated through many interviews. Sometimes family connections and resources were stretched too thin, and people snapped or relationships cooled. One hard-working mother struggled with her feelings of guilt because her daughter's lupus fatigue looked a lot like lethargy to her, and it annoyed her terribly. Similarly, Rosa, who has long had tenuous relationships with her extended family, claims she can no longer count on them for help as she fears their judgment and annoyance. Yet her inability to count on them seems to rankle and disappoint her, pointing to the emotional connections that she thinks ought to be there, even if they are not.

As Rosa's case also highlights, family finances are often seriously affected by lupus. Difficult choices have to be made about what medical interventions are absolutely necessary and what sacrifices will be made to afford them. Women without any health insurance coverage enter a world of constant negotiation between their pocketbooks, their well-being, their family's priorities, and their physicians' advice, no doubt adding to their social stress and their illness burdens. Some women worried about and lamented the financial sacrifices made by their families and wondered how that money could be better spent elsewhere. One newly diagnosed young woman, Susana, who works in the informal economy and has no health insurance, spent our entire interview crying and worrying about how she could continue to afford the medications her physician prescribed and care for herself and her mother, with whom she lives. Her married sister promised to help, but with children and a home of her own, there are limits to the help she can give but also limits to the sacrifices that Susana will allow her nieces and nephews to experience because of her.

Encounters with the health care system left some of the most well-off women fairly optimistic about their health and their futures, and others vaguely suspicious that because of their economic means or social status that they were not receiving the very best care. Rosa's long-standing suspicions of elites carries over into her relationships with physicians, which are characterized by passive compliance in their presence and jaded cynicism about them in private. A few women, mostly those who are doing pretty well or who are well connected socially, are grateful for the services they received in the Social Security system, while others less well connected and without easy alternatives in the private sector find that the problems with the pharmacy, the crowded hospital wards, and the out-of-pocket expenses for tests disrupts their care and creates needless anxiety. Always alert for social-class differences, several women have the nagging feeling that some unfairness might be occurring, even at IESS.

A further concern throughout this book has been to reveal the complex interplay between a biomedical category, lupus, and cultural knowledge. We have seen here how lupus is nuanced so that the etiology, treatment, and consequences of the disease are put in terms that are locally meaningful. Lupus is understood to be a biomedically managed medical problem, yet that does not suspend culturally variable speculation about its origins, how best to manage it through diet, or how to prevent social stigma over fears of contagion or suspicions of moral laxity. The distinction between "folk" and biomedical become blurred along the margins as women and their doctors seek ways to manage and comprehend lupus. Moreover, contestations over biomedical authority are woven throughout these narratives, as women and the family members assert their abilities to "know" about their health and their bodies and to challenge both their physicians and the chronic illness label.

Although every woman I spoke to was under the supervision of a physician and some, like Monica, who has a transplanted kidney, are highly dependent on high-tech biomedicine, many women expressed skepticism about western medicine. Sometimes their skepticism sprang primarily from their suspicions discussed above that good care was simply inaccessible to them for economic or social reasons. In other cases, as we have seen, women sought explanations outside of biomedicine for why they had lupus or what to do about it. Pushing biomedical explanations aside, Mercedes and her mother continue to speculate about how her female labors, the dirty money, toxic household cleaners, and frigid wash water likely contributed to her illness, while Jessica and her mother ponder the possibilities of the "bad" blood associated with her conception. Similarly, Paula extols the virtues to be found in the pristine air of the high mountains and the healing powers of both the landscape and the people who live there, while her mother, educated and elite, wonders if her dead father's spirit has not somehow brought health to Paula. Finally, despite their daily dependence on biomedicine, both Monica and Sonia speak of true healing as coming from themselves, through mental or physical discipline.

"HAY QUE SEQUIR ADELANTE"

It is probably safe to assume that as diagnostic techniques become better and less expensive and as record-keeping practices improve, the documented incidence rates in Ecuador for autoimmune disorders such as lupus will rise. Moreover, as time goes by, Ecuadorian physicians will probably become better trained to spot lupus earlier, and perhaps, with some luck, improvements will be made in the drug supply system in the MPH and IESS. I think it would be too much to hope that the price of biologic therapy will be reduced enough anytime soon to make them a truly viable option for most patients. Pharmaceutical companies already offer them at much lower prices than in the United States, but they are still out of the reach of most lupus patients. Cuenca, however, may be in a better position than most Ecuadorian cities to improve the health outcomes of lupus patients, as it has a large base of physicians, many of them the best trained in the country, and many of them have substantial interests in improving both research and services to lupus patients. One physician has plans to start a lupus research program at the Hospital Universitario del Río with the collaboration of a nephrologist. This center would ideally be the home to both biological and social science research on lupus.

Sadly, as we have seen with Monica's plans for a lupus support group, often the best laid plans can be stymied by lack of funds or changes in regulations and laws that seriously derail honest efforts to provide services or that promise to fix one problem while in reality just creating another. Indeed, when I returned to Ecuador briefly in 2009 I learned that IESS had instituted several new changes in their appointment system for patients. However, while it would seem that any change in the appointment policy of IESS would be an improvement, as it turns out, these efforts to streamline the system, eliminate corruption, and keep a better eye on the workloads and especially the working hours of physicians, have created other equally frustrating problems for patients. In 2008 IESS centralized its appointment system so that every IESS patient anywhere in the country must call the Quito office of IESS to make an appointment at their local hospital. The phone lines are open 24 hours a day. In theory this sounds like a very good idea.

In practice, however, patients found the system unnecessarily cumbersome. Several patients reported that they always have a great deal of difficulty getting through to the Quito number or that their cell phones were charged for what is supposed to be a toll-free call. In the end, patients are still getting up in the middle of the night to make an appointment, only now they get up to make a phone call. One woman said that even then, she is not guaranteed to get through. While all my informants had phones, this systemic change also assumes that all IESS members have access to a phone 24 hours a day, which may not be the case, especially for more rural residents. I can only imagine the problems this has caused them. Moreover, and somewhat inexplicably, a patient can only make one appointment per phone call, and so if she wishes to see several physicians during the same trip to the clinic, she is required to make several phone calls.

Changes have also been made at IESS to monitor patient appointments and directly link them to the disbursement of medications. Prescriptions are valid now only if the date on them corresponds to the date of an officially scheduled appointment. One patient reported that in the past, if she only needed to have her physician reissue a prescription, she could stop by the office briefly, catch her doctor between patients, and get a quick prescription. Now if she does that, she is barred from filling that prescription at the IESS pharmacy because that office visit was not "official," in other words, it was not scheduled through the central system.

In 2009 I learned of another casualty of the well-meaning tax reforms that had stymied Monica's efforts at forming a lupus foundation in Cuenca. In this case, an already established foundation dedicated to helping patients with rheumatoid arthritis (RA) suddenly found itself without funds to operate its newly constructed educational and rehabilitation clinic. On the urging of two Cuencan physicians who volunteer for the foundation, I visited Ibarra, a small city two hours north of Quito, to meet with an RA sufferer there who had, on her own initiative, established the clinic. The physicians thought it was important for me to meet and write about María's efforts, as a vivid symbol of what is possible. Unfortunately, I am not sure that is the message I ultimately walked away with. Located on a nondescript street in Ibarra, the facility she has constructed, but has no funds to operate, contains state-of-the art exercise and water therapy equipment, abundant space for patient consultations, and hospital rooms. The goal of clinic is to provide medical care, including physical therapy and education, to RA sufferers.

The impressive three-story facility has been financed exclusively through María's fund-raising efforts, which have ranged from selling locally produced chocolates in Quito to harnessing substantial contributions through the previous foundation allocation tax law. She has held several RA "campaigns" locally, seeking out fellow sufferers from all walks of life and offering the best available medical care from volunteer physicians. María's long-term vision, ideally, is to open the hospital full time and accept patients for daily rehabilitation, treatment, and education as well as provide living facilities for longer-term medical "tourists." The tourism idea is a relatively new one put in place after the tax law changes with the hopes that the money generated from tourism would offset the significant tax-allocation losses. Ibarra is not far from the thermal baths of Papallacta, touted for their healthful benefits, and she is hoping to capitalize on this already popular tourist destination.

María is a tiny woman with incredibly big ambitions. Her own case of RA is very serious, and although she receives the best possible medical care, she still walks with difficulty. What she has accomplished to date is a testament to her will and her ability to carry others along on her enthusiasm. Her husband is her closest collaborator, but she also is well connected socially, and she has support from local and national level politicians and important physicians. While I was astounded by what she has accomplished so far, I also could not help wondering how her endeavor could ever really get off the ground and sustain itself over the long term. What makes it so heart-breaking is that María has thought of everything and her intentions are quite noble. She wants to help the very poor who she says "suffer alone in their poverty," and she spared nothing in an effort to provide the poor with the best facilities available. She has thought of everything and has even included a small apartment and a roof-top barbeque for visiting volunteer physicians. But how she will find the funds to finish the work and to staff the facility now that her steady source of income from taxes has ended is not at all clear. Much of the clinic still lacks basic equipment, and most of the outer buildings, including administrative offices and an auditorium for educational campaigns, are still unfinished. When I met with her she was regrouping as best she could, but it was clear that she was worried. The facility stands empty, its halls echoing as we walked down them, as she scrounges as best she can to find new sources of funding.

The efforts of people like María are often difficult for critical medical anthropologists to fully come to terms with. On the one hand, her work is undoubtedly inspirational and only the most cynical observer could not admire her dedication to filling the gaps in care for sufferers of RA. Her motivations are clearly altruistic, and she wants to do what the public services do not, that is, offer state-of-the art care for all, regardless of the ability to pay. Suffering as she does with pain and immobility, she is deeply concerned for those who have far fewer options than herself. She wonders what their anguish must be like without the latest medications, without physical therapy, and without the support of family and doctors.

On the other hand, a more critical reading of María's efforts might point out the "system maintaining" or "nonreformist" nature of the endeavor (see Singer 1995:90). By this I mean that the care that María wants to provide for the poor is solely dependent on the goodwill and "charity" of the wealthy, rather than being part of a comprehensive public health strategy. Some have argued that such "band-aid" approaches may serve to temporarily mask problems and ultimately further delay real structural reform. While I certainly understand the logic of this critique and agree that there is much right about it, I also cannot help but wonder whether it is always really better to do nothing while we wait for the revolution to begin. Indeed, it does not look like the public health facilities will improve substantially anytime soon. While recent changes by the government have sought to eliminate patient costs in the public health system, they have enacted these cost changes without increasing health care staff or improving equipment and facilities. The lower costs have served to flood the system with patients seeking tests and procedures they could not afford earlier. One doctor told me in 2011 that she thought the public health hospital in Cuenca was on the verge of "collapsing" because of the increase in patient demand unaccompanied by an increase in staff and equipment.

While the public system shudders under the weight of good intentions, María's unfinished facility echoes with a ghostly quiet; the clinic opens only for outpatient care less than once a month, when volunteer doctors, many of them from Cuenca, can be rounded up. A victim of unforeseen, and perhaps long needed, changes in social policies, the future of the facility is now unknowable. María has ideas for funding the hospital that range from renting "vacation" cabins to requesting Peace Corps volunteers to staff administrative positions, but for now these are just hopeful possibilities that have yet to be tested.

Indeed, for this and other reasons, to me, María's hospital with its empty, gleaming corridors and locked front gate seems like a brick-and-mortar symbol of the struggles of the women I interviewed with lupus. Like so many lupus patients, the hospital is sadly vulnerable, and it has been buffeted by circumstances that are unpredictably changeable and seemingly outside of anyone's immediate control. Built in a flood of hope and optimism, today it sits in its own state of functional and structural liminality, trying to figure out how to survive, if not flourish, under constantly changing conditions. Now there is nothing left to do, María says, but to continue to *seguir adelante* ("move forward") into an unclear future.

Notes

1. Remittances from abroad are an increasingly important source of revenue for Ecuador. Jokisch (n.d.) writes that "the Inter-American Development Bank estimated that Ecuador received $2.0 billion in remittances in 2004, equivalent to 6.7 percent of its GDP and second only to oil exports; 14 percent of adults in Ecuador receive remittances regularly" (http://www.migrationinformation.org/Profiles/display.cfm?ID=575).

2. Mortality statistics in general are poor in Ecuador (Waters 2006). While there are no statistics on lupus there, both heart disease and diabetes are major causes of morbidity and mortality (PAHO 2007).

3. I refer here to an idea that will be explained in much greater detail in Chapter Two. Lock and Nguyen (2010) argue that culture, environment, and biology intermingle in multiple ways, including impacting the physical body in particular, but not exclusively in subjective ways. Their concept of local biologies includes the idea that there are "biosocial" differences that emerge between populations (90). Both evolutionary and historical time can produce these biosocial differences.

4. Hahn (1985) critiqued the term "culture bound" as juxtaposed to biomedical as a "false division" that too often makes others appear to have conditions that are "cultural," while westerners have illnesses that are more truly "biomedical," reifying the differences between them.

5. Informed consent procedures for this project were approved by Western Michigan University's Institutional Review Board. I have used pseudonyms throughout for all participants to protect their privacy. For more details about the sample, see Miles 2011. Most of what is described here covers the research period from 2005 to 2007, with some updates from 2009 after populist President Rafael Correa instituted significant changes to the health care delivery system.

6. Charon (2006) takes a more literary position vis-à-vis the analysis of illness narratives and examines five aspects of text construction: frame, form, time, plot, and desire. Frame includes parsing the author's intention and determining what is

and is not included in the text; form concerns analyzing the genre and structure of the narrative, including metaphor and allusions; an analysis of time considers how the temporality of illness is related in the narrative; plot is what happens; and desire asks what "appetite" has been satisfied by writing and reading the text.

CHAPTER TWO

1. In 2000 Ecuador began the process of converting their currency from the *sucre* to the U.S. dollar. Dollarization of the economy was done in an effort to stabilize rising inflation and interest rates (see Larrea 2004). All prices quoted in the book are in dollars (the local currency) and are current as of 2007.

2. While the words *cholo* (m.) or *chola* (f.) are common throughout Latin America and are often derogatory terms of address, in Cuenca the *Chola Cuencana* (f.) is a more complex and ambiguous figure. The *Chola Cuencana* represents primarily rural styles of female dress and comportment typical to the province of Azuay. The *Chola Cuencana* is usually a monolingual Spanish speaking mestiza who resides in the rural areas or who works in urban markets. The *Chola Cuencana* has important symbolic meanings in Cuenca, as she stands as a symbol of the mixing of the Spanish and Indigenous cultures in the region and is the living embodiment of the regional folklore. A statue of the *Chola Cuencana* graces the southern entrance to the city and the song "The *Chola Cuencana*" is taught to school children and sung at civic events, school programs, and private family gatherings. She is an ambivalent figure since she is most admired when she remains in the rural areas and becomes a figure of suspicion or disdain when she enters the urban landscape and demands access to public services and spaces. (See Miles 2004; Weismantel 2001.)

3. It is difficult to ascertain statistically exactly how Cuenca has grown in recent decades because much of the population increase has occurred in the burgeoning neighborhoods that are just outside the city limits. The city of Cuenca solves this dilemma by reporting on its website population data about the Canton of Cuenca, composed of twenty-one parishes, including the city of Cuenca. Some parishes are designated as "urban" and some "rural." This city website, which does not yet report results from the 2010 census, indicates that the urban population of the canton has grown from 152,406 in 1980 to 331,028 in 2000 (Cuenca Alcaldía 2010). But there is a noticeable drop in the rural population between 1990 and 2000 (136,047 to 86,604 respectively), reflecting the redesignation of some parishes near the city from rural to urban. The Ecuadorian Census Institute (INEC) reports the canton population (rural and urban) was 505,000 in 2010 (INEC 2012), and the city population (which does not include all "urban" residents) is at 331,888 inhabitants (*El Mercurio* 2011).

4. The growing literature on health disparities and race points to the complex ways that racism (and not biological race) and inequality can contribute to poorer health outcomes in the U.S. Among the concerns are how living as a minority race in a dominant white society creates stress (see Dressler 1993; Geronimus et al. 2010), how living in conditions of inequality and not just poverty can negatively impact

health (see Nguyen and Peschard 2003), and how the healthcare system operates under conditions of entrenched racism (Malat et al. 2010).

5. In *The Culture of Pain*, Morris wonders if all pain and illness in the "modern" contexts has the potential to become "meaningless" pain. According to Morris, pain is "an event that demands interpretation" (Morris 1991:18). Morris worries that as biomedical explanations for chronic pain increase, pain becomes a solely biological event and is therefore at risk of being stripped of its social and cultural significance. On the other hand, Sontag (1990) welcomes the move away from metaphoric meanings of illness towards more biomedical and, in her estimation, less morally and socially charged explanations of illness. Commenting on the meanings of cancer in the 1970s, Sontag argues that the cancer victim was "blamed" for his or her condition and that a "cancer"-prone personality existed. While there still may be some stigma attached to certain cancers, including rectal and colon, for the most part cancer no longer carries with it the same moral interpretations as it did in the 1970s. Other diseases, like HIV/AIDS for example, still stigmatize their sufferers (Sontag 1990).

6. There is an extensive literature in the United States that shows that women's illness complaints are often not taken as seriously as men's and even that women are less likely to receive aggressive treatment for the same symptoms as men since medical professionals are less likely to give credence to women's expressions of distress (Avanian and Epstein 1991; McMurray 1991).

7. African Americans are also at higher risk for lupus nephritis than non-Hispanic white populations (Alarcón 2001).

8. The Lupus Foundation of America reports that annual direct costs for lupus care in the United States are $12,643. When direct costs are combined with indirect costs, including lost wages, the total is $20,924 (http://www.lupus.org/webmodules/webarticlesnet/templates/new_newsroomreporters.aspx?articleid=247&zoneid=60; see also Clarke et al. 2000).

9. In addition to an expanding formal health care system, Ecuador has also seen significant growth in the marketing of over-the-counter drugs and medications (see Euromonitor International 2011) and in the promotion of "natural" and herbal medicines (see Miles 1998a and 1998b).

CHAPTER THREE

1. There is also a military health care system that provides care for military personnel, police, and their family members. However, the military health services are slightly more costly than the MPH services and nationally are used by only about 1% of the population (Fretes Ciblis et al. 2003:308). There are also a number of municipal clinics focused primarily on maternal and early childhood preventive care. The 20% figure for IESS coverage is anecdotal; it was reported to me by two physicians who work in the hospital. Nationally, the coverage rate is lower; Fretes-Ciblis et al. (2003) reports that only 18% of the Ecuadorian population as a whole is covered by IESS.

2. This changed in 2008, after a series of government reforms led to greater monitoring of doctor's schedules. Several doctors long accustomed to putting in half a day's work on a full salary were forced to accept only half-time salaries.

3. Fretes-Ciblis et al. report that as of 2003 it was the poorest of the poor who most suffered from the increases in user fees. Among the poorest, health expenditures reached close to 40% of income, while the middle classes spent closer to 5% of their income on health care.

4. While public health services in cities such as Cuenca are generally available (if not all that their users would desire), the system is least effective in rural areas where services are often sporadic or unavailable. Fully two-thirds of the population (much of it rural) has no health insurance and "the Ministry of Public Health and other public institutions are incapable of providing health care to this 30% of the population . . ." (Fretes-Ciblis et al. 2003:301).

Rafael Correa, Ecuador's populist President, began an initiative in 2008 to significantly increase the funding of the Ministry of Public Health. By reallocating money originally earmarked to pay down Ecuador's foreign bonds, Correa announced a $40 million infusion into the public health system, including a one-year-only increase of 4,500 health personnel.

5. Included in this category is SOLCA (Sociedad de Lucha Contra Cáncer), the Ecuadorian cancer institute that has hospital facilities in major cities in the country. SOLCA services are considered better and more advanced than those of the public sector, but they can also be quite costly.

6. The Hospital Universitario del Río officially opened in May 2009. At that time, it was under the management of the American Hospital Management Company, a U.S.-based hospital management outsourcing company that operated several hospitals in Ecuador, including the Hospital Metropolitano in Quito, one of the most prestigious hospitals in the country. By 2012 the Hospital Universitario del Río no longer appeared to be managed by the American Hospital Management Company, but I could find no evidence in the local newspaper, *El Mercurio*, for when or why the hospital management changed hands; nor were any of my local contacts able to provide details of the administrative shifts. The hospital is now heavily promoted to the growing ex-pat community in Cuenca, many of whom are retirees from the United States, and new insurance schemes have been developed that are specific to their needs.

7. Other published reports offer more mixed results from biologic therapies (see Schröder and Zeuner 2009; Bruce 2010).

CHAPTER FOUR

1. S. J. Williams (2005) provides an excellent review of the sociological critiques of Parsons' formulation, including its inapplicability to chronic illness, but he also argues that much of what Parsons wrote has left an important imprint on how we understand the sick body and the medical encounter. See also Varul (2010), who dis-

cusses how the sick role is challenged by chronic illness, which threatens a loss of approval and then esteem that is acquired through completion of social roles and relations of reciprocity.

2. Parsons also discusses the idea that, generally, sick people are not considered responsible for their condition, especially if they follow the requisite "rules" of the sick role, which entails seeking proper expert help (Parsons 1951).

3. Becker writes of a similar case in the United States, where a woman with chronic illness interprets her pregnancy as a sign of her own "normalcy." Even when she loses the baby through miscarriage, she interprets her ability to conceive and the four months she was pregnant as a sign that she is "like other women"—something she doubted previously (Becker 1997:35).

4. This is similar to Foucault's argument in *Birth of a Clinic* (1994) about the power and consequence of the medical "gaze." The medical gaze, that only trained specialists have, sees past the individual symptomology penetrating below the surface to reveal the underlying pathology.

CHAPTER FIVE

1. Rosa sold the SUV soon after my visit to pay some of the hospital bills.

2. A study published in 2005 reports that 47% of urban Ecuadorian women of all ages are "economically active," compared with 70% of men (Pérez and Gallardo 2005:74). Adult urban women between the ages of eighteen and sixty-four report spending between 30 and 45 hours a week taking care of the home and children in comparison with men who report only 12–15 hours (Pérez and Gallardo 2005:69).

3. Scientific research is increasingly clear that social stress negatively impacts immune and endocrine functions, which can have "severe" effects on health, including resistance to infections, vaccine responses, and "the development and progression of cancer" (Webster Marketon and Glaser 2008; see also Glaser and Kiecolt-Glaser 2005).

4. Research on lupus conducted in the United States shows that, as women's social networks contract over the course the illness, there is a measurable impact on both psychological and physical well-being (Keller 1999). In other words, women do worse on both measures as their social-support networks become smaller (Keller 1999). Studies suggest that social support can help mitigate the physical distress of lupus and that women with strong and more supportive networks have less depression and a greater sense of well-being, even when they have significant illness burdens (Keller 1999). Similarly, loss of social roles can create greater disease and distress (Karasz and Ouellete 1995); moreover, the ability to perform social roles at work and at home acts as a mediating factor between disease activity and perceived distress (Karasz and Ouellete 1995). In other words, strong social support and the ability to continue important social roles and connections are linked to overall psychological and physical well-being. The stress induced by the loss of vital social relationships contributes to depression and greater disease activity.

5. Charmaz (1991) briefly discusses the ways in which chronic illness can have an impact on and affect the sufferers understanding of and relationship to time. Time often "slips away" (90) while ill, and while it does, "existence and self also slip away." Valentina's sense of self is partially destabilized because she cannot keep track of the past in her head. She has literally lost time, both real and metaphoric.

6. Both Chant (2002) and Arriagada (2006) point out that the liberalization of divorce laws, increased economic opportunities for women, and changes in values and mores have resulted in a significant increase in the number of households headed by single females throughout Latin America.

CHAPTER SIX

1. Cheney (2005a) reports that 89% of Ecuadorians are Catholic and, in the diocese of Cuenca, 95% of the population is Catholic (Cheney 2005b). Roberts (2006) argues that in Quito most Ecuadorians today practice a "baroque" Catholicism. Roberts describes "baroque" Catholicism as one that fosters personalistic relationships between individuals and the divine, rather than strict adherence to sanctioned orthodoxy and bureaucratic rules. So, for example, Roberts explains, despite papal bans, Ecuadorian physicians who practice in-vitro fertilization feel little contradiction between their faith and their occupations, and they interpret their work as being well within their understandings of God's relationship with man. In this pragmatic Catholicism, individuals are free to interpret their own actions and life events within a broad framework that presumes a certain flexibility in the relationship between humans and the divine.

2. Cuencanos' passion for Virgins reached a feverish pitch in 1988, when a young woman from a well-to-do family claimed to have seen an apparition of the Virgin, who asked her to build a sanctuary for her in Cajas, a nearby high-altitude wilderness park just outside Cuenca. In 1989 it was reported in local newspapers that nearly 100,000 people had made the pilgrimage to Cajas, where it was believed the Virgin would make an appearance.

3. An extensive literature in medical anthropology, much of it focused on the Andes, links female suffering, bodily distress, emotions, and morality (Tousignant 1984; Tapias 2006; Darghouth et al. 2006). While the specifics of how bodily distress and "morality" intersect differ considerably from place to place, this body of work suggests that women (and not men) in the Andes are prone to illnesses whose origins lie in moral distress. In some cases, the moral laxity of others sickens women who depend upon them (Darghouth et al. 2006; Tousignant 1984), while in the case of nursing mothers in Bolivia, they face moral disapprobation when their own anger (caused by conditions of social suffering) spoils their milk and sickens their children (Tapias 2006). Taken as a whole, this literature affirms the connection between women's bodily distress, their social connections to others, and concepts of interpersonal morality.

4. I agree with Young (1981), who wrote that the ill often have multiple ways of

thinking about their conditions and that it is not always possible to connect all their negotiated thoughts into a single, coherent narrative.

5. Throop discusses the ways that those who experience chronic pain in Yap also tap into deeply held notions about personal and cultural virtues (Throop 2010). Throop highlights the tentative nature of virtuous suffering and writes that "moments of virtuous suffering are subjective and intersubjective accomplishments that may be realized, even if momentarily, before resolving back into instances of non-virtuous and unwanted forms of 'mere suffering' and vice versa" (Throop 2012:265).

CHAPTER SEVEN

1. I use the term "Western thought" here to refer broadly to the influences of Judeo-Christian teachings (see Escalante Gonzalbo 2006). That is not to say that such thinking does not occur outside western influence but rather to point out what an essential part it has played in Judeo-Christian thinking.

2. Hawkins (1993:1) also examined what he termed "pathographies," "a form of autobiography or biography that describes personal experiences of illness, treatment and sometimes death." In this work, Hawkins examines a wide range of English-language texts and argues that the transformation "myth" figures large as illness often signals a kind of rebirth. Hawkins also points out the frequency of "battle and journey" metaphors in pathographies, which also often result in transformation.

3. LIVESTRONG n.d.

4. Becker writes about the emplotment of illness narratives, noting that they are culturally constructed and also individually mediated. "When we think of memory as the representation and embodiment of loss rather than simply retrospective continuity, it becomes clearer how memory is utilized in a cultural way" (Becker 1997:182).

5. http://lilwolff.com/Embrace/sanctuary.htm (accessed September 29, 2004).

6. Both Ehrenreich and Lochmann Jain point out that there is intense cultural pressure on the ill to become "survivors," not "victims," and to accept the challenge to "battle" cancer with "hope" rather than critique the social causes and inequalities that contribute to cancer incidence, inhibit treatment options, or bankrupt families (Ehrenreich 2001; Lochmann Jain 2010). Both also point out that there are considerable corporate interests behind "supporting" cancer survivorship and that races, products, and advertisements are often underwritten by corporations who profit from cancer treatment, from engaging in cancer "awareness" publicity, or from having attention distracted away from corporate responsibility for cancer-provoking products and wastes (see also Sulick 2010).

7. Like lupus, rheumatoid arthritis (RA) is primarily a clinical diagnosis based on a patient's presenting symptoms. Sonia is probably referring here to a rheumatoid factor test, which looks for RA antibodies. The test is "positive" in about 80% of RA patients and would have been available in the 1970s and 1980s.

8. Although I asked Sonia she could not elaborate on or name the test. I assume it was an antinuclear antibody test, which was developed in the 1950s.

9. The notion of discipline is central to Adventist thinking. The General Council of the Seventh Day Adventist Church writes in their document "Fundamental Beliefs" that "because our bodies are the temples of the Holy Spirit, we are to care for them intelligently. Along with adequate exercise and rest, we are to adopt the most healthful diet possible and abstain from the unclean foods identified in the Scriptures. Since alcoholic beverages, tobacco, and the irresponsible use of drugs and narcotics are harmful to our bodies, we are to abstain from them as well. Instead, we are to engage in whatever brings our thoughts and bodies into the discipline of Christ, who desires our happiness, joy, and goodness" (http://www.adventist.org/beliefs/fundamental/index.html; accessed May 2012).

References

ALARCÓN, G.S.

2001   "Of Ethnicity, Race, and Lupus." *Lupus* 10:594–596.

ALARCÓN, G.S., G. MCGWIN JR., M. PETRI, J.D. REVEILLE, R. RAMSEY-GOLDMAN, AND R.P. KIMBERLY

2002   "Baseline Characteristics of a Multiethnic Lupus Cohort: PROFILE." *Lupus* 11(9) 95–101.

ALLEN, CATHERINE

2002   *The Hold Life Has: Coca and Cultural Identity in an Andean Community.* Washington, DC: Smithsonian Press.

ANDERSON, JEANINE

2000   "Narrativas de Aflicción de Mujeres Andinas." *Allpanchis* 56:75–106.

APPADURAI, ARJUN

1991   "Global Ethnoscapes: Notes and Queries for a Transnational Anthropology." In *Recapturing Anthropology: Working in the Present.* Richard G. Fox (ed.), pp. 191–210. Santa Fe, NM: School of American Research Press.

1996   *Modernity at Large: Cultural Dimensions of Globalization.* Minneapolis: University of Minnesota Press.

ARCHETTI, EDUARDO P.

1997   *Guinea-pigs: Food, Symbol, and Conflict of Knowledge in Ecuador.* Oxford: Berg.

ARKFELD, D.G.

2008   "The Potential Utility of B-cell Directed Biologic Therapy in Autoimmune Diseases." *Rheumatology International* 28:205–215.

ARRIAGADA, IRMA

2006   "Changes and Inequality in Latin American Families." *Journal of Comparative Family Studies* 37(4):511–537.

ASAD, TALAL

1993   *Genealogies of Religion: Discipline and Reasons of Power in Christianity and Islam.* Baltimore: Johns Hopkins University Press.

AVANIAN, JOHN Z., AND ARNOLD M. EPSTEIN

1991 "Differences in the Use of Procedures between Women and Men Hospitalized for Coronary Heart Disease." *New England Journal of Medicine* 325(4):221–225.

BAE, SANG-CHEOL, HIDEKI HASHIMOTO, ELIZABETH K. KARLSON, MATTHEW H. LIANG, AND LAWREN H. DALTROY

2001 "Variable Effects of Social Support by Race, Economic Status, and Disease Activity in Systemic Lupus Erythematosus." *The Journal of Rheumatology* 28(6):1245–1251.

BALSHEM, MARTHA LEVITTAN

1993 *Cancer in the Community: Class and Medical Authority.* Washington, DC: Smithsonian Institution Press.

BARKER, KRISTIN K.

2005 *The Fibromyalgia Story: Medical Authority and Women's World of Pain.* Philadelphia, PA: Temple University Press.

BASTIAN, H. M., J.M. ROSEMAN, G. MCGWIN JR., G.S. ALARCÓN, A.W. FRIEDMAN, B.J. FESSLER, B.A. BAETHGE, AND J.D. REVEILLE

2002 Systemic Lupus Erythematosus in Three Ethnic Groups: Risk Factors for Lupus Nephritis after Diagnosis. *Lupus* 11(3):152–160.

BEARD, LAURA J.

2003 "Whose Life in the Mirror? Examining Three Mexican Telenovelas as Cultural and Commercial Products." *Studies in Latin American Popular Culture* 22:73–88.

BECKER, GAY

1997 *Disrupted Lives: How People Create Meaning in a Chaotic World.* Berkeley: University of California Press.

BENEDEK, THOMAS G.

2002 "Historical Background of Discoid and Systemic Lupus Erythematosus." In *Dubois' Lupus Erythematosus.* Daniel Wallace and Bevra Hahn (eds.), pp. 3–16. Philadelphia, PA: Lippincott.

BIEHL, JOÃO, BYRON GOOD, AND ARTHUR KLEINMAN

2007 "Introduction: Rethinking Subjectivity." In *Subjectivity.* João Biehl, Byron Good, and Arthur Kleinman (eds.). Berkeley: University of California Press.

BOURDIEU, PIERRE

1977 *Outline of a Theory of Practice.* Cambridge: Cambridge University Press.

BRIGGS, CHARLES

1986 *Learning How to Ask: A Sociolinguistic Appraisal of the Role of the Interview in Social Science Research.* Cambridge: Cambridge University Press.

BORQUE, SUSAN, AND KAY B. WARREN

1981 *Women of the Andes: Patriarchy and Social Change in Two Peruvian Towns.* Ann Arbor: University of Michigan Press.

BROWNER, CAROLE

1996 "The Production of Authoritative Knowledge in American Prenatal Care." *Medical Anthropology Quarterly* 10(2):141–156.

BROWNRIGG, LESLIE ANNE

1972 "The Nobles of Cuenca: The Agrarian Elite of Southern Ecuador." Ph.D. dissertation, Columbia University, New York, Department of Anthropology.

BUTLER, JUDITH

1999 *Gender Trouble: Feminism and the Subversion of Identity.* New York: Routledge.

BRUCE, IAN

2010 "Re-evaluation of Biologic Therapy in Systemic Lupus Erythematosus." *Current Opinion in Rheumatology* 22(3):273–277.

CHAKRAVARTY, ELIZA F., THOMAS M. BUSH, SUSAN MANZI, ANN E. CLARKE, AND MICHAEL M. WARD

2007 "Prevalence of Adult Systemic Lupus Erythematosus in California and Pennsylvania in 2000: Estimates Obtained Using Hospital Data." *Arthritis and Rheumatism* 56(6):2092–2094.

CHANT, SYLVIA

2002 "Researching Gender, Families, and Households in Latin America: From the 20th into the 21st Century." *Bulletin of Latin American Research* 21(4):545–575.

CHARMAZ, KATHY

1991 *Good Days, Bad Days: The Self in Chronic Illness and Time.* New Brunswick, NJ: Rutgers University Press.

CHARON, RITA

2006 *Narrative Medicine: Honoring the Stories of Illness.* New York: Oxford University Press.

CLARKE, ANN E., JOHN PENROD, YVAN ST. PIERRE, MICHELLE A. PETRI, SUSAN MANZI, DAVID A. ISENBERG, CAROLINE GORDON, JEAN-LUC SENECAL, PAUL R. FORTIN, NURHAN SUTCLIFFE, ET AL.

2000 "Underestimating the Value of Women: Assessing the Indirect Costs of Women with Systematic Lupus Erythematosus." *The Journal of Rheumatology* 27(11):2597–2604.

COHN, SIMON

1999 "Taking Time to Smell the Roses: Accounts of People with Chronic Fatigue Syndrome and their Struggle for Legitimization." *Anthropology and Medicine* 6(2):195–214.

COLSON, AUDREY BUTT, AND CESAREO DE ARMELLADA

1983 "An Amerindian Derivation for Latin American Creole Illnesses and Their Treatment." *Social Science and Medicine* 17(17):1229–1248.

CRANDON-MALAMUD, LIBBET

1993 *From the Fat of Our Souls: Social Change, Political Processes and Medical Pluralism in Bolivia.* Berkeley: University of California Press.

DANCHENCKO, N., J.A. SATIA, AND M.S. ANTHONY

2006 "Epidemiology of Systematic Lupus Erythematosus: A Comparison of Worldwide Disease Burden." *Lupus* 15:308–318.

DARGHOUTH, SARAH, DUNCAN PEDERSON, GILES BIBEAU, AND CECIL ROUSSEAU
2006 "Painful Languages of the Body: Experiences of Headache among Women in Two Peruvian Communities." *Culture, Medicine, and Psychiatry* 30(3):271–297.

DAVIS-FLOYD, ROBBIE
1996 Intuition as Authoritative Knowledge in Midwifery and Home Birth. *Medical Anthropology Quarterly* 10(2):237–269.

DEMAS, KRISTINA L., AND KAREN H. COSTENBADER
2009 "Disparities in Lupus Care and Outcomes." *Current Opinion in Rheumatology* 21:102–109.

DIGIACOMO, SUSAN M.
1992 "Metaphor as Illness: Postmodern Dilemmas in the Representation of Body, Mind, and Disorder." *Medical Anthropology* 14:109–137.

DRESSLER, WILLIAM
1993 "Health in the African American Community: Accounting for Health Inequalities." *Medical Anthropology Quarterly* 7(4): 325–345.

EHRENREICH, BARBARA
2001 "Welcome to Cancerland." *Harper's Magazine* 303(818): 43–53.

EHLERS, TRACY BACHRACH
1991 "Debunking Marianismo: Economic Vulnerability & Survival Strategies among Guatemalan Wives." *Ethnology* 30(1):1–14.

ESCALANTE, AGUSTÍN, AND INMACULADA DEL RINCÓN
2001 "Epidemiology and Impact of Rheumatic Disorders in the United States Hispanic Population." *Current Opinion in Rheumatology* 13:104–110.

ESCALANTE GONZALBO, FERNANDO
2006 *In the Eyes of God: A Study on the Culture of Suffering.* Austin: University of Texas Press.

ESTROFF, SUE
1993 "Identity, Disability, and Schizophrenia: The Problem of Chronicity." In *Knowledge, Power, and Practice: The Anthropology of Medicine in Everyday Life.* S. Lindenbaum and M. Lock (eds.), pp. 247–286. Berkeley: University of California Press.
2001 "Transformations and Reformulations: Chronicity and Identity Politics, Policy and Phenomenology." *Medical Anthropology* 19:411–413.

FINERMAN, RUTHBETH
1989 "The Burden of Responsibility: Duty, Depression and Nervios in Andean Ecuador." *Health Care for Women International* 10(23):141–157.

FINKLER, KAJA
1994 *Women and Pain: Gender and Morbidity in Mexico.* Philadelphia: University of Pennsylvania Press.

FISCHER, MICHAEL M.
2007 "Epilogue. To Live with What Would Otherwise Be Unendurable: Return(s) to Subjectivity." In *Subjectivity,* João Biehl, Byron Good, and Arthur Kleinman (eds.), pp. 434–446. Berkeley: University of California Press.

FOSTER, GEORGE M.

1953 "The Relationship between Spanish and Spanish-American Folk Medicine." *Journal of American Folklore* 66(261):201–217.

FOUCAULT, MICHEL

1994 *Birth of a Clinic: An Archaeology of Medical Perception*. New York: Vintage Books.

FRANK, ARTHUR

1991 *At the Will of the Body: Reflections on Illness*. Boston: Houghton Mifflin.

FRETES-CIBLIS, VICENTE, MARCELO M. GIUGALE, AND JOSÉ ROBERTO LÓPEZ-CÁLIX

2003 *Ecuador: An Economic and Social Agenda in the New Millennium*. Washington, DC: World Bank.

GARCÍA, BRÍGIDA, AND ORLANDINA DE OLIVEIRA

1997 "Motherhood and Extradomestic Work in Urban Mexico." *Bulletin of Latin American Research* 16(3):367–384.

GARCÍA-GONZÁLEZ, A. ET AL.

2008 "Treatment Adherences of Patients with Rheumatoid Arthritis and Systemic Lupus Erythematosus." *Clinical Rheumatology* 27(7):883–889.

GARRO, LINDA C., AND CHERYL MATTINGLY

2000 "Narratives as Construct and Construction." In *Narrative and the Cultural Construction of Illness and Healing*, Cheryl Mattingly and Linda C. Garro (eds.). Berkeley: University of California Press.

GERONIMUS, ARLINE T., MARGARET T. HICKEN, JAY A. PEARSON, SARAH J. SEASHOLS, KELLY L. BROWN, AND TRACEY DAWSON CRUZ

2010 "Do US Black Women Experience Stress-Related Accelerated Biological Aging? A Novel Theory and First Population-Based Test of Black-White Differences in Telomere Length." *Human Nature* 1(22):19–38.

GLADMAN, DAFNA D., AND MURRAY B. UROWITZ

2002 "Prognosis, Mortality and Morbidity in Systemic Lupus Erythematosus." In *Dubois' Lupus Erythematosus* (6th ed.), Daniel J. Wallace and Bevra Hannahs Hahn (eds.), pp. 1255–1273. Philadelphia, PA: Lippincott Williams and Wilkins.

GLASER, RONALD, AND JANICE K. KIECOLT-GLASER

2005 "Stress-Induced Immune Dysfunction: Implications for Health." *Nature Reviews Immunology* 5:243–251.

GOFFMAN, ERVING

1963 *Stigma: Notes on the Management of Spoiled Identity*. Englewood Cliffs, NJ: Prentice Hall.

GOLDSTEIN, MELISSA ANNE

2000 *Travels with the Wolf: A Story of Chronic Illness*. Columbus: Ohio State University Press.

GOOD, BYRON J.

1994 *Medicine, Rationality and Experience: An Anthropological Perspective*. Cambridge: Cambridge University Press.

GREENSTEIN, B.D.

2002 "Lupus: Why Women?" *Journal of Health and Gender Based Medicine* 10(3): 233–239.

HAHN, ROBERT A.

1985 "Culture-Bound Syndromes Unbound." *Social Science and Medicine* 21(2): 165–171.

HALE, E.P., ET AL.

2006 "'Concealing the Evidence': The Importance of Appearance Concerns for Patients with Systemic Lupus Erythematosus." *Lupus* 15:532–540.

HAMPTON, TRACY

2007 "Researchers Probe Lupus Causes, Treatments." *Journal of the American Medical Association* 297(2):141–142.

HASSAUREK, FRIEDRICH

1967 *Four Years among the Ecuadorians.* Edited and with an Introduction by C. Harvey Gardiner. Carbondale: Southern Illinois University Press.

HAWKINS, ANNE HUNSAKER

1993 *Reconstructing Illness: Studies in Pathography.* West Lafayette, IN: Purdue University Press.

HILLBERT, RICHARD A.

1984 "The Acultural Dimensions of Chronic Pain: Flawed Reality Construction and the Problem of Meaning." *Social Problems* 31(4):365–378.

HIRSCHKIND, LYNN

1980 "On Conforming in Cuenca." Ph.D. Dissertation. University of Wisconsin, Madison, Department of Anthropology.

HONKASALO, MARJA-LIISA

1999 "What Is Chronic Is Ambiguity." *Suomen Antropology* 24(4):75–92.

2001 "Vicissitudes of Pain and Suffering: Chronic Pain and Liminality." *Medical Anthropology* 19: 319–353.

HOUGHTON, AZULA A., AND FREDERIC J. BOERSMA

1988 "The Loss-Grief Connection in Susto." *Ethnology* 27(2):145–154.

JACKSON, JEAN E.

2000 *"Camp Pain": Talking with Chronic Pain Patients.* Philadelphia: University of Pennsylvania Press, Philadelphia.

2005 "Stigma, Liminality and Chronic Pain: Mind-Body Borderlands." *American Ethnologist* 32(3):332–353.

JAIN, S. LOCHLANN

2010 "Be Prepared." In *Against Health: How Health Became the New Morality.* Jonathan M. Metzl and Anna Kirkland (eds.), pp. 170–182. New York: New York University Press.

JOHANSSON, EVA E., KATARINA HAMBURG, GOREN WESTMAN, AND GERD LINDGREN

1999 "The Meanings of Pain: An Exploration of Women's Descriptions of Symptoms." *Social Science and Medicine* 48(12):1791–1802.

KAPFERER, BRUCE

2008 "Beyond Symbolic Representation: Victor Turner and Variations on the Themes of Ritual Process and Liminality." *Suomen Antropologi* 33(4): 5–25.

KARASZ, ALISON, AND SUZANNE C. OUELLETTE

1995 "Role Strain and Psychological Well-Being in Women with Systemic Lupus Erythematosus." *Women and Health* 23(3):41–59.

KELLER, SHIRLEY M.

1999 "Social Support and Psychological Distress in Women with Systemic Lupus Erythematosus." Ph.D. dissertation, Case Western Reserve University, Department of Social Work.

KLEINMAN, ARTHUR

1988 *The Illness Narratives: Suffering, Healing and the Human Condition.* New York: Basic Books.

KLEINMAN, ARTHUR, PAUL BRODWIN, BYRON J. GOOD, AND MARY JO DELVECCHIO GOOD

1992 "Pain as Human Experience: An Introduction." In *Pain as Human Experience: An Anthropological Perspective.* Mary Jo DelVecchio Good, Paul E. Brodwin, Byron J. Good, and Arthur Kleinman (eds.), pp. 1–28. Berkeley: University of California Press.

KLEINMAN, ARTHUR, VEENA DAS, AND MARGARET LOCK

1997 "Introduction." In *Social Suffering.* Arthur Kleinman, Veena Das, and Margaret Lock (eds.), pp. ix–xxxvii. Berkeley: University of California Press.

LANE, KRIS

2003 "Haunting the Present: Five Colonial Legacies for the New Millennium." In *Millennial Ecuador: Critical Essays on Cultural Transformations and Social Dynamics.* Norman E. Whitten (ed.), pp. 46–74. Iowa City: University of Iowa Press.

LARREA, CARLOS MALDONADO

2004 *Dolarización, crisis y pobreza en el Ecuador.* Quito: Abya-Yala/IEE/FLACSO/ILDIS.

LATEEF, AISHA, AND MICHELLE PETRI

2010 "Biologics in the Treatment of Systemic Lupus Erythematosus." *Current Opinions in Rheumatology* 22(5):504–509.

LIM, SAM S., AND CRISTINA DRENKARD

2008 "Epidemiology of Systemic Lupus Erythematosus: Capturing the Butterfly." *Current Rheumatology Reports* 10(4):265–272.

LOCK, MARGARET, AND VINH-KIM NGUYEN

2010 *An Anthropology of Biomedicine.* Malden, MA: Wiley Blackwell.

MALAT, JENNIFER ET AL.

2010 "White Doctors and Nurses on Racial Inequality in Health Care in the USA: Whiteness and Colour-blind Racial Ideology." *Ethnic and Racial Studies* 33(8):1431–1450.

MANDERSON, LENORE

2010 "Half a Woman: Embodied Disruptions and Ideas of Gender among Australian Women." In *Chronic Conditions, Fluid States: Chronicity and the Anthropology of Illness.* Lenore Manderson and Carolyn Smith-Morris (eds.), pp. 96–112. New Brunswick, NJ: Rutgers University Press.

MANDERSON, LENORE, AND CAROLYN SMITH-MORRIS

2010 "Introduction: Chronicity and the Experience of Illness." In *Chronic Conditions, Fluid States: Chronicity and the Anthropology of Illness*. Lenore Manderson and Carolyn Smith-Morris (eds.), pp. 1–18. New Brunswick, NJ: Rutgers University Press.

MANN, THOMAS

1996 *Magic Mountain*. New York: Vintage International.

MANZI, SUSAN

2001 "Epidemiology of Systemic Lupus Erythematosus." *American Journal of Managed Care* 7(16):474–479.

MARCUS, GEORGE E.

1998 *Ethnography through Thick and Thin*. Princeton, NJ: Princeton University Press.

MATTINGLY, CHERYL

1998 *Healing Dramas and Clinical Plots: The Narrative Structure of Experience*. Cambridge: Cambridge University Press.

2000 "Emergent Narratives." In *Narrative and the Cultural Construction of Illness and Healing*. Cheryl Mattingly and Linda C. Garro (eds.), pp. 181–211. Berkeley: University of California Press.

MAXWELL-SCOTT, MARY MONICA

1914 *Gabriel Garcia Moreno, Regenerator of Ecuador*. Help of Christians Publications. 3rd edition. London: R & T Washbourne Ltd.

MCMURRAY, RICHARD J. ET AL.

1991 "Gender Disparities in Clinical Decision Making." *Journal of the American Medical Association* 266(4): 559–562.

MENDELSON, CINDY

2009 "Diagnosis: A Liminal State for Women Living With Lupus." *Health Care for Women International* 30:390–407.

MERLEAU-PONTY, MAURICE

1962 *Phenomenology of Perception*. Translated by Colin Smith. New York: Humanities Press.

MILES, ANN

1998a "Radio and the Commodification of Natural Medicine in Ecuador." *Social Science and Medicine* 47(12):2137–2138.

1998b "Science, Nature and Tradition: The Mass-Marketing of Natural Medicines in Urban Ecuador." *Medical Anthropology Quarterly* 12(2):206–225.

2000 "Poor Adolescent Girls and Social Transformations in Cuenca, Ecuador." *Ethos* 28(1):54–74.

2004 *From Cuenca to Queens: An Anthropological Story of Transnational Migration*. Austin: University of Texas Press.

2009 "Of Butterflies and Wolves: Enacting Lupus Transformations on the Internet." *Anthropology and Medicine* 16(1):1–12.

2011 "Emerging Chronic Illness: Women and Lupus in Ecuador." *Health Care for Women International* 32(8):651–668.

MITCHELL, WINIFRED

1994 "Women's Hierarchies of Age and Suffering in an Andean Community." *Journal of Cross-Cultural Gerontology* 9:179–191.

MOL, ANNEMARIE

2002 *The Body Multiple: Ontology in Medical Practice.* Durham, NC: Duke University Press.

MONGEY, ANNE-BARBARA, AND EVELYN V. HESS

2002 "The Role of Environment in Systemic Lupus Erythematosus." In *Dubois' Lupus Erythematosus.* Daniel Wallace and Bevra Hahn (eds.), pp. 33–64. Philadelphia, PA: Lippincott, Williams and Wilkins.

MORRIS, DAVID B.

1991 *The Culture of Pain.* Berkeley: University of California Press.

MOSS, PAMELA, AND ISABEL DYCK

2002 *Women, Body, Illness: Space and Identity in the Everyday Lives of Women with Chronic Illness.* Lanham, MD: Rowman and Littlefield.

MURPHY, ROBERT

1990 *The Body Silent.* New York: Norton.

NAPIER, A. DAVID

2003 *The Age of Immunology: Conceiving a Future in an Alienating World.* Chicago: University of Chicago Press.

NASH, JUNE

1990 "Gender Studies in Latin America." In *Gender and Anthropology: Critical Reviews for Research and Teaching.* Sandra Morgan (ed.), pp. 228–245. Washington, DC: American Anthropological Association.

NICHTER, MARK

1981 "Idioms of Distress: Alternatives in the Expression of Psychological Distress: A Case Study from South India." *Culture, Medicine and Psychiatry* 5:379–408.

NGUYEN, VINH-KIM, AND KARINE PESCHARD

2003 "Anthropology, Inequality and Disease." *Annual Reviews of Anthropology* 32:447–474.

ORTNER, SHERRY

2005 "Subjectivity and Cultural Critique." *Anthropological Theory* 5(1):31–52.

OTS, THOMAS

1990 "Angry Liver, the Anxious Heart and the Melancholy Spleen: The Phenomenology of Perceptions in Chinese Culture." *Culture, Medicine and Psychiatry* 14(1):21–58.

PAN AMERICAN HEALTH ORGANIZATION (PAHO)

2007 *Health in the Americas,* Volume 2. Washington, DC: Pan American Health Organization.

PARISH, STEVEN M.

2008 *Subjectivities and Suffering in American Culture.* New York: Palgrave MacMillan.

PARSONS, TALCOTT

    1951   *The Social System.* New York: Free Press.

PÉREZ, ALBA, AND CLAUDIO GALLARDO

    2005   *Mujeres y hombres del Ecuador en cifras II.* Quito, Ecuador: CONAMU.

PETRI, MICHELE, SUSANNE PEREZ-GUTTHAN, J. CRAIG LONGENECKER, AND
MARC HOCHBERG

    1991   "Morbidity of Systemic Lupus Erythematosus: Role of Race and Socioeco-
nomic Status." *American Journal of Medicine* 19(4):345–354.

POLLACK, ANDREW

    2010   "F.D.A. Panel Backs Drug for Lupus." *New York Times.* November 17, B1.

PORTES, ALEJANDRO, AND KELLY HOFFMAN

    2003   "Latin American Class Structures: Their Composition and Change during
the Neoliberal Era." *Latin American Research Review* 38(1):41–82.

PRIBILSKY, JASON

    2007   *La Chulla Vida: Gender, Migration, and the Family in Andean Ecuador and
New York City.* Syracuse, NY: Syracuse University Press.

QUINN, NAOMI

    2005   "How to Reconstruct Schemas People Share, from What They Say." In
Finding Culture in Talk: A Collection of Methods, Naomi Quinn (ed.),
pp. 35–81. New York: Palgrave Macmillan.

REBHUN, LINDA ANN

    1994   "Swallowing Frogs: Anger and Illness in Northeast Brazil." *Medical An-
thropology Quarterly* 8(4):360–382.

ROBERTS, ELIZABETH F.S.

    2006   "God's Laboratory: Religious Rationalities and Modernity in Ecuadorian
In-Vitro Fertilization. *Culture, Medicine and Psychiatry* 30(4):507–536.

RUS, VIOLETA, AND MARC C. HOCHBERG

    2002   "The Epidemiology of Systemic Lupus Erythematosus." In *Dubois' Lupus
Erythematosus,* Daniel Wallace and Bevra Hahn (eds.), pp. 65–83. Philadelphia, PA: Lippincott, Williams and Wilkins.

SACKS, J.J., ET AL.

    2002   "Trends in Death from Systemic Lupus Erythematosus–United States
1979–1998." Morbidity and Mortality Weekly Report 51(17):371–374.

SARIS, JAMIE A.

    1995   "Telling Stories: Life Histories, Illness Narratives, and Institutional Land-
scapes." *Culture, Medicine and Psychiatry* 19(1):39–72.

SCHEPER-HUGHES, NANCY

    1992   *Death without Weeping: The Violence of Everyday Life in Brazil.* Berkeley:
University of California Press.

SCHOENFELD, NAOMI, AND TERESA C. JUARBE

    2005   "From Sunrise to Sunset: An Ethnography of Rural Ecuadorian Women's
Perceived Health Needs and Resources." *Health Care for Women International* 26:957–977.

SCHRÖDER, JOHANN O., AND RIANALD A. ZEUNER

2009 "Biologics as Treatment for Systemic Lupus: Great Efforts, Sobering Results, New Challenges." *Current Drug Discoveries Technologies* 6:252–255.

SELDIN, M.F., L. QI, H.R. SCHERBARTH, C. TIAN, M. RANSOM, G. SILVA, J.W. BELMONT, S. GAMRON, A. ALLIEVI, S.A. PALATNIK ET AL.

2008 "Amerindian Ancestry in Argentina Is Associated with Increased Risk for Systemic Lupus Erythematosus." *Genes and Immunity* 9:389–393.

SIEGEL, BERNIE S.

1986 *Love, Medicine, and Miracles: Lessons Learned about Self-Healing from a Surgeon's Experience with Exceptional Patients.* New York: Harper and Row.

SINGER, MERRILL

1995 "Beyond the Ivory Tower: Critical Praxis in Medical Anthropology." *Medical Anthropology Quarterly* 9:1(80–106).

SMITH-MORRIS, CAROLYN

2006 *Diabetes among the Pima: Stories of Survival.* Tucson: University of Arizona Press.

2010 "The Chronicity of Life, the Acuteness of Diagnosis." In *Chronic Conditions, Fluid States: Chronicity and the Anthropology of Illness.* Lenore Manderson and Carolyn Smith-Morris (eds.), pp. 21–37. New Brunswick, NJ: Rutgers University Press.

SONTAG, SUSAN

1990 *Illness as Metaphor and AIDS and Its Metaphors.* New York: Doubleday.

SONTHEIMER, RICHARD D., AND DANIEL MCAULIFFE

2002 "Cutaneous Manifestations of Lupus Erythematosus." In *Dubois' Lupus Erythematusus,* Sixth Edition. Daniel J. Wallace and Bevra Hannahs Hahn (eds.), pp. 573–618. Philadelphia, PA: Lippincott, Williams and Wilkins.

STEVENS, EVELYN P.

1973 "Marianismo: The Other Face of Machismo in Latin America." In *Male and Female in Latin America.* Ann Pescatello (ed.), pp. 89–101. Pittsburgh, PA: University of Pittsburgh Press.

STØLEN, KRISTI ANNE

1991 "Gender, Sexuality and Violence in Ecuador." *Ethnos* 56(1–2):82–100.

STOLLER, PAUL

2004 *Stranger in the Village of the Sick.* Boston: Beacon Press.

SULICK, GAYLE

2010 *Pink Ribbon Blues: How Breast Cancer Culture Undermines Women's Health.* New York: Oxford University Press.

SULLIVAN, MARK

1986 "In What Sense Is Contemporary Medicine Dualistic?" *Culture, Medicine and Psychiatry* 10(4):331–350.

TAPIAS, MARIA

2006 "Emotions and Intergenerational Embodiment of Social Suffering in Rural Bolivia." *Medical Anthropology Quarterly* 20(3):399–415.

TATE, JULEE

2007 "The Good and Bad Women of Telenovelas: How to Tell Them Apart Using a Simple Maternity Test." *Studies in Latin American Popular Culture* 26:97–111.

THROOP, C. JASON

2010 *Suffering and Sentiment: Exploring the Vicissitudes of Experience and Pain in Yap.* Berkeley: University of California Press.

TOUSIGNANT, MICHEL

1984 "Pena in the Ecuadorian Sierra: A Psychoanthropological Analysis of Sadness." *Culture, Medicine and Psychiatry* 8(4):381–398.

1989 "Sadness, Depression and Social Reciprocity in Highland Ecuador." *Social Science and Medicine* 28(9):899–904.

TURNER, EDITH

2008 "Exploring the Work of Victor Turner: Liminality and Its Later Implications." *Suomen Antropologi: Journal of Finnish Anthropological Society* 33(4):26–44.

TURNER, VICTOR

1969 *The Ritual Process: Structure and Anti-Structure.* Ithaca, NY: Cornell University Press.

1974 *Dramas, Fields and Metaphors.* Ithaca, NY: Cornell University Press.

VARUL, MATTHIAS ZICK

2010 "Talcott Parsons, The Sick Role and Chronic Illness." *Body and Society* 16(2):72–94.

VIGH, HENRIK

2008 "Crisis and Chronicity: Anthropological Perspectives on Continuous Conflict and Decline." *Ethnos* 73(1):5–24.

VON HILDEBRAND, DIETRICH

2007 *The Heart: An Analysis of Human and Divine Affectivity.* South Bend, IN: St. Augustine Press.

VOS, ROB, JOSÉ CUESTA, MAURICIO LEÓN, RUTH LUCIO, AND JOSÉ ROSERO

2004 *Ecuador: Creating Fiscal Space for Poverty Reduction: A Fiscal Management and Public Expenditure Review Vol. II.* Report No. 28911-EC. Washington DC: World Bank and InterAmerican Development Bank.

WALSH, S.J., AND A. GILCHRIST

2006 "Geographical Clustering of Mortality from Systemic Lupus Erythematosus in the United States: Contributions of Poverty, Hispanic Identity and Solar Radiation." *Lupus* 15(10):662–670.

WANG, JUN, ASHLEY B. KAY, JEREMIAH FLETCHER, MARGARET K. FORMICA, AND TIMOTHY E. MCALINDON

2008 "Is Lipstick Associated with the Development of Lupus Erythematosus (SLE)?" *Clinical Rheumatology* 27(9):1183–1187.

WARD, MICHAEL

2001 "Examining Health Disparities in Systematic Lupus Erythematosus." *Arthritis and Rheumatism* 44(12):2711–2714.

WARE, NORMA

1999 "Toward a Model of Social Course in Chronic Illness: The Example of Chronic Fatigue Syndrome." *Culture, Medicine and Psychiatry* 23(3):303–331.

WATERS, WILLIAM F.

2006 "Salud, transición y globalización: La experiencia del Ecuador." *In Estudios Ecuatorianos: Un aporte a la discusión.* Ximena Sosa-Bucholz and William F. Waters (eds.), pp. 103–132. Quito, Ecuador: Ediciones ABYA-YALA.

WEBSTER MARKETON, JEANETTE L., AND RONALD GLASER

2008 "Stress Hormones and Immune Function." *Cellular Immunology* 252(1–2): 16–26.

WEINSTEIN, ARTHUR, AND VASILEIOS KYTTARIS

2003 "Lab Tests." *The Lupus Newslink* 6:1, 4–5, 12.

WEISMANTEL, MARY J.

2001 *Cholas and Pishtacos: Stories of Race and Sex in the Andes.* Chicago: University of Chicago.

WERNER, ANNE, LISE WIDDING ISAKSEN, AND KIRSTI MALTERUD

2004 "'I Am Not the Kind of Woman Who Complains of Everything': Illness Stories on Self and Shame in Women with Chronic Pain." *Social Science and Medicine* 59:1035–1045.

WHITEHEAD, KATE, AND JENNIE WILLIAMS

2001 "Medical Treatment of Women with Lupus: The Case for Sharing Knowledge and Decision-Making." *Disability and Society* 16(1):103–121.

WHYTE, SUSAN REYNOLDS

2009 "Health Identities and Subjectivities: The Ethnographic Challenge." *Medical Anthropology Quarterly* 23(1):6–15.

WILLIAMS, BRIAN, AND DAVID HEALY

2001 "Perceptions of Illness Causation among New Referrals to a Community Mental Health Team: 'Explanatory Model' or 'Exploratory Map'?" *Social Science and Medicine* 53(3):465–476.

WILLIAMS, DEREK

2001 "Assembling the "Empire of Morality": State Building Strategies in Catholic Ecuador, 1861–1875." *Journal of Historical Sociology* 14(2):149–174.

WILLIAMS, S.J.

2005 "Parsons Revisited: From the Sick Role to . . ." *Health* 9(2):123–144.

WINNICOTT, D.W.

1975 *Through Pediatrics to Psycho-Analysis.* New York: Basic Books.

YOUNG, ALLAN

1980 "The Discourse on Stress and the Reproduction of Conventional Knowledge." *Social Science and Medicine* 14B(3):133–146.

1981 "When Rational Men Fall Sick." *Culture, Medicine and Psychiatry* 5(4):317–335.

ZOUALI, MONCEF

2005 "Taming Lupus." *Scientific American* 292(2):71–77.

WEBSITES

ALCALDÍA CUENCA
2010 Estadísticas de la Ciudad. http://www.cuenca.gov.ec/?q=page_estadis
      ticasciudad (accessed 5/17/2012).

CAMMINO NEOCATECUMENALE
2000 "Historical note and some data about the Neocatechumenal Way."
      http://www.camminoneocatecumenale.com/new/papa.asp?id=159&a=13
      (accessed 5/21/2012).

CHENEY, DAVID M.
2005a Statistics by Country by Percentage Catholic. http://www.catholic-hier
      archy.org/country/sc3.html (accessed 5/21/2012).
2005b Ecuador Statistics by Diocese. http://www.catholic-hierarchy.org/coun
      try/scec3.html (accessed 5/21/2012).

EUROMONITOR INTERNATIONAL
2011 "Herbal/traditional products in Ecuador." http://www.marketresearch
      .com/Euromonitor-International-v746/Herbal-Traditional-Products-Ec
      uador-6537506/ (accessed 5/18/2012).

IESS [INSTITUTO ECUATORIANO DE SEGURIDAD SOCIAL]
2008 "Historia." Instituto Ecuatoriano de Seguridad Social. http://www.iess
      .gob.ec/site.php?content=292-quienes-somos (accessed 5/18/2012)

INEC [INSTITUTO NACIONAL DE ESTADÍSTICA Y CENSOS]
2012 Resultados del Censo 2012. Canton Cuenca. http://www.inec.gob.ec/cpv
      /index.php?option=com_wrapper&view=wrapper&Itemid=49&lang=es
      (accessed 5/17/2012).

JEAN (A.K.A. WOLFLADY)
1997 "Jean's World of Reality." http://wolflady.pspbuddies.com/peace/lupus
      .html (accessed 5/30/2012).

JOKISCH, BRAD
N.d. "Ecuador: Diversity in Migration." Migration Information Source. http://
      www.Migrationinformation.org/Profiles/display/cfm?ID=575 (accessed
      5/16/2012).

LIVESTRONG
N.d. The LIVESTRONG Manifesto. http://www.livestrong.org/who-we-are
      /our-strength/livestrong-manifesto (accessed 5/29/2012).

EL MERCURIO
2007a "Diá mundial de lupus." http://www.elmercurio.com.ec/hemeroteca
      -virtual?noticia=74614, 2007/05/09 (accessed 5/15/12).
2007b *Farmasol capta interés de la ciudadanía.* http://www.elmercurio.com.ec
      /hemeroteca-virtual?noticia=76935, 2007/07/05 (accessed 5/22/2012).
2011 "Azuay con 712,127 habitantes." http://www.elmercurio.com.ec/299803
      -azuay-con-712–127-habitantes.html, 2011/09/24.

PLEDGER, GAYLA L.
1998 "I'm Really Not Crazy." http://wir2.tripod.com/Lupus/gaylapledger.htm.

Index

Weismantel, Mary J., 19, 49, 156
Werner, Anne, Lise Widding Isaksen, and
    Kirsti Malterud, 36
Whitehead, Kate, and Jennie Williams, 27
Whyte, Susan Reynolds, 60
Williams, Brian, and David Healy, 104, 117
Williams, Derek, 106
Williams S. J., 60, 158
Winnicott, D. W., 64

wolf, as symbol, 22, 127–128, 161
World Bank, 48

Young, Allan, 5, 9, 138, 160

Zouali, Moncef, 23

CPSIA information can be obtained at www.ICGtesting.com
Printed in the USA
BVOW08s0045030816

457735BV00001B/22/P